Experts Answer
95 New Practice Management Questions

Mary Mourar, MLS

Consulting editors:
Kenneth T. Hertz, FACMPE, CMPE
Cynthia L. Dunn, FACMPE
Nick A. Fabrizio, PhD, FACMPE
Jeffrey B. Milburn, MBA, CMPE

Medical Group Management Association
104 Inverness Terrace East
Englewood, CO 80112-5306
877.275.6462

www.mgma.com

Production Credits
Content Manager: Marti A. Cox, MLIS
Editorial and Production Manager: Anne Serrano, MA
Copyeditor: Erica Nikolaidis
Compositor: Virginia Howe
Proofreader: Mary Kay Kozyra
Cover Design: Ian Serff, Serff Creative Group, Inc.
Indexer: Sonja Armstrong

Library of Congress Cataloging-in-Publication Data
Mourar, Mary.
 Experts answer 95 new practice management questions / Mary Mourar ; consulting editors, Kenneth T. Hertz ... [et al.].
    p. ; cm.
 Includes bibliographical references and index.
 Summary: "A great resource for medical practice executives, the 95 questions in this book review many frequently asked questions received by the MGMA Information Center over the years, as well as questions that address current issues and emerging trends in our ever-changing and complex healthcare environment"--Provided by publisher.
 ISBN 978-1-56829-384-4
 I. Hertz, Kenneth T., CMPE. II. Medical Group Management Association. III. Title.
 [DNLM: 1. Practice Management, Medical. 2. Office Management. W 80]

  610.68--dc23
                    2011037380

Item 8369

ISBN: 978-1-56829-384-4

Printed in the United States of America

10 9 8 7 6 5 4 3 2

ABOUT THE AUTHOR

Mary Mourar, MLS, is a healthcare information professional, freelance writer, and developmental editor. While working for MGMA more than 11 years as a librarian and information specialist in the Information Center, Mary assisted MGMA members and staff with a plethora of medical practice management questions, addressing current trends and issues across the healthcare industry. She received a master's degree in library science from the University of California, Los Angeles, and a bachelor of arts from The Colorado College.

ABOUT THE
CONSULTING EDITORS

Cynthia "Cindy" L. Dunn, RN, FACMPE, is a principal consultant in the MGMA Health Care Consulting Group. Cindy has 34 years of experience in healthcare, including 25 years in management, 18 as the administrator of two medical private practices, and 6 years in nursing management for a hospital-owned physician practice. The last 10 years of her private-practice work focused exclusively on an orthopedic practice. She has also managed the planning and construction of a medical office building and ambulatory surgery center. This experience offers clients practical and efficient solutions utilizing technology in both business and clinical management.

Nick A. Fabrizio, PhD, FACMPE, FACHE, has more than 20 years of practice management and health system experience in private physician and large medical group practices; for-profit and nonprofit hospitals and health systems; academic medical centers; physician faculty practice plans; and ambulatory care networks. His primary expertise is in physician practice management and managing complex physician–hospital relationships and clinical enterprises. A principal consultant with the MGMA Health Care Consulting group, Nick also authored the MGMA books *Goals into Gold: Strategic Planning for Healthcare Professionals* and *Integrated Delivery Systems: Ensuring Successful Physician–Hospital Partnerships.*

Kenneth T. Hertz, FACMPE, a principal consultant in the MGMA Health Care Consulting Group, has 30 years of management experience. He has held leadership positions in both small and large healthcare organizations, including primary care, multispecialty, and large integrated systems. His healthcare consulting work has encompassed a broad range of services, including operational improvement, practice analysis, strategic planning, organizational development, and strategic marketing. A popular conference speaker, he has also authored or provided expertise on articles addressing strategic planning, physician leadership, and governance issues.

Jeffrey B. Milburn, MBA, CMPE, former senior vice president and interim CEO for a 90-physician multispecialty group, has nearly 30 years of healthcare financial management experience. He has served as chief financial officer and was responsible for his organization's payer contracting and management. He focuses on physician compensation plans, financial management, and payer contracting for MGMA consulting clients. A former member of the MGMA Board of Directors, he is active on the MGMA Survey Advisory Committee. Jeff is a frequent presenter at conferences and author of articles on practice financial management.

CONTENTS

ACKNOWLEDGMENTS

My thanks to the many excellent staff members of the Medical Group Management Association, including Craig Wiberg, Charlyn Treese, and Carol Knee; and to the MGMA Government Affairs staff, including Amy Nordeng and Rob Tennant. Special thanks to Marti Cox for her assistance in research and handling of my many requests related to this book.

Finally, thanks to my husband, Tom, for his understanding, patience, and support, without which I would not have been able to complete this project.

INTRODUCTION

Since its founding in 1972, the library at the Medical Group Management Association (MGMA) has been a primary information resource for professionals in medical practice management. Practice executives, administrators, physicians, and others have turned to the MGMA librarians for help in dealing with practice management issues. Requests for information can be as simple as "What is the average operating cost for my specialty?" and as complex as "What can I do for my practice to succeed in this changing healthcare environment?"

The MGMA librarians are adept at answering questions dealing with all aspects of medical practice management, from business operations to human resources to strategic planning. They have helped with issues representing ongoing concerns (such as financial ratios) and emerging trends (including quality outcomes measurement and physician pay for performance). Whether a request for information arrives via telephone, Web portal, or e-mail, the librarians draw on a variety of resources to provide an answer — from MGMA surveys, industry research, and other tools and resources to industry consultants and think tanks, and the collection of industry literature and Internet resources.

The questions presented in this book review many of the most frequently asked questions received by the MGMA Information Center. Included are questions commonly asked throughout the years, as well as questions addressing current issues and emerging trends. This publication updates the content covered in *Experts Answer 101 Tough Practice Management Questions*, and it also adds many new questions reflecting the changes that continue to evolve in our ever complex and changing healthcare environment.

As in the first book, these questions were compiled, researched, answered, and then reviewed by MGMA staff and the experts in the MGMA Health Care Consulting Group for content, validity, and accuracy.

Arrangement of the 95 questions is according to the key subject domains (major areas of responsibility) as identified in the *Body of Knowledge for Medical Practice Management, 2nd Edition,* developed by the American College of Medical Practice Executives, the certification body of MGMA. The domains, which also have evolved are:

➤ Business Operations;

➤ Financial Management;

➤ Human Resources Management;

➤ Information Management;

➤ Organizational Governance;

➤ Patient Care Systems;

➤ Quality Management; and

➤ Risk Management.

Medical practice executives will find answers to some very pressing and frequently asked questions of their colleagues. Executives will also glean knowledge and resources from this title, either for help with an existing issue in the practice or for a problem that might soon require a response.

CHAPTER ONE

Business Operations

QUESTION 1 The physicians in my practice asked me to evaluate our practice operations and if we would gain anything by outsourcing some of our business operations, including billing. What are the pros and cons of outsourcing, and what are other practices doing?

There are many functions in medical practices that can be outsourced, including transcription, EHRs and other information systems, billing, collections, human resource functions, and laundry and janitorial services. The decision over contracting for services versus keeping them in house is a complicated one, and you must carefully weigh the pros and cons. An important issue is the size of your practice and the staff expertise that it can support. For example, small practices may not be able to fund an information technology expert to manage the complicated EHRs and practice management systems in today's environment.

The first step is to determine the goals of outsourcing. Is it to save costs or gain outside expertise? Are the physicians concerned about the time you're spending on certain functions, and the fact that you're needed in other areas to take the practice in a new direction?

Then consider the various benefits and disadvantages of outsourcing. The potential benefits include

➤ The increased knowledge and experience of a company that specializes in one function, which could enhance performance and quality control;

➤ The possibility of reducing expenses;

➤ Increased time to devote to other operations; and

➤ Other value-added services that the company may offer.

Factors to consider for keeping operations within the practice include

➤ Increased control over functions for quality control and compliance;

➤ Quicker implementation of changes in practice policies
   and procedures;

➤ Concerns regarding trust in contracted personnel and
   their expertise; and

➤ Cost of contracted services compared to total expenses for
   performing the function in house.

To assess the potential costs for outsourced versus in-house processes, gather as much data as you can. Investigate what the company will charge for the service and exactly what will be included
in that charge. Charges will vary depending on your specialty,
the services you request, and the rate you negotiate, but obtain
as accurate a figure as possible. Compare this figure with your
staff salary and benefit expenses for the function and the related
costs for space, supplies, and other overhead. Find out what other
practices are doing.

For example, billing services typically charge practices 6 percent
to 10 percent of collections, again depending on your specialty.
Salary expenses for patient accounting staff in multispecialty
practices average 2.7 percent of total practice net medical
revenue plus benefits, according to the *MGMA Cost Survey
for Multispecialty Practices: 2010 Report Based on 2009 Data*.
However, in a recent MGMA analysis of better-performing
medical practices, only 2.7 percent contracted out to billing
services compared with 10 percent of other surveyed practices
(*Performance and Practices of Successful Medical Groups: 2010
Report Based on 2009 Data*).

If choosing to investigate a contracting service, develop a list of
questions to ask and compare different services. Questions to ask
and items to review should include

➤ What is the company's background information, such as
   number of years in business, number of clients, and size
   and makeup of client practices?

➤ What are the terms and the length of the contract? For
   which reasons can it be terminated? Are there specific
   performance standards for the company, and what are the
   consequences if they aren't met?

➤ Does the company assume liability and the expenses related to negligent actions of its employees? Is the contractor insured?

➤ What exactly is included in the fee the company charges, and are there additional charges for record storage, account follow-up, reports, extra requests, and so on?

➤ How is communication with the practice handled? Ask to see sample reports and find out their frequency. Will one person be assigned to your practice's account? If yes, meet with that person, if possible. Does the company emphasize customer relations?

➤ How does the company train its personnel on the current issues and laws including infection control, patient and work safety, and HIPAA's regulations on privacy and confidentiality?

➤ Does the company operate with the latest technology? What backup or redundancy is in place in case of system failure or a disaster?

You will also need to draft questions specific to the function to be outsourced. For example, if you're reviewing a billing service, consider

➤ How will the practice be billed: per transaction or as a percentage of revenue or amount collected?

➤ Will the billing service's technology and reports enable comparison of reimbursements with contractual agreements, track your claims, and provide electronic error reports?

KEY POINT

 MGMA healthcare consultant Kenneth T. Hertz, FACMPE, warns, "One of the key points for me with outsourcing is the ongoing need for the administrator to 'manage' the outsource companies by establishing goals, timelines, and holding them accountable. I find too many administrators who outsource and then don't manage the process. It doesn't work that way."

Prior to contracting with a service, conduct a site visit to meet with service employees, review the software and operations, understand how the service and its employees maintain compliance, and discuss details in the contract. It's always wise to ask for and check several references for the company.

Detailed questions and ideas for the selection process are available on the MGMA Web site (www.mgma.com), including the *Selecting a Billing Service* tool.

Sources:

Jack H. Humphrey, MSHA, FACMPE, "Selection of a Medical Billing Service: Due Diligence Process," ACMPE Fellowship Paper, October 2007, www.mgma.com/WorkArea/DownloadAsset.aspx?id=23024 (accessed November 26, 2010).

Janet Marcus, CPC, "Know-How: (Billing) Help Wanted: A Guide to Selecting a Third-Party Biller," *MGMA Connexion*, February 2008, www.mgma.com/WorkArea/DownloadAsset.aspx?id=16432 (accessed November 26, 2010).

Leigh Ann Simms, CCSP, "Practice Context Determines Appropriateness of Outsourced Billing," *MGMA e-Source*, June 2007, www.mgma.com/article.aspx?id=13438 (accessed January 6, 2011).

Medical Group Management Association, *Cost Survey for Multispecialty Practices: 2010 Report Based on 2009 Data* (Englewood, CO: Medical Group Management Association, 2010).

QUESTION 2 How many physicians should there be to serve a community of our size?

The answer to your question is not as readily accessible as you would like. With the exception of government-sponsored research, there have been limited studies on the ideal physician to population ratios in the United States, and many were conducted in the 1980s and 1990s. The studies reflected the impact of market characteristics (high managed care or not) and the ideas of the authors (emphasis on primary care or specialists).

The following is a brief summary of the most frequently cited studies:

> ➤ **Graduate Medical Education National Advisory Committee (GMENAC)** — Published in 1980, this government-sponsored study remains the most widely cited.

Its physician-to-population ratio of one physician to 522 people tends to be higher than studies that take into account managed care. It concluded that primary care physicians should make up 36 percent of the physician pool and that specialists should handle 64 percent of cases.[1]

➤ **Hicks-Glenn** — In this 1989 study, physician needs were calculated by multiplying the average annual physician encounters (the population using a specialty) by the population to be served and dividing that number by the annual number of patient encounters that the specialty generally handles as determined by benchmarking data.[2]

➤ **Weiner** — This 1994 study compares traditional healthcare to a managed care environment. It provides adjusted ratios that take into account managed care population statistics such as age, gender, and Medicaid or uninsured status; patients who choose out-of-network services; and physician productivity. This study determined the lowest physician-to-population ratio of all the studies: one primary care physician per 1,538 people, and up to 30 percent fewer specialists than other models recommend.[3]

➤ **The U.S. Health Resources and Services Administration (HRSA)** — Assessment of demand-based requirements for physicians incorporating a physician supply model and requirement models. The requirement model is based on physician-to-population ratios, use patterns of physician services, and expected trends in demographics, insurance coverage, and patterns in use of health services. The Physician Workforce Report predicted an increase in demand for all specialties from 2005 to 2020 — from 9 percent for pediatrics and 30 percent for urology to 33 percent for cardiology — with most specialties needing a 20 to 25 percent increase in the number of physicians. In the year 2000, the authors predicted a need of 95 primary care physicians per populations of 100,000 and 158 nonprimary care physicians. The report was published prior to the passing of healthcare reform, which is predicted to increase the demand for primary care providers.

The HRSA report found several additional points of interest, including the increasing number of female physicians and their impact on physician requirements because of their preference for primary care and urban settings plus their different work patterns than their male counterparts. The report also concluded that increases in the number of minorities in the United States is increasing the need for minority physicians, especially African American and Hispanic physicians.[4]

Primary care physicians needed per 100,000 population by study

HRSA	Weiner	Hicks-Glenn	GMENAC
95	69 to 84 with nonphysician providers	64	69

Patient population required to support one physician

Specialty	GMENAC and Hicks-Glenn	Weiner HMO study
Family practice	3,000	6,400–10,800
Internal medicine	3,500–5,700	3,500–6,000
Pediatrics	6,700–7,800	6,700–10,800
Anesthesiology	12,000	12,000–28,000
Cardiology	16,000–31,000	34,000–62,000
General surgery	7,300–10,000	15,000–24,000
OB/GYN	9,000–10,000	9,000–11,400
Orthopedics	16,000–18,000	15,000–26,000
Radiology	14,000	13,000–23,000

Because of their age, these studies may not reflect current healthcare demands and services, and they should be used with caution. Another method is to conduct a larger analysis of the health-manpower need of your community. Follow these five steps to determine the physician need for your community:

➤ Define the geographic region that you serve. Depending on the community and your goals, you may want to include areas beyond your immediate neighborhood or community. You may need to obtain data from hospitals or local health organizations to identify the geographic perimeters of the population that seeks health services within your community.

➤ Calculate the population within the medical service area using the local chamber of commerce data or U.S. Census Bureau (www.census.gov).

➤ Identify the providers and specialties within the area using information from local business directories or your state medical board. Use only the number of active physicians, and identify the number that are 55 years of age or older whose activity level will begin to decline. The HRSA workforce studies Web site offers the Health Resources County Comparison Tool, which includes a current number of specialists per population and county demographic summaries (www.arf.hrsa.gov/arfwebtool).

➤ Gather information from your local hospitals regarding their physician staff development plans.

➤ Apply calculations from physician-to-population ratio studies, including HRSA's report.

Physician-to-population ratios are frequently used to develop a physician-needs assessment or plan for growth opportunities or other changes. Because of the debate over the studies, you should also look at additional information including

➤ Utilization of nonphysician providers and alternative medical services, including retail clinics or alternative and complementary healthcare providers;

➤ Impact of healthcare reform legislation. Massachusetts experienced an increase in demand for health services when the insured population increased after their reform was implemented;

➤ Changes in demands among your patients to identify what services they are looking for and what services are less in demand;

➤ The demographics of your community to help identify how demands may change healthcare services in the future. A young-adult population may mean an increase in births or orthopedic services, while an aging population will be looking for other services;

➤ Information from hospitals and health plans showing their recommendations for the populations they are serving; and

➤ Analysis of the competition to identify their strengths that you may not want to compete against and their weaknesses that might provide you with a competitive edge.

References:

1. Uwe E. Reinhardt, "The GMENAC Forecast: An Alternative View," *American Journal of Public Health*, V. 71, No. 10 (1981): 1149–57.

2. L. Hicks and J. Glenn, "Too Many Physicians in the Wrong Places and Specialties? Populations and Physicians from a Market Perspective," *Journal of Healthcare Marketing*, V. 9, No. 4 (1989): 18–26.

3. J.P. Weiner, "Forecasting the Effects of Health Reform on U.S. Physician Workforce Requirement," *Journal of the American Medical Association*, V. 272, No. 3 (1994): 222–30.

4. U.S. Department of Health and Human Services, Health Resources and Services Administration, Bureau of Health Professions, *The Physician Workforce: Projections and Research into Current Issues Affecting Supply and Demand*, December 2008, http://bhpr. hrsa.gov/healthworkforce/reports/physwfissues.pdf (accessed May 6, 2011).

Sources:

Daniel P. Stech, MBA, "Physician-to-Population Ratios: What Are We Really Talking About?" in *Performance and Practices of Successful Medical Groups: 2003 Report Based on 2002 Data*, Medical Group Management Association, 24–27 (Englewood, CO: Medical Group Management Association, 2003).

Randy Edwards, "Access," *H&HN: Hospitals & Health Networks*, August 2010, V. 84, No. 8, August 2010.

Stephen P. Sales, FACMPE, "Determining Provider Panel Size in a Staff-Model HMO," ACMPE Fellowship Paper, October 2006, www.mgma.com/WorkArea/DownloadAsset. aspx?id=12424 (accessed December 27, 2010).

Todd Grages, "Developing a Physician Needs Assessment," *MGMA Journal*, V. 48, No. 3, May/June 2001.

QUESTION I have just been hired as the practice administrator of a multispecialty practice. I'd like to conduct a practice assessment to see what's working and what needs to be updated. Is there any advice or tools to help me?

Conducting a practice assessment is an excellent way to review practice plans, financials, and operations. Unfortunately, practice leaders rarely conduct an assessment because day-to-day operations and putting out fires demand so much time. Conducting one now will provide you with a detailed look at the practice. Reviewing the strategic, business, and marketing plans will also provide insight into the mission, culture, and desired image of the practice.

Financial indicators and ratios are discussed in Question 10 (Financial Management, Chapter 2). However, it is also important to track several nonfinancial areas to ensure a successful practice. With the increasing emphasis on reimbursement based on quality, monitoring the practice's quality measurements is equally important (discussed in Question 77).

An excellent tool for conducting practice assessments is the *Assessment Workbook for Medical Practices, 5th Edition*. This MGMA publication walks you through the internal and external environments, the financial picture, and all operational aspects of your medical group.

The workbook provides advice on reviewing the strategic, business, and marketing plans, an excellent means of learning about a practice. Too often these guiding plans are forgotten as soon as they're written. Evaluating the plans and their implementation is an opportunity to review the practice's mission, vision, and commitment and to identify opportunities for new directions. It will also help you identify the priorities and goals of your new position. You should proceed carefully, though, as a new employee, to not challenge what some practice members may hold dear.

STRATEGIC PLANS

The strategic plan should be the groundwork for everything the practice does; it aligns the practice with its vision, mission, and how it will implement other plans and operations. Goals and objectives are keys to determining the direction of the organization. You should review the following key questions related to the strategic plan and its effectiveness with the physician leadership:

➤ Do the mission and vision statements provide direction to the practice's desired future, as stated by the leadership and stakeholders?

➤ Are goals defined targets that orient the practice's activities?

➤ Do the objectives align with the goals and define measures of success?

➤ Is the plan current, and are practice activities in line with meeting goals and objectives?

➤ Was development of the strategic plan based on a SWOT analysis (strengths, weaknesses, opportunities, and threats)?

Practices should periodically review the strategic plan to ensure that the goals and objectives are current and valid, that practice activities are directed toward meeting the goals and objectives, and that the practice culture supports the plan and objectives.

BUSINESS PLANS

Business plans support the strategic plan and are directed by the mission and vision statements. There are several types of business plans: operational, financial, feasibility, and financing. Feasibility plans analyze a proposed new service and should include a SWOT analysis, market analysis, and detailed financial analysis and address legal and regulatory issues, referrals, and payers.

Business plans and operational plans should be developed with participation and consensus of interested stakeholders. The board or appropriate practice leadership approves them. If there is a business plan in place, review the following questions:

➤ When was the plan last reviewed and updated?

➤ Does the practice budget reflect the priorities specified in the plan?

➤ Are activities in the plan directed toward meeting strategic plan goals and objectives?

➤ Is the leadership committed to the business plan?

➤ Are practice operations following the business plan?

Success of business and operational plans requires the following features:

➤ Governance and management structures are in place to implement the plan;

➤ Action items are identified;

➤ Responsibilities are assigned, including follow-up assignments;

➤ Reasonable timelines have been developed; and

➤ Operations are reviewed and redirected toward the plan, or the plan is adjusted as necessary.

MARKETING PLANS

Each practice should have a marketing plan; it ensures that the practice identifies and remains focused on its customers and vocalizes that focus to the community and the employees. Marketing is identifying and communicating value to the customer. Conducting market analyses and developing the marketing plan ensures connectivity to the community and its potential customers.

Developing the customer focus starts with the following:

➤ Identifying potential market segments and understanding their motivation related to healthcare services.

➤ Identifying key relationships including referring physicians, payers, vendors, and hospitals.

➤ Ensuring that service and outcomes meet or exceed customer expectations.

Contents of the marketing plan:

➤ Reference to and alignment with the mission, vision, and strategic plan.

➤ Competitive analysis that identifies key and potential competitors and their strengths and weaknesses.

➤ Demographic analysis to identify market segments, their needs, and their buying decisions.

➤ Strengths of the practice and unique characteristics or services.

➤ Review of patient satisfaction or outcomes measures.

➤ Development of a marketing message that is clear and distinctive.

➤ Assessment of advertising and promotion options, including electronic media, and their effectiveness for the market and customers.

➤ Timeline for testing and reviewing the effectiveness of messages and promotions.

A component of marketing efforts is developing the brand and image for the practice. Did the practice bring in a consultant to identify the practice image? Is it still effective and true for the practice? Are the brand and image reflected consistently in promotional materials?

Previous efforts at public relations should be evaluated, including the use of press releases to announce new physicians, services, or facilities. Providers should also be aware of the value of participating in community organizations and events, including local boards and health fairs and providing educational events.

If done properly, reviewing these plans and their related activities should provide an assessment of the organization's mission and goals and the operational success in reaching these goals.

Sources:

Carolyn Pickles, MBA, FACMPE, and Alys Novak, MBA, *Assessment Workbook for Medical Practices, 5th Edition* (Englewood, CO: Medical Group Management Association, 2011).

QUESTION How do I determine the fair market value of my medical practice?

4

The value of a medical practice is determined for several different reasons: inclusion in a buy/sell agreement, to sell or buy another practice, or in legal issues such as those related to divorce or taxes. The reason for the valuation will affect the calculation, but the general concepts are the same. As Reed Tinsley, consultant, and Mark Dietrich, medical practice appraiser, state

➤ The strength of the practice's income stream and what it produces for the owner(s) is what creates true value in a medical practice; and

➤ The key to a successful valuation is deciding whether the practice's future income stream will mirror its present one.

There are many experienced practice appraisers or consultants to help in your practice valuation. Based on the reason for the valuation, they can advise on the best method for determining valuation, have access to comparable sales data, and assess the practice's characteristics, patient demographics, community need, and other factors to assist in calculating the fair market value.

The IRS defines fair market value as the price at which property would change hands between a buyer and a seller, neither having to buy nor sell, and both having reasonable knowledge of all necessary facts. Therefore, there is no additional incentive or stress affecting the valuation.

There are three major categories of valuation methodologies applicable to medical practices:

1. Income based, determined by cash flow or earnings;

2. Cost or asset based, calculated by determining the value of the assets minus the liabilities; and

3. Market based, which incorporates data from sales of comparable practices.

Market-based valuations are difficult in medical practices because of limited sales data and the variety of factors affecting practice sales.

For asset-based valuations, an appraiser will look at hard assets (furniture, building, and equipment), accounts receivable (A/R), and intangible assets or goodwill. Hard assets can be calculated using book value or appraised values. Many buyers are no longer interested in purchasing accounts receivable and expect the practice seller to collect it. Physicians buying into a practice shouldn't be required to pay for A/R unless the collections will be distributed to them equally, and only A/R less than six months old should be included.

Medical records and the practice's expected continued reputation have been used in determining goodwill; however, the use of goodwill in medical practice valuations has declined. Physicians are wary of using goodwill in buy-in agreements since it raises the value and the difficulty for new physicians to buy in. The IRS has declared a value for medical records ($12–$22), so a greater value for expected business can't be developed. Hospitals won't consider goodwill when purchasing a practice because of anti-kickback and Stark regulations, and the future performance of the practice will be paid to the hospital under the agreement with the physician.

Some accountants and appraisers prefer income-based approaches. Two methods can be applied: (1) the capitalization of earnings and (2) the capitalization of excess earnings. Income from ancillary services should be included in the total income for valuation purposes.

Sources:

1. Reed Tinsley, CPA, "How Much Is a Medical Practice Worth?" *MGMA e-Source*, July 28, 2009, www.mgma.com/article.aspx?id=29774 (accessed November 29, 2010).

2. Bob Redling, "Appraisals: What's Your Practice Worth?" *Physicians Practice*, V. 18, No. 11, July 15, 2008.

Becky L. Ayers, FACMPE, "Shopping for Size: To Buy or Not to Buy," *MGMA Connexion*, December 2008, www.mgma.com/WorkArea/DownloadAsset.aspx?id=24340 (accessed November 29, 2010).

Hobart Collins, MA, CMPE, "Grabbing — or Releasing — the Brass Ring: Strategic Buy/ Sell Agreement Considerations," *MGMA Connexion* special article reprint, 2008, www. mgma.com/WorkArea/DownloadAsset.aspx?id=16348 (accessed November 29, 2010).

Mark O. Dietrich, "Medical Practices: A BVRx," *Journal of Accountancy*, V. 200, No. 5 (November 2005): 45–50.

QUESTION 5 I'm looking for ways to increase patient volume and get more out of our marketing efforts. Are the Internet and social media the way to go?

The importance of your practice Web site and Internet social media will continue to grow as Americans' use of the Internet increases, including seeking information about physicians and their services. However, it is just one tool and should be incorporated into your total marketing plan and effort.

Before jumping from one new marketing effort to the next, you need to identify the marketing strategies and your audience. Marketing plans should be based on strategic plans and should identify the vision for the practice, your target audience, and future plans or new growth areas. Identify what makes your practice unique in your marketplace, either in types of services or quality of care, and how to use that in your marketing efforts. (See Question 3.)

Marketing goals should be developed that are measurable and include specific time periods. For example: increase by 5 percent the number of female patients who are 25 to 35 years of age within one year of implementing the plan. Goals may include increasing awareness of the practice, growing the market share for your specialty, expanding the number of referring physicians, or increasing patients from a favorable payer.

The majority of medical practices' promotional efforts rely on maintaining current patients and referrals and using their recommendations to increase patients and referrals. Relying on these tried-and-true methods doesn't mean maintaining the status quo. Look for ways to improve customer service to ensure patients stay with the practice and refer their friends and family to your practice. Use various means to promote other services to your patients, including signs around the practice or comments made by receptionists and providers. You don't want patients going to other locations for services that your practice offers.

Referring physicians should be surveyed to identify any potential issues that would impact their relationship with your practice. Difficulty in contacting your practice and scheduling appointments or delays in hearing the results of the referral can decrease satisfaction. Build the relationship with referring physicians by responding quickly and sharing information about new services, new physicians, and new medical information.

INTERNET PROMOTIONS

The Internet and social media are tools to increase patient and referring-physician satisfaction and to gain new patients and referrals. Web sites are the Yellow Pages of the future — directory listings that advertise practices' hours, locations, and services. Web sites are convenient ways to provide more information and services beyond an ad or promotional brochure. They should include helpful, solid information and opportunities to engage users. As Web sites for other types of businesses expand their functionality, patients will expect more from their physicians' sites, including interactivity and even live scheduling through a patient portal.

The style of the Web site should match other promotional efforts through consistent use of logos and messages. The content and opportunity to build trust are more important than the flashiness. Relationship building can be done through

> ➤ **Blogging.** Its conversational style is an appealing way to share information with a personal spin.

> ➤ **Videos.** Patients' testimonial videos will connect more to other patients, but physicians discussing new procedures or research may appeal to other physicians.

> ➤ **Q&A areas.** These encourage participation and share information. Place additional Q&A areas near specialty or procedure information. Make sure questions are checked and answered regularly.

The Web site should be designed with your patient population in mind. Specific groups within your population can be reached by using links on the home page. Patients from different ethnic groups, age groups, or with chronic-care conditions will appreciate that you recognize their special needs and interests. Note if your providers speak other languages. Provide a separate link for referring physicians to view different information than patients.

Work with your Web site manager or provider to ensure your site is search engine optimized (SEO). This includes registering it with the largest search engines (Google, Bing, Yahoo, and so on) and formatting the site with your practice's name in the meta title and on every page. Make sure your Web site is located using key words such as your specialty, city or region, and services that you provide. Have your Web site provider or manager study the use of your Internet site to identify points of access, frequently viewed pages, occasional problem areas, and so on to constantly improve the site. You should also be investigating how to develop a patient portal as part of your Web site to improve interaction with your patients (discussed more in Question 42).

E-mail can be used appropriately to remind patients of annual appointments and promote new services or physicians and upcoming events. There is a danger in being accused of sending spam, so use e-mail on a limited basis and only with permission from recipients. Modify current patient registration or other forms, and develop a Web page for obtaining patients' e-mails and their permission. Then include options to opt out of e-mail communication within your e-mails.

The Internet's social media can also be used to connect to current patients and reach out to others in a more accepting way. There's no guarantee these efforts will increase the number of patients or referrals, but they can increase the traffic to your Web site. Engaged customers will remain satisfied customers and are more apt to refer others to you. Participants should always be cautious to ensure medical advice is not inappropriately provided in social media communications. With care, the Internet can be a great tool.

KEY POINT

MGMA Health Care consultant Kenneth T. Hertz, FACMPE, reminds us that "Practices need to understand that maintaining the Web site and social media requires resources: people, time, expertise, and in some cases, money. In order for these tools to be successful, they must have ongoing attention, [be] kept fresh and current, and [be] used as components of a thoughtful marketing plan."

Start with the basic social media: Facebook, with its hundreds of millions of participants, Twitter, and YouTube. Current staff members or providers may already be active users and can assist in using Twitter or setting up a Facebook page. Identify physicians within the practice interested in participating and contributing information. Twitter is used to share information, publicize events, such as open houses or free screenings, and connect with patients in "tweets" limited to 140 characters. Facebook offers options for setting up pages for places of business or the usual individual's page. Group practices currently use Facebook to

➤ Share medical and procedure information, including links to relevant articles;

➤ Post photos of providers, the employee of the month, interiors of the practice, and practice events;

➤ Encourage patients to post photos, including photos of children delivered by the practice's OB/GYN physicians;

➤ Develop a "fitness challenge" with a weekly activity and photos of patients participating in last week's challenge;

➤ Present questions and answers with valuable content and timely responses; and

➤ Link patients' YouTube videos to their testimonials.

Social media is a great way to reach your audience, but it can also be used to spread dissatisfaction and negative experiences.

Someone in your practice should monitor the social media to identify issues before they "go viral." It is possible to counter the posts by asking the person to contact the practice so the situation can be rectified and commenting that the practice will be implementing necessary changes. The practice's respondent should always be upfront about their identity and not pretend to be a patient with a counter impression.

The Internet and social media are constantly growing and changing, providing people with new opportunities to participate, promote, and connect. Medical practices must be aware of and use the new media to maintain customer relationships and change with the population.

Case Studies

North Florida Women's Care in Tallahassee, Fla., developed a practice Facebook page with a practice newsletter, a photo album of the providers, photos of employees of the quarter, upcoming events, and special recognitions for the practice. The page now has over 500 fans, and a tweet is sent automatically when the page is updated. They created a Facebook ad to drive business to the page and were able to target specific demographics. CEO Bill Hambsh plans on adding discussions on health topics. He confesses "I am a Facebook junky. I love it as much as my Blackberry."

Source: Bill Hambsh, via e-mail communication with author, January 23, 2011.

Henry Ford Health System in Detroit used a combination of Internet-based techniques to increase patient visits and revenue during the recent recession. Practice providers began sending tweets during live surgeries. The effort was picked up by the online and general media and led to wide publicity.

The public relations department used blogs with videos and edgy titles like "Baby Blunders, Secrets of Spit, and Can Viagra Rewire Your Brain?" The most popular blog was from a physician who posted comments and photos while volunteering in Haiti after the 2010 earthquake.

(continued)

A campaign to increase mammograms used a Facebook application urging women to schedule appointments and share the push with their friends and family. The Facebook page included news articles, upcoming events, testimonials, and photos related to breast cancer. A link to the Henry Ford Web site was included as well as an online scheduling function. The total campaign increased mammogram appointments by 161 percent over the previous year.

Source: Rose Glenn, "Growth in a Parched Economy," *Marketing Health Services*, V. 30, Issue 2 (2010): 10–13.

Sources:

Andrew Neitlich, "Why Marketing Is Not a Dirty Word," *MGMA Connexion*, January 2007, www.mgma.com/WorkArea/mgma_downloadasset.aspx?id=11016 (accessed January 20, 2011).

Andrew Roberts, "Tomorrow Has Arrived," *Marketing Health Services*, V. 30, No. 2 (2010): 30–31.

Bret Pollard, "5 of the Best Facebook Medical Practice Fan Pages," *Alert Presence* blog, February 8, 2010, www.alertpresence.com/2010/02/08/5-of-the-best-facebook-medical-practice-fan-pages (accessed January 21, 2011).

Caren Baginski, "Tips to Increase Your Medical Practice Web site's SEO," MGMA *In Practice* blog, May 4, 2009, http://blog.mgma.com/blog/bid/20325/Tips-to-increase-your-medical-practice-Web-site-s-SEO (accessed March 11, 2011).

David Duchek, "Web Marketing Is More Than Just an Online Brochure," *Ophthalmology Times*, October 15, 2008, www.modernmedicine.com/modernmedicine/Practice+Management/Web-marketing-is-more-than-just-an-online-brochure/ArticleStandard/Article/detail/559879 (accessed January 21, 2011).

Jamie Verkamp, "Social Media as a Way to Connect with Patients," *MGMA Connexion*, July 2010.

Patrick T. Buckley, MPA, "Your Practice's Marketing Toolkit," *Medical Economics*, December 17, 2010, www.modernmedicine.com/modernmedicine/Modern+Medicine+Now/Your-practices-marketing-toolkit/ArticleStandard/Article/detail/700596 (accessed January 20, 2011).

Robin Segbers, "Go Where the Customers Are," *Marketing Health Services*, V. 30, No. 1 (2010): 22–25.

QUESTION Several of the physicians in my practice are complaining that our facility isn't big enough. What resources are available for comparing square footage, number of exam rooms, and other facility data for medical practices?

MGMA offers three resources with information on medical group practice facilities:

1. *Information Exchange* #3410, "Space Planning," is an informal questionnaire asking medical groups about their number and size of exam and treatment rooms. The results from the questionnaire show that the typical number of rooms per physician is two to three rooms. This document also includes sample floor plans from several responding practices.

2. The annual *Cost Survey Reports* include data on total square footage and square feet per full-time-equivalent (FTE) physician. The report includes information for multispecialty practices and many individual specialties. The following table is an example of the data from the *Cost Survey: 2010 Report Based on 2009 Data*:

Practice type	Median number of square feet per FTE physician
Multispecialty	2,170
Family practice	2,132
Pediatrics	1,722
Anesthesiology	109
Cardiology	1,931
Gastroenterology	1,860
Orthopedic surgery	2,749
Obstetrics and gynecology	1,912
Urology	2,189

3. *Medical and Dental Space Planning: A Comprehensive Guide to Design, Equipment, and Clinical Procedures,*

3rd Edition, by Jain Malkin, provides detailed space requirements and floor plans, along with interior design and layout ideas for pleasant and efficient medical facilities.

If your facility has less square footage than the above medians, it may be time to expand your current facility or move to a new facility. If the facility is within the medians, you should evaluate the current floor plan and space utilization. There may be a means of using your current space more efficiently to improve operational flows. Analyze your current processes, work flows, staffing, and scheduling related to the layout. Are there ways of modifying the schedule or adjusting work flows to increase efficiency of the space? Are all of the exam rooms fully utilized? Does the practice offer new services with new technology that demand more room? Is the complaint related to the lack of *office* space or *clinical* space? Is renovating your current facility an option? Renovation can be very disruptive, but it may be beneficial in the long run and doesn't require your patients to follow you to a new location.

A CLOSER LOOK . . .

Evidence-Based Design

Is dissatisfaction with the current facility related to space requirements or interior design and functionality? Evidence-based design (EBD) is influencing the design of healthcare facilities. The intent is to design spaces to improve clinical outcomes, economic performance, productivity, patient satisfaction, and cultural considerations. Some recommendations for incorporating EBD include

- ➤ Using natural light;
- ➤ Allowing natural ventilation;
- ➤ Incorporating nature throughout and among buildings (gardens, courtyards, indoor plants, windows, and so on);
- ➤ Building with local, natural materials;
- ➤ Using aquariums, fountains, and other water features;
- ➤ Reducing environmental stressors like noise and glare; and

➤ Incorporating features that provide privacy and space for patient visitors.

Sources:

Center for Health Design, "Challenges Aside, EBD Promises to Help Organizations Meet Health Care Demands through the Application of Solutions Based on Research," www.healthdesign.org (accessed January 22, 2011).

Kathi Levell, FACMPE, "Evidence-Based Design: Facilities Promote Safety, Health for Patients and Staff," *MGMA e-Source*, June 24, 2008, www.mgma.com/article. aspx?id=20064 (accessed January 22, 2011).

Sources:

Jain Malkin, *Medical and Dental Space Planning: A Comprehensive Guide to Design, Equipment, and Clinical Procedures, 3rd Edition* (Hoboken, NJ: John Wiley & Sons, 2002).

Medical Group Management Association, *Cost Survey for Multispecialty Practices: 2010 Report Based on 2009 Data* (Englewood, CO: Medical Group Management Association, 2010).

Medical Group Management Association, *Cost Survey for Single-Specialty Practices: 2010 Report Based on 2009 Data* (Englewood, CO: Medical Group Management Association, 2010).

Robert I. Freedman, Esq., "Planning a New Medical Office Space," *Medscape Business of Medicine*, April 13, 2007, www.medscape.com/viewarticle/554115 (accessed January 22, 2011).

QUESTION 7 We'd like to add ancillary services or a new service line to increase the practice revenue. What should we do to get started in the process?

Many medical practices seek additional revenue opportunities by expanding the services they provide, including offering ancillary services or developing new service lines. Success in pursuing these options will only come with the right strategy, physician buy-in, and a carefully planned approach. Open discussions should occur among physicians and practice leadership regarding the decision to offer a new service line. A planned approach calls for an in-depth feasibility study with an honest assessment of the potential risks and rewards prior to making a decision.

Start by discussing options with practice physicians and leadership. Compose a list of options gained from industry knowledge and research. Don't jump on ideas that a physician heard about from a colleague. Ask, "What types of services are consistent with our core specialties and business activities that we're not delivering today?" Are there services that aren't being offered in your community or area at this time? What is the reason for adding the service line: just to increase revenue, or is it filling a needed niche in the marketplace? Will it improve continuity of care? What is the future of the service and payment for it? You should consider the ongoing shift in payment for healthcare services, discussion within the Centers for Medicare and Medicaid Services (CMS) for any changes, and whether new technology and demographics will shift away from the service or increase demand for it.

Opportunities include diagnostic services, in-office clinical laboratories, ambulatory or specialty surgery centers, urgent care or retail health centers, and alternative or complementary therapies. Primary care practices may add MRI, CT, echocardiography, bone densitometry, and other imaging services. Specialty practices may also choose imaging and diagnostic services in addition to new procedures. Some examples include physical therapy, nuclear medicine, in-office catheterization, bariatric surgery, cosmetic services, and vein clinics.

The MGMA Web site includes a checklist to assess the legal, regulatory, and other issues involved in the development of new services. "The Entrepreneurial Health Care — A Checklist for Legal Compliance and Business Success," developed by Bruce A. Johnson, Esq., of the MGMA Health Care Consulting Group, addresses such issues as who will own the venture, who will provide the services, what services will be provided, and how the start-up will be funded. The checklist is located at mgma.com under "Member Benefits and Communities" and "Risk Management Tools" or under "Consulting" and tools.

FEASIBILITY STUDY

If the initial discussions convince everyone to pursue the idea, then you will need to develop a feasibility study to determine its viability. The study should be a thorough analysis that will raise serious questions and determine the potential for the venture's financial and business success. It will also aid in the later development of a business plan. MGMA and medical associations can be sources of financial data including compensation figures, operating costs, and total charges.

The feasibility study will address several issues, including

➤ Organizational structure and governance of the practice and potential management and staffing of the new service. What can be handled within the current structure and staffing, and what additions will be needed? What structure is needed for compliance with state and federal regulations?

➤ What are the applicable state and federal regulations related to reimbursement, ownership, licensing, and certificates of need? Is there any discussion of changes that could impact reimbursement or operating the service or specialty clinic? Medicare and other payers are investigating the growth in physician office diagnostic imaging services and may implement changes.

➤ What new technology will be needed, and what are the purchase and operational costs? Include computer hardware along with medical equipment.

➤ Are specialized providers and technicians needed? What is their availability and compensation range? If a current physician is receiving training, will the expected licensure or certificate and experience be in place with the planned opening?

➤ What are the trends for the service and related medical research? Is it approaching market saturation? Will new medical techniques and healthcare reform measures increase or decrease the demand for the service? What about changes in the population and economics of your area? Don't expect past trends to carry into the future.

➤ Conduct a market analysis to ensure there will be enough demand for the service:

➤ How many times do you refer patients to other locations for the service? Have staff record the number of times a patient asks about a service.

> ➤ Do competitors currently offer the same service? Do you have advantages over the competitor, or is there demand for more services in the area?

> ➤ Analyze the demographics of your community and surrounding area. Will there be an expanding population, especially in the population that requests this service? How far away is the next community with the service?

> ➤ Discuss the idea with referring physicians to see if they would refer patients to you for the service. Approach major employers in the area about services to which they may refer employees.

> ➤ Develop a worst case, best case, and most likely case in developing utilization numbers. Be aware that there is a tendency to exaggerate the predicted utilization rate.

➤ Look at the reimbursement issues. Who are the major health payers in your market, and what are their reimbursement policies for the service? Do they already have preferred providers for the service, or will they include your service in their network? Will you need new contracts? Do they require accreditation? What services are not covered by Medicare? Will there be enough demand from non-Medicare patients or self-pay patients?

➤ Develop a financial analysis to determine the start-up and operating costs, expected revenue over several years, and financing requirements. Do your research and be realistic with these figures. Be sure to calculate operating costs, such as staff salaries and benefits, which will occur until the break-even point. What are the costs to retrofit a currently owned facility or lease or purchase a new building?

➤ How much financing will be needed to fund the start-up and initial operations? Will the funding come from current equity or credit sources? Lenders will need accurate predictions including actual reimbursement rates, not what you plan on charging.

Once you've completed the feasibility study with a detailed market analysis and financial projections, it's time to carefully review the assumptions that were made. Were they realistic? Do the projections show a steady increase in income over expenses? What are the risks versus rewards for building the service line? Be prepared for a negative result and the decision not to proceed.

Sources:

Courtney Price, *Medical Practice Ultimate Feasibility & Pre-Planning Workbook* (Englewood, CO: Medical Group Management Association, 2008).

Donna K. Knapp, MA, FACMPE, "Sleep Medicine: No Sleeper When It Comes to Profits," *MGMA Connexion*, October 2010, www.mgma.com/WorkArea/mgma_downloadasset. aspx?id=39567.

Judy A. Montgomery, MBA,CPA, FACMPE, "Developing a Heart Surgery Program," *MGMA e-Source*, January 8, 2008, www.mgma.com/article.aspx?id=15938 (accessed February 11, 2011).

Ken Brockman, CPA, "How to Perform a Feasibility Study and Market Analysis to Determine if an Ancillary Service Makes Sense," in *Orthopedic Ancillary Services: A Guide to Practice Management*, by Jack M. Bert, MD, 5–10 (New York: Elsevier, Inc., 2008).

Trip Kinmon, FACMPE, "The Imaging Dilemma: Is This Service Line Worth the Money?" *MGMA Connexion*, April 2010, www.mgma.com/WorkArea/mgma_downloadasset. aspx?id=33268 (accessed February 11, 2011).

Case Studies

An orthopedic practice considered three options for providing physical therapy and decided on the physician-owned option by integrating it into the practice. Benefits included greatest control over the service and fiscal decisions and implementing a management structure aligned with the practice's culture and expectations. Steps in implementing the decision included

- ➤ Hiring a qualified manager;

- ➤ Conducting site visits of similar practices with physical therapy (PT) services;

- ➤ Learning about the intricacies of billing and reimbursement for PT; and

- ➤ Understanding federal, Medicare, and state regulations and requirements.

Lessons learned included careful deliberation of the options leading to a better model rather than the initial, rushed idea.

(continued)

Source: Harry W. Cartwright Jr., FACMPE, "Developing and Implementing Physical Therapy Services in a Medical Practice Setting," ACMPE Paper, October 2009, www.mgma.com/WorkArea/mgma_downloadasset. aspx?id=30744 (accessed February 11, 2011).

The Urology of Indiana practice developed bladder-control centers after experiencing a growth in demand. A service line committee manages the strategic development; the service line director implements the strategies; and medical and clinical directors oversee the operations, training, and quality programs. The practice promoted the clinics directly to referring physicians and to patients using local TV commercials. Increases in total charges averaged almost 30 percent each year in the first four years of operation.

Source: Matthew Vuletich, "Bladder-Control Centers Bolster Practice's Charges, *MGMA e-Source*, August 14, 2007, www.mgma.com/article. aspx?id=14122 (accessed February 11, 2011).

Many physicians choose to open sleep disorder clinics. The American Academy of Sleep Medicine (AASM) accredited more than 2,000 centers in 2010, and the American Board of Medical Specialties (ABMS) recognizes sleep medicine as a subspecialty. However, there are several factors affecting the future of sleep disorder clinics:

➤ Development of home sleep testing impacting the need for centers;

➤ Shift in requiring centers to show results from treatment not just effective diagnosis;

➤ Shortages of qualified personnel;

➤ Increased scrutiny by payers and regulating and accrediting bodies; and

➤ Patients' search for alternative treatments.

Similar factors could affect revenue for other specialty clinics and services.

Source: Donna K. Knapp, MA, FACMPE, "Sleep Medicine: No Sleeper When It Comes to Profits," *MGMA Connexion*, October 2010, www.mgma. com/WorkArea/mgma_downloadasset.aspx?id=39567 (accessed February 11, 2011).

QUESTION

8

I've heard of other practices starting urgent care centers or retail clinics to bring in additional revenue. What's involved in starting one, and what's the expected return?

Starting any new business or service requires analysis of the goals of the practice in starting the service, the costs related to startup and operation, and the expected return. Many practices are considering opening new service lines, such as urgent care centers (UCCs) or retail clinics, for additional revenue and to increase patient volume.

The National Association for Ambulatory Care defines UCCs as

> "walk-in ambulatory care centers, generally open seven (7) days each week often 13 or more hours each day. No appointment is required for a patient to receive care. These centers have a broad array of diagnostic and therapeutic services, often including x-ray, laboratory testing, on-site pharmacy, procedure rooms for laceration and fracture care, exam rooms, and specialized corporate services for employee health and workers' compensation cases."

Retail clinics are also walk-in clinics, but they are located within grocery stores, drugstores, and general retailers, including Wal-Mart, Target, CVS/Pharmacy, and Walgreens. They offer a variety of diagnostic and treatment services for common medical conditions, as well as preventive and wellness services, but retail clinics are usually more limited in services than UCCs. Nurse practitioners (NPs) and, occasionally, physician assistants (PAs) frequently staff retail centers. Their numbers have grown rapidly, and reimbursement has shifted from an initial emphasis on cash-based services to insurance coverage.

Prior to deciding to open an urgent care or retail clinic, several planning steps are recommended:

> ➤ **Develop a strategic plan identifying the goals and action plans for the clinic.** Is it to increase revenue, build patient volume by reaching another audience, improve

quality of medical services for a specific population, or build one before a competitor does? Conduct a market analysis on competing services in place, typical patient volume, types of services, and average fees. Develop a marketing plan.

Will you offer occupational medical services to nearby businesses? Possible occupational medicine services include pre-placement exams, drug screening, and health promotion services along with nonemergency injury and illness visits. The center's medical director and administrator can meet with business representatives to promote services.

➤ **Develop a pro forma for the business.** Determine start-up costs: Will you buy or lease a facility or convert part of your practice? Total the expenses for information and communications equipment and programs, medical equipment, furniture, supplies, and marketing. If a retailer has space for your retail clinic, what will be the rent and the expected budget for renovating the space? Calculate the ongoing expenses.

Depending on the services you plan to offer, what kind of staff will you need, and what are the average salaries? Determine the coverage needed for extended hours, including evenings and weekends.

What revenue can you expect? Determine average patient visits and services from industry resources. UCCs typically charge 150 percent to 200 percent of Medicare's fee schedule but investigate the reimbursement rates of major payers' in your area. Fees at retail clinics vary by market and service, from $25 for vaccinations to $110 for more involved services. What are the clinics in your market charging? How many self-pay patients will there be, and will you offer cash discounts? The National Association for Ambulatory Care (www.urgentcare.org) and Urgent Care Association of America (www.ucaoa.org) offer resources.

Compare the expected costs and revenue to determine the feasibility of the clinic. If needed, can you increase revenue by offering additional services? Retail clinics have been less successful at generating a profit but may provide benefit in increasing referrals. Be reasonable in your expectations.

➤ **Assess the federal, state, and local regulations and requirements for your type of clinic.** Check state regulations for license and marketing requirements and regulations affecting the corporate practice of medicine. California, Colorado, Illinois, Iowa, New Jersey, New York, and Texas require a physician owner. UCCs are exempt from the Emergency Medical Treatment and Active Labor Act (EMTALA) unless the center is hospital owned or on the campus of a hospital.

Retail clinics will be restricted by a state's scope of practice regulations. Forty-three states now enable nurse practitioners (NPs) to practice independently or in remote collaboration with physicians. All states provide NPs with some authority to write prescriptions. Check your state's requirements for scope of practice and requirements for physician supervision.

➤ **Prepare to open the clinic.** Negotiate with payers and initiate the provider credentialing process. Select a director, implement the marketing plan, prepare the facility, and purchase the equipment and supplies; purchase the information systems; and hire and train the staff.

Keys to a successful UCC include

➤ **Being located in a high-profile, high-traffic area.** Patients are more apt to visit if they've seen the facility prior to wanting the service. The location needs easy access and plenty of parking. If offering occupational medical services, is the location convenient to several large employers?

➤ **Offering a variety of services expands options, potential referrals, and reimbursement.** Typical visits to UCCs are for injuries from recreation and construction activities in the summer and illnesses during the flu and allergy seasons.

➤ **Extending appropriate pricing for population and competition.** Charges should be lower than emergency room rates but at a level that is in line with insurers' reimbursements. Self-pay or cash-paying customers will appreciate discounts or bundled payments.

➤ **Developing a successful advertising program that identifies target markets and effective means to reach them.** Pediatric audiences can be reached at locations where children and parents gather. Local construction or recreation publications can be targeted for seasonal injuries. A Web site should be developed and social media should be utilized to promote the center.

➤ **Employing professional and customer-service-oriented staff and physicians.** This includes providers who are experienced and comfortable dealing with a variety of cases, and choosing front-desk staff members with excellent customer relation skills. Word of mouth will become a major recruiting tool if customers are impressed with the quality of care and service.

➤ **Optimizing patient flow to minimize wait times.** Although difficult to manage and predict with walk-in appointments, it is important to customer satisfaction. Consider cross-training staff to handle a variety of responsibilities and minimize wait time. Part-time staff can assist during high-traffic times. The waiting area should be welcoming and include entertainment (TV, magazines, and so on) to relieve the wait.

➤ **Ensuring collections at the time of service, and checking insurance coverage for UCCs.** Some insurance plans specify "no urgent care benefit." Negotiate with payers and employers on contracted rates.

Case Study

An MGMA member practice decided to open a retail clinic after negotiating with several retailers in the community. An NP was hired, and a physician agreed to serve as the NP's supervisor. Initially a cash-only operation, the clinic had to include insurance billing after several patients complained, but the increased costs were offset by the increased volume. The practice realized an increase in referrals from the clinic and received $75,000 in net profits the first two years the retail clinic was open.

Source: J. Travis Dowell, MBA, FACMPE, "How a Retail Clinic Can Make Money for the Medical Group Practice," ACMPE Fellowship Paper, October 2007, www.mgma.com/WorkArea/mgma_downloadasset.aspx?id=16248 (accessed February 11, 2011).

Sources:

Alan A. Ayers, MBA, "Minding Your Urgent Care Ps and Qs," *Journal of Urgent Care Medicine*, June 2008, 26–29, http://viewer.zmags.com/publication/734bc2ad#/734bc2ad/28 (accessed February 9, 2011).

Alan A. Ayers, MBA, "Playing to Win: Maximizing Profits in Urgent Care," *Journal of Urgent Care Medicine*, April 2008, http://viewer.zmags.com/publication/534d82a9#/534d82a9/34 (accessed February 9, 2011).

Amer Kaissi, "Hospital-Affiliated and Hospital-Owned Retail Clinics: Strategic Opportunities and Operational Challenges," *American Journal of Healthcare Management*, V. 55, No. 5 (2010): 324–37.

Daniel P. Stech, MBA, Darrell L. Schryver, DPA, and Bruce A. Johnson, JD, MPA, "Checklist for New Practice Start-Up," Medical Group Management Association, www.mgma.com/WorkArea/mgma_downloadasset.aspx?id=5566 (accessed February 9, 2011).

Donna Lee Gardner, RN, MS, "Creating a Health Surveillance Product Line," *Journal of Urgent Care Medicine*, April 2008, www.jucm.com/magazine/index.php?mid=534d82a9&page=30 (accessed February 9, 2011).

Kaj Rozga, "Retail Health Clinics: How the Next Innovation in Market-Driven Healthcare is Testing State and Federal Law," *American Journal of Law & Medicine*, V. 35, No. 1 (2009): 205–231. (accessed February 9, 2011).

National Association for Ambulatory Care, "Frequently Asked Questions," 2011, www.urgentcare.org/FAQs/tabid/135/Default.aspx

Urgent Care Association of America, www.ucaoa.org

QUESTION 9

One of my physicians is thinking of leaving to develop a retainer or concierge practice. Do you have information to help him get started?

Some primary care physicians, growing increasingly frustrated over dealing with the bureaucracy of health insurance plans and Medicare and decreasing time with patients, are looking for alternatives that enable them to concentrate on patients without the overhead of payers' demands.

Cash-only practices require patients to pay at the time of service either with cash, check, or debit or credit cards. Claims are not submitted to insurance companies, although patients can file their own claims. Practices have lower operating costs since they don't process and submit claims, follow up on denied claims, or bill for the patient's charges. Payers and state regulations may limit the ability to directly bill insured patients. Medicare regulations prohibit providers from charging cash-only patients in excess of the usual charges, so many physicians choose to opt out of Medicare.

A version of a cash-only practice is a concierge or retainer practice. These practices have fewer patients who usually pay just an annual "retainer" fee or an annual fee and a fee for each service. Patients receive extra services, including house calls and access to the physician at any time. Concierge practices may bill insurers for covered services. They see a variety of patients: more health-conscious patients, urban professionals, patients with complicated health conditions that demand more time, and the affluent. Noncovered services that may be provided by a concierge practice include wellness planning, smoking cessation, exercise management, and nutrition.

The Government Accountability Office conducted a survey of concierge practices in 2004. It identified only 146 practices at that time, with the majority located on the East and West coasts. The majority charged annual fees between $1,500 and $2,000 for same-day or next-day appointments, 24-hour telephone access, and preventive care examinations. Two-thirds of the respond-

A LOOK AT THE NUMBERS . . .

1
2
3

Results from a 2006 survey of 144 retainer or concierge practices:

➤ Mean patient panel size: 898 patients versus 2,303 for non-retainer practices

➤ Patients seen per day (mean): 11 versus 22 for nonretainer practices

➤ Percentage of former patients included in patient panel: 12 percent

➤ Percentage offering charitable care: 84 percent

➤ Services offered:
  – 24-hour direct physician access
    91 percent of respondents
  – Coordinated hospital care
    86 percent of respondents
  – House calls
    63 percent of respondents
  – Accompanied specialist visits
    30 percent of respondents

Source: G. Caleb Alexander, MD, MS, Jacob Kurlander, BA, and Matthew K. Wynia, MD, MPH, "Physicians in Retainer ('"Concierge'") Practice: A National Survey of Physician, Patient, and Practice Characteristics," *Medscape*, January 10, 2006, www.medscape.com/viewarticle/521083 (accessed January 14, 2011).

ing physicians billed the patient's health insurance for covered services.

Prior to starting a cash-only or concierge practice, physicians should investigate the marketplace and ask other questions:

➤ Does your community have a large number of affluent patients or uninsured patients who may be willing to pay cash? Are there other concierge or retail practices in your area? What benefits do the top employers in your area cover?

➤ How many of your current patients would willingly become cash-only patients? Conduct an informal survey to find out.

➤ What services would you offer to make the concept appealing to patients? Would you provide 24-hour, 7-days-per-week coverage? Will you have a partner or nonphysician provider to help with the extended coverage and during vacations?

➤ What would your charges be? Hire a practice consultant or conduct a literature search to aid in determining rates. Use your current costs and desired total revenue to help in the calculation.

➤ How would the transition occur? How will you keep some insured patients for a while until the self-pay practice is established? Review your current payer contracts to understand your obligations to current patients and the requirements to notify them of your planned withdrawal.

Case Study

Two family physicians in California decided to devote half of their new practice to concierge patients and the remaining half to patients in need. They calculated the annual retainer fee by starting with the total revenue goal for the year divided by the number of available visits per year at 30 minutes per visit and 5 visits per patient per year. The payment schedule became $500 per year for children, $1,200 for middle-aged adults, and $1,500 per year for seniors. The annual fee includes same-day extended visits and direct access via e-mail and cell phone 24 hours a day. The practice provides several services for the benefactors, including basic lab tests, ECG, spirometry, vaccinations, and casting and splinting, plus hospital, home, and skilled nursing-facility visits as needed. Half of the office visits were reserved for indigent patients who receive free care. St. Luke's Family Practice began with 250 enrolled patients (benefactors) and grew to 550 within four years, reaching their goal in net revenue.

Sources:

Bruce Steinwald, "Physician Services: Concierge Care Characteristics and Considerations for Medicare: GAO-05-929." *GAO Reports*, August 12, 2005.

Gwendolyn Roberts Majette, "From Concierge Medicine to Patient-Centered Medical Homes: International Lessons and the Search for a Better Way to Deliver Primary Health Care in the U.S.," *American Journal of Law & Medicine*, V. 35, No. 4 (2009): 585–619.

Robert A. Forester, MD, "A New Model of Charitable Care: The Robin Hood Practice," *Family Practice Management*, February 2008, www.aafp.org/fpm/2008/0200/p12.html (accessed January 14, 2011).

Trevor J. Stone, "Cash-Only Practice: Could It Work for You? *Family Practice Management,* V. 13, No. 2 (2006): 61–63, www.aafp.org/fpm/2006/0200/p61.html (accessed January 14, 2011).

CHAPTER 2

Financial Management

QUESTION **What are the best financial ratios and reports I should use to monitor the financial health of my practice?**

There are almost as many opinions on what the key financial ratios are for medical practices as there are calculations. Also, there are ratios and reports that need to be monitored on a monthly basis, while others are part of the year-end report and review. The ratios you choose to analyze regularly will depend on the type of practice (community health center, hospital owned, or specialty center) and its goals. By selecting a few key performance indicators to review frequently, you will be able to concentrate efforts on areas key to financial success and be able to observe trends or spot potential issues in a timely manner. Also, the indicators you choose for one period of time may not be as relevant in the future. Re-evaluate your key indicators from time to time.

David N. Gans, MSHA, FACMPE, has identified the key financial performance indicators applicable for most practice types:

Revenue cycle indicators	Total accounts receivable per physician
	Percentage of total accounts receivable 120+ days old
	Days in accounts receivable
	Adjusted fee-for-service collection percentage
Financial performance	Total medical revenue per physician
	Total operating cost per physician
	Total medical revenue after operating cost per physician
Efficiency	Total operating cost as a percentage of total medical revenue

Medical groups identified by an MGMA survey as better performers typically generate the following reports monthly and annually to evaluate financial performance:

➤ Financial reports:

➤ Accounts receivable aging report;

➤ Cost reports by department, provider, and location;

➤ Income statement;

➤ Balance sheet; and

➤ Statement of cash flow.

➤ Practice management reports:

➤ Collections system summary analysis;

➤ Untracked encounter forms report;

➤ Unbilled revenue report;

➤ Billing summary;

➤ Procedures analysis; and

➤ Managed care plan profitability (capitation analysis).

You may choose to develop a dashboard or flash report to present to physicians and staff. These one-page reports will show key indicators in a format that is easy to understand. Along with key financial information (revenue, expenses, A/R, available cash, and so on), it will also include key performance indicators, such as number of visits, procedures, or work RVUs.

The key to successful financial management is using the reports and indicators effectively. Besides benchmarking with other practices, they should enable you to compare the practice's status with annual budgets and organizational goals.

Sources:

David N. Gans, MSHA, FACMPE, "Data Mine: What Matters and What Doesn't," *MGMA Connexion*, September 2010, www.mgma.com/WorkArea/DownloadAsset.aspx?id=39295 (accessed November 26, 2010).

Gregory Feltenberger, MBA, FACMPE, FACHE, CPHIMS, and David N. Gans, MSHA, FACMPE, *Benchmarking Success: The Essential Guide for Group Practices* (Englewood, CO: Medical Group Management Association, 2008).

Medical Group Management Association, *Performance and Practice of Successful Medical Groups, 2008 Report Based on 2007 Data* (Englewood, CO: Medical Group Management Association, 2008).

Timothy E. Krause, MT, FACMPE, CPA, *Meaningful Financial Statements and Reports for the Medical Practice*, ACMPE Fellowship Paper, October 2007.

QUESTION 11 I am analyzing the accounts receivable for my practice. How does my A/R compare with other practices?

You are right to be concerned about accounts receivable (A/R); it is one of the key indicators of whether or not a practice is on the right financial track. The longer the accounts go uncollected, the more revenue is lost and the more your practice's resources are spent in ongoing collection efforts. Accounts receivable aging and days or months outstanding should be included in a monthly key indicator financial report.

However, knowing your practice's A/R doesn't help without knowing how your numbers compare with other practices. To compare your A/R numbers, refer to the annual MGMA *Cost Survey Report* or the *Performance and Practices of Successful Medical Groups Report.*

MGMA uses the following definition for calculating A/R in its two reports:

> **A/R** is the summation of the amounts owed to the practice by patients, third-party payers, employer groups, and others for fee-for-service (FFS) activities before bad debt or contractual adjustments. Assigning a charge into A/R begins at the time an invoice is submitted to the payer or patient for payment.

Months of gross fee-for-service charges in accounts receivable =

$$\frac{(\text{Total accounts receivable})}{(\text{Gross FFS charges}) \times (1/12)}$$

Accounts receivable key performance indicators

	Percentage of total A/R 120+ days		Months gross FFS charges in A/R	
	Better Performers	All Respondents	Better Performers	All
Primary care	10.34%	19.17%	0.93	1.34
Medicine specialties	9.52%	16.12%	0.86	1.24
Surgical specialties	9.02%	16.55%	0.97	1.39
Multispecialty practices	10.23%	17.76%	1.00	1.28

Note: FFS = fee for service

Source: Medical Group Management Association, *Performance and Practices of Successful Medical Groups: 2010 Report Based on 2009 Data* (Englewood, CO: Medical Group Management Association, 2010).

If your accounts receivable numbers do not compare favorably with the better-performing groups studied in the MGMA report, you should investigate aspects of your payment and collection processes to identify problem areas. Steps might include

➤ **Analyzing collections by payer.** Which payers are slower to pay and which ones have more denials?

➤ **Assessing collections from patients.** Is the practice collecting all the copayments, prepayments, and outstanding payments at the time of service? Is the payment process explained to patients before or at the time of service? Some practices employ a financial counselor to advise and assist patients.

➤ **Calculating the frequency of errors that delay collections.** Repeated errors in gathering patient data, coding, billing, or in other processes are signs of where changes need to be made.

➤ **Investigating means to leverage the practice management or billing program.** These systems should have automated means of notifying staff when accounts are past due or follow-up steps should be taken.

> ➤ **Involving staff.** Seek their suggestions; assign individu-
> als to track specific payers; and have regular meetings to
> discuss A/R status, collection techniques that work, or
> potential problem areas.

Besides using better-performing groups to benchmark against,
you can also look to them for ideas and techniques. Compared
with other groups, better-performing groups collected a greater
percentage of copays at the time of service, had face-to-face
contact with patients regarding payments, and assisted patients
with making financial arrangements. These groups also had more
detailed bills, which included telephone numbers for questions
and options for credit card payment.

Sources:

Chris Plemons, MS, and Doral Davis-Jacobsen, MBA, CMPE, "Making A/R Results
A-OK: A Case Study of 11 Process Improvements You Can Make in Your Practice,"
MGMA Connexion, April 2008, 28–29, www.mgma.com/WorkArea/DownloadAsset.
aspx?id=17566 (accessed November 24, 2010).

David N. Gans, MSHA, FACMPE, "Getting Paid for What You Do: How Better-
Performing Practices Minimize Bad Debt and Maximize Patient Collections," *MGMA
Connexion*, May/June 2010, 23–24, www.mgma.com/WorkArea/DownloadAsset.
aspx?id=33796 (accessed November 24, 2010).

Deborah Walker Keegan, Elizabeth W. Woodcock, and Sara M. Larch, *The Physician
Billing Process: 12 Potholes to Avoid in the Road to Getting Paid, 2nd Edition*, 183–87
(Englewood, CO: Medical Group Management Association, 2008).

QUESTION **12** I would like to get the bad debt for my practice under control. How can we manage our bad debt to ensure it is not out of line with the industry average?

There are two kinds of bad debt: (1) bad debt from commercial
payers (health insurance, for example) and self-pay patients,
and (2) inappropriate contractual write-offs and denied claims
by payers (denials are discussed in Question 13). The MGMA
benchmarks for bad debt from commercial payers and patients
follow.

Bad debts due to fee-for-service activities per FTE physician

	Better performers	All respondents
Primary care practices	$5,535	$12,408
Medicine specialties	$14,035	$19,564
Surgical specialties	$15,888	$27,977

Source: Medical Group Management Association, *Performance and Practices of Successful Medical Groups: 2010 Report Based on 2009 Data* (Englewood, CO: Medical Group Management Association, 2010).

If your practice is experiencing higher bad debt than the benchmarks, you will need to identify the source of the problem and then implement solutions. To identify the source, you will need to review several operational issues and financial ratios.

Start by analyzing the bad debt and your A/R. Is the chief culprit self-pay patients or payers? Is there one payer that leads the pack for denying payments? (See Question 11 for help with A/R.) If the bad debt is related to payers, what are the reasons for the lack of payment? Review the contract, claims completion and submission processes, and reasons for denials and rejections.

If bad debt is largely caused by self-pay patients, is it related to inaccurate patient information or inadequate steps to ensure payment? Review front-office and billing-department procedures to identify improvements in collecting copays, coinsurance, deductibles, and noncovered charges at the time of service. For larger payments, meet with patients to discuss payment options (including cash, checks, credit and debit cards) and payment plans. Do you offer installment plans? Include employees in suggestions and training to increase time-of-service payments. For instance, encourage employees to ask, "How would you like to pay today?" instead of "Would you like to pay now?"

Bad debt may be caused by little or no follow-up to claims, whether or not the payer is a managed care company or patient. What processes are in place if a claim is denied, rejected, or otherwise not paid within a designated period? Are there adequate personnel to follow up on claims, and do they have the training and resources needed to complete the process?

If your practice has insufficient resources for adequate follow-up or has exhausted its abilities to collect, you may choose to turn over outstanding accounts to collection agencies. The older an account is, the less chance that it can be collected even by a collection agency. After 90 days, a business has only a 69.6 percent probability of collecting its money. By six months, the odds drop to 52.1 percent. Develop policies specifying at what age an account will be sent to collection agencies, and streamline the process to minimize delays and expenses.

A CLOSER LOOK . . .

Forty-eight percent of the better-performing practices collected more than 90 percent of their patient copayments at the time of service, compared to 35 percent of the other responding practices.

Source: Medical Group Management Association, *Performance and Practices of Successful Medical Groups: 2010 Report Based on 2009 Data* (Englewood, CO: Medical Group Management Association, 2010).

Sources:

Brian Roth, MBA, CPA, "Bad-Debt Blues: Change Your Tune by Attending to Small Percentages," *MGMA Connexion*, October 2008, 16–17, www.mgma.com/WorkArea/DownloadAsset.aspx?id=22166 (accessed November 26, 2010).

Commercial Collection Agency section of the Commercial Law League of America, www.ccaacollect.com/10-18-04COLLECTABILITYCHART.pdf (accessed December 8, 2010).

Deborah Walker Keegan, Elizabeth W. Woodcock, and Sara M. Larch, *The Physician Billing Process: 12 Potholes to Avoid in the Road to Getting Paid, 2nd Edition*, 183–87 (Englewood, CO: Medical Group Management Association, 2008).

Donn Sorenson, MBA, FACMPE, and Henry Bird, MBA, "Up Front and Personal: How Front-End Collections Can Improve Your Revenue Cycle — and Patient Satisfaction," *MGMA Connexion*, February 2008, 34–37, www.mgma.com/WorkArea/DownloadAsset.aspx?id=16442 (accessed November 26, 2010).

James Margolis, MPA, FACMPE, and Christina Pope, "Perspective on Patient Payments," *MGMA Connexion*, April 2010, 36–41, www.mgma.com/WorkArea/DownloadAsset.aspx?id=33267 (accessed November 26, 2010).

QUESTION **My practice is suffering from an increasing number of claims being rejected by payers. Do you know what the average is for the percentage of claims denied? What can I do to reverse this trend?**

A LOOK AT THE NUMBERS . . .

The ideal is to have claim denials at 5 percent or less of the total claims submitted. Better-performing groups typically had 4 percent of claims denied on the first submission, according to the MGMA *Performance and Practices of Successful Medical Groups: 2010 Report Based on 2009 Data.*

The cost of reworking a denied claim is approximately $15 per claim including staff time, interest, and overhead, according to Deborah Walker Keegan, Elizabeth W. Woodcock, and Sara M. Larch in *The Physician Billing Process: 12 Potholes to Avoid in the Road to Getting Paid, 2nd Edition* (MGMA, 2009).

Many practices choose to ignore denied claims with the idea that they aren't worth the effort to follow up. You are smart to realize that accepting rejected claims is denying money that your practice is due. There are several steps you can take to assess and correct the issue:

Step 1. Study the Explanation of Benefits to determine the reasons for denied claims. This involves deciphering the explanations and codes used by different payers and Medicare.

Step 2. Categorize the reasons for denials and tabulate the totals by category. Separate the data by payer and department or even by physician. Identify the most frequent reasons for claim rejection and whether specific payers, departments, or physicians have higher rates than others.

The most frequent reasons for denied claims are

➤ Patient registration errors, including missing data;

➤ Lack of insurance verification;

➤ Inappropriate code or modifiers;

➤ Incomplete information relating to referrals and pre-authorizations;

➤ Duplicate bills for the same services;

➤ Medical necessity claims and documentation;

➤ Incomplete documentation for the medical services provided; and

➤ Incorrectly bundling services.

Step 3. Set up processes for resubmitting claims. Denied claims should be adjusted based on the reason for the denial and then resubmitted. When resubmitting the claim, include a letter to the payer explaining the reason for the second submission. Identify the claim and include additional documents to support the claim, providing information or data not included with the first submission.

Identify one or two employees who will lead the effort, and ensure that they have adequate training to understand the billing processes and payers' techniques and have the right resources to accomplish the goals. The employee should be familiar with correct coding policy, including Medicare's National Correct Coding Initiative (NCCI). Leverage your practice management or billing system to automate as much as possible.

If claims are denied a second or third time, learn about the payer's appeal policies and other options. Medicare's policy is available at www.cms.hhs.gov/OrgMedFFSappeals.

Step 4. Use the reasons for rejected claims to correct errors within practice operations. Minimizing the problems before claim submission will decrease the number of rejections and increase practice efficiency and revenue. If patient registration errors were a major reason for denials, how can front-office efforts be improved to minimize errors? If lack of documentation is a problem, include a step or checklist prior to claim submission to ensure that all documentation is in place. Problem payers may require a telephone call or face-to-face meetings with company representatives.

Step 5. Keep on it. After processes are in place to minimize rejections, don't assume the problem will go away. Continue to monitor denial rates and implemented changes to ensure the rates decrease and the corrective measures remain effective.

A CLOSER LOOK . . .

Total Account Ownership — Elizabeth W. Woodcock, practice consultant and speaker, proposes another option for managing claim submission and follow-up: total account ownership (TAO). Employees are assigned by payer to handle claims from start to finish — reviewing and submitting claims, posting payments, making contractual adjustments, correcting and resubmitting rejected claims, and transferring claim responsibility to second parties or patients if appropriate. Employees are assigned one or more payers, depending on the number of claims and difficulty of working with that payer. The advantages are the in-depth knowledge and sense of ownership the employee has of the claims and the payer. Supervisors can easily review data to assess payer and employee performance but must ensure that the workload is equitably distributed.

Source: Elizabeth W. Woodcock, MBA, FACMPE, CPC, "Total Account Ownership: A New Model for Streamlining Your Business Office Staff," *MGMA Connexion*, January 2007, 28–33.

Sources:

Jeffrey B. Milburn, CMPE, "Mining for Gold: Extract Revenue from Unprocessed Claims Denials," *MGMA Connexion*, January 2007, 38–41, www.mgma.com/WorkArea/DownloadAsset.aspx?id=11022 (accessed November 28, 2010).

Laurie Desjardins, "Manage Your Claim Denials: Fight for Revenue You've Justly Earned," *MGMA Connexion*, October 2009, 13–14, www.mgma.com/WorkArea/DownloadAsset.aspx?id=30439 (accessed November 28, 2010).

"What's Causing Claim Denials?" *Healthcare Collector*, V. 19, No. 1 (2005): 1, 4–5.

QUESTION **I need to renegotiate some payer contracts that have not been in our best interest. What steps can I take prior to and during the negotiation process?**

14

A regular review and comparison of your managed care and other health plan contracts is a good idea. It's often too easy to renew a contract without an in-depth analysis of the payer's performance and the contract's terms. Allow several months for adequate time to gather and review data and negotiate the contract prior to the termination of the current contracts.

Step 1. Pull together your current contracts and develop a matrix with the following information:

➤ Payer name;

➤ Termination clauses and termination or anniversary date;

➤ Notification period prior to giving notice to terminate or renegotiate a contract;

➤ Representative's contact information; and

➤ Reimbursement terms.

Step 2. Analyze the current reimbursement by payer. Record the actual reimbursement (contractual allowable, not the payment) and frequency for at least 20 of your practice's most common procedures (the more the better) from the last 6 to 12 months. Using total RVUs and allowables for the selected procedures, divide the sum of the allowables by the total RVUs to arrive at a frequency-weighted reimbursement per total RVU. Divide this number by the current Medicare conversion factor to determine the payers' reimbursement as a percentage of current Medicare. You will then be able to compare reimbursement for all of your payers regardless of the terms of the contract.

Step 3. Compare your charges with the usual, customary, and reasonable (UCR) charge data and Medicare rates. (See Question 15 on fee schedules for UCR data sources.) Ensure that you are within expected ranges, keeping in mind that the UCR can be as high as 250 percent to 350 percent above Medicare for some specialties.

Analyze the denial or rejection rates, and quantify the administrative costs for claims follow-up or unique authorization, documentation, and carve-out or coding rules.

Step 4. Assess your practice's and the payer's position in your market. How does your practice stand out compared to others? Look at the access, specialties, services, and procedures you offer. Gather data on your market share and quality measurements. Look at the payers' data for your marketplace, including

> ➤ Contracted hospitals;

> ➤ Number of insured in your area;

> ➤ Other contracted physicians in your area; and

> ➤ Contracted employer groups in your area.

Step 5. Start the negotiation process by submitting a written notice asking for a new agreement. Ask for one medical group agreement so you don't have to deal with several agreements. Research the payer's rate increases to employers in your area. Don't accept delaying tactics; set deadlines during the negotiation process. For underperforming payers, you might want to include an intent-to-terminate notice if new terms aren't agreed upon. This will provide you with more leverage. If the payer refuses to negotiate, evaluate its percentage of your net revenue, factor in the extra expenses related to managing its claims, and determine if you are willing to cancel the contract. You may be able to increase revenue by seeing more patients from better-performing payers.

Step 6. Review the contract and its language with your attorney. Confirm state regulations regarding offset rules, timely payment requirements, periods for notifying payers of errors, and other health insurance regulations. MGMA member Cecelia Bartz has an extensive contract checklist that she has found useful:

> ➤ The carrier's rates compared with Medicare's rates and the practice's procedure costs. Don't accept rates based

on current or prevailing Medicare rates in case of future Medicare reductions;

➤ Termination clauses;

➤ Amendment clauses (Are they mutual, or do they allow amendments to be made only by the carrier?);

➤ Policies for billing noncovered services to identify whether you can have the patient sign a waiver agreeing to pay for services the plan won't cover;

➤ Hold-harmless clauses (replace these with "responsibility for own acts" clauses);

➤ Timely filing limits (should be at least 180 days);

➤ Timely payment provisions (review state requirements);

➤ Denial appeal limits;

➤ Time allowed to recoup overpayments (one year is recommended from the date of service, and require 45 days' notice before the "take-back" date);

➤ Precedence (What's the priority reference — the manuals or the contract?);

➤ Compliance with CPT guidelines;

➤ Adherence to NCCI edits;

➤ Opt-in and opt-out provisions;

➤ Practice locations covered by the contract;

➤ Time limits for providing notification about claims that are ineligible for payment and why; and

➤ Quality-of-care requirements (or replace these with "Physicians shall endeavor to provide care of the same quality that prevails in the community").

Also, watch out for terms regarding binding arbitration or other means of solving disputes. The payer may require that you not join any class-action lawsuits. Another red flag is multiyear agreements without adequate increases in the following years. Ensure they're based on industry indexes, such as the Consumer Price Index or medical cost index, from the U.S. Bureau of Labor Statistics.

A CLOSER LOOK . . .

New Trends

The U.S. healthcare industry is changing based on demand for reduced costs and increasing quality leading to new reimbursement methods. The "pay me right" concept coordinates the efforts of payers, financial leaders, and providers to ensure coordination with clinical management and contractual and financial processes. The goal is to reduce costs while offering rewards for premium performance.

Many payers are following Medicare's lead and developing pay-for-performance (P4P) reimbursement methods. Negotiating contracts based on P4P will require an understanding of the selected quality measures, the reimbursement methodology based on those measures, and the processes within your practice for tracking your quality measures. See Question 76 for more P4P information.

Sources:

Cecelia Bartz, "Create a Checklist for Reviewing Payer Contracts," *MGMA e-Source*, May 13, 2008, www.mgma.com/article.aspx?id=18774 (accessed January 8, 2011).

Michael E. Nugent, "Beyond the 'Pay Me More' Strategy," *Healthcare Financial Management*, V. 63, No. 6 (2009): 62–70.

Peggy Noyes, "Payer Contracting Tips for Medical Practice Administrators: Novices to Pros," Medical Group Management Association. MGMA Buyer's Guide 2010, www.mgma.com/WorkArea/mgma_downloadasset.aspx?id=34328 (accessed January 8, 2011).

Randy Cook, MPH, CMPE, "Know How: Payer Negotiations: You Have More Power than You Think," *MGMA Connexion*, February 2007, www.mgma.com/WorkArea/mgma_downloadasset.aspx?id=11568 (accessed January 8, 2011).

A CLOSER LOOK . . .

Payer Lawsuits

A class-action lawsuit against Aetna, CIGNA, Prudential, Anthem/WellPoint, and Humana led to a 2007 settlement. The lawsuit, known as *In re. Managed Care Litigation or Multidistrict Litigation (MDL)*, required the insurance payers to comply with fairer business practices including

➤ Improved payment schedules and processes;

➤ Adherence to the American Medical Association CPT;

➤ Physician contracts, billing, and compliance disputes, including gag clauses; and

➤ Medical necessity definition.

In 2005, lawsuits against three insurers, Health Net, Prudential, and WellPoint, led to settlements in which the insurers agreed to

➤ Modify the definition of medical necessity;

➤ Cease using claims-processing software that modifies claims from the original service-code designations;

➤ Pay electronic claims within 15 days of receipt and paper claims within 30 days; and

➤ Provide an electronic fee schedule.

Previous concerns and lawsuits led several states to pass prompt-payment legislation requiring insurers to pay within a set number of days (usually 30 to 45 days) upon receipt of claims.

Monitor your contracts and payer responses to ensure their compliance with the state laws and lawsuit agreements. Assign a staff member to review payers' Web sites for medical-necessity payment policies and other changes in payment policies.

Sources:

MGMA Government Affairs, "Recent Activity in Managed-Care Litigation," *MGMA Connexion*, February 2007, www.mgma.com/WorkArea/linkit.aspx?LinkIdentifier =id&ItemID=11586 (accessed February 7, 2011).

MGMA Government Affairs, "Washington Report: Additional Settlements Reached in Managed Care Litigation," *MGMA e-Connexion*, Issue 82, August 25, 2005.

QUESTION

15

I have been hired as an administrator of a new practice. How do I ensure that the fee schedule will optimize revenue for the practice?

There are several techniques and resources for medical practice fee schedules. Since you are new to the practice, a comprehensive review of the schedule is called for, but subsequent reviews should occur on an annual basis.

The first step is to investigate if your current fee schedule actually covers the costs of providing the procedures. To compare costs with your charges, select the most-frequently used codes in the practice and those that bring in the most revenue. Use RVUs to calculate and compare the cost per CPT code and the net or gross charges per procedure. If the net or discounted charges don't exceed the costs, it's time to adjust your fee schedule. Keep in mind that it is collections or net revenue, not charges, that pay the overhead expenses and providers. Adjusting charges upward to cover costs may be an answer, but you may also have to look at improving your payer contracts and/or reducing expenses.

The Medicare physician fee schedule can be used as a basis for your practice's fee schedule. The schedule, based on the resource-based relative value scale (RBRVS), is published annually in the *Federal Register* or is available online at the Centers for Medicare & Medicaid Services Web site: www.cms.hhs.gov/physicianfeesched.

A CLOSER LOOK . . .

The Medicare fee schedule is based on the concept of relative value units (RVUs), defined as the "relative units of measure that indicate the value of healthcare services." They assign relative values or weights to medical procedures for determining reimbursement. The resource-based relative value scale (RBRVS) was implemented in the Medicare payment system in 1992. The scale is based on an RVU of 1.0 for CPT 99213, and all other RBRVS values are determined relative to 99213.

RBRVS values are comprised of three components:

➤ Work RVU — "The relative time, effort, and skill needed by a provider in the provision of a procedure or service."

➤ Practice expense RVU — "The costs associated with maintaining a practice, such as rent, equipment, supplies, and staff."

➤ Professional liability insurance or malpractice RVU — Incorporates the relative level of risk in performing any given procedure.

To adjust for regional differences in health service costs, geographic practice cost indices (GPCIs) are used for each of the three RVU components. The conversion factor (CF) converts the RVU into a dollar figure, and it is announced for each year. The reimbursement amount for each CPT code is calculated by:

$$[(wRVU \times wGPCI) + (peRVU \times peGPCI) + (mRVU \times mGPCI)] \times CF = \text{reimbursement value}$$

Source: Kathryn P. Glass, MBA, MSHA, PMP, *RVUs: Applications for Medical Practice Success, 2nd Edition* (Englewood, CO: Medical Group Management Association, 2008).

You may need to set your fees at a certain percentage above the Medicare schedule to ensure that your costs are covered. Also, the RBRVS tends to place a relatively higher value on the E&M services, giving lower values to procedures. If your group performs many surgical procedures, you may want to use another system or set a higher conversion factor for surgical services.

You will also need to compare your charges with the reimbursement you have been receiving from insurance companies. You may want to increase your charges if you've been receiving full reimbursement from any payers; your charges should be above their reimbursement rate to ensure that you are receiving the maximum allowable. If the payer's fee schedule is based on Medicare's, find out if they use the current year's conversion factor and how geographic locale is factored in.

Most payers are now using their own fee schedules, which payers may not release to you in their entirety. Request information from the payer starting with the CPT codes with the greatest volume or charges. You may need to submit several requests until you have enough codes to conduct an adequate comparison of charges versus costs. Conduct this analysis for every payer and type of service, including E&M codes, medicine, and surgery.

Whatever method you use to set your fee schedule, review it and payers' reimbursement on a regular basis, annually or biannually, to ensure that your fees reflect changing costs and reimbursements.

A LOOK AT THE NUMBERS . . .

1
2
3

What is the primary method you use to establish and/or maintain your fee schedule?

    a. Ratio of Medicare = 46.2 percent

    b. RBRVS = 20.3 percent

    c. Based on payer contract amounts = 11.9 percent

    d. Surveys and published lists = 6.8 percent

    e. Other = 9.9 percent

    f. Cost plus markup = 2.9 percent

Source: Frank Cohen, survey conducted for the National Association of Health Care Consultants, January 2010, www.frankcohengroup.com, personal communication with the author, March 2, 2011. Reprinted with permission, www.frankcohengroup.com.

FOR MORE INFORMATION . . .

Detailed steps for calculating costs and charges can be found in *RVUs: Applications for Medical Practice Success, 2nd Edition*, by Kathryn Glass (Englewood, CO: Medical Group Management Association, 2008).

There are many consultants and businesses that provide information on average fees or will consult with you to develop a fair fee schedule for your practice and location. The following list contains a few contacts:

Contact	Web site	Telephone
Ingenix	Ingenix.com	800.464.3649
MagMutual Healthcare Solutions	Coderscentral.com	800.253.4945
Practice Management Information Corporation	PMIConline.com	800.med.shop
EMC Captiva UCR Databases	www.emc.com/captiva	858.320.1100
MGMA Health Care Consulting Group	MGMA.com	888.275.6462

Sources:

Cindy L. Jones, FACMPE, "The Art and Science of Physician Practice Fee Schedule Development and Maintenance," ACMPE Fellowship Paper, October 2006.

Kathryn P. Glass, MBA, MSHA, PMP, "Know Your Fee Schedules," *MGMA e-Source*, June 10, 2008.

QUESTION
16

We are trying to decide if we should centralize our billing when we merge with another practice. What are other practices doing?

A frequent question in medical practices is whether or not to have centralized or decentralized billing and business offices. The issue is becoming complicated with the increasing number of merging practices and physicians aligning with hospitals.

Advantages of the centralized business office include

> ➤ Economies of scale to reduce costs;
> ➤ Standardization of processes, data collection, and reports;
> ➤ Centralized compliance monitoring;
> ➤ Development of expertise with increased employee specialization;
> ➤ Opportunities to share knowledge in one office;
> ➤ One location for managing patients' requests; and
> ➤ Leverage to purchase and manage one information system.

Advantages of a decentralized office include

> ➤ Closer relationship with physician and nonphysician providers;
> ➤ Easier communication among staff with diverse functions within one practice;
> ➤ More ownership of processes with closer connections to physicians and patients;
> ➤ Improved collections from patients; and
> ➤ Opportunity for more direct communication with patients.

Many practices have adopted hybrid models that centralize some functions but decentralize others. Those at the locations where patients are seen can easily handle charge entry and time-of-service collections. Claims submission and payer follow-up may be handled in the central office.

Elizabeth W. Woodcock, MBA, FACMPE, and Loc Nguyen compared the operating costs and collections of practices with centralized billing offices to those with decentralized billing offices (see the following table). Those with centralized operations had lower business office expenses than those without. However, collections took longer in centralized offices, and the collection percentages were mixed. Their conclusion was that a hybrid centralized/decentralized billing office may be best, "allowing the practice to capture the economies that are possible while retaining the relationships, communication, productivity, and control that are essential to success."

Comparison between decentralized and centralized billing offices

	Decentralized	Centralized
Business office expenses (median per physician)		
Single specialties	$22,571	$17,455
Multispecialties	$19,962	$16,873
Collection percentage		
Single specialties	96.02%	97.59%
Multispecialties	98.50%	97.56%
A/R days outstanding		
Single specialties	56.0	57.5
Multispecialties	52.8	57.4

Source: Elizabeth W. Woodcock and Loc Nguyen, "The Economics of Central Billing Offices," *MGMA Journal,* V. 47, No. 3, May 2000.

Factors that will affect your decision include your practice's current situation. If you're a recently merged practice, you may want to centralize at least part of the billing functions to contribute to the sense of unity within the new practice. For integrated delivery systems (IDS), the decision will depend on the model: directly employed physicians frequently transfer the billing function to the hospital's centralized business office or office specific to managing the practices. Subsidiary models may continue to operate the business office within the practice or adopt a hybrid model with some functions within the practice and others in the IDS' centralized office.

A LOOK AT THE NUMBERS . . .

1
2
3

Practice's billing function structure

Centralized	72.58%
Decentralized	11.37%
Both/Hybrid	13.04%
Other	3.01%

Source: Medical Group Management Association, *Performance and Practices of Successful Medical Groups: 2010 Report Based on 2009 Data* (Englewood, CO: Medical Group Management Association, 2010).

Nick Fabrizio, MGMA healthcare consultant, describes the potential benefits for hospital-affiliated practices to modify their billing processes, especially for primary care practices with large Medicare populations. Switching to a provider-based setting enables the hospital to bill Medicare for the hospital facility payment as well as for the physician services. The total may be higher than if the practice billed as a separate clinic. Prior to moving in this direction, you should research current Medicare regulations and definitions for provider-based billing, the reimbursement rates for the two options at your location, and the processes for notifying patients of the change.

If the decision is made to centralize or partially centralize billing operations in a merged system, the difficulty is in the transition. Form a work group with staff members from all of the involved organizations to review current procedures and structure. Identify the final structure that is desired and develop a transition plan, including training. Establish performance and communication expectations and accountability standards. Monitor after implementation to ensure a successful and complete transition, and monitor procedures and training as needed. During transition, a claims clearinghouse or billing service might be used to provide a central location and identification number for the different offices until the new office is operational and IDs are in place.

Sources:

Deborah Walker Keegan, Elizabeth W. Woodcock, and Sara M. Larch, *The Physician Billing Process: 12 Potholes to Avoid in the Road to Getting Paid, 2nd Edition*, 319–24 (Englewood, CO: Medical Group Management Association, 2008).

Donn Sorensen, MBA, FACMPE, and Henry Bird, MBA, "Up Front and Personal: How Front-End Collections Can Improve Your Revenue Cycle — and Patient Satisfaction," *MGMA Connexion*, February 2008, www.mgma.com/WorkArea/mgma_downloadasset. aspx?id=16442 (accessed January 7, 2011).

Nick A. Fabrizio, PhD, FACMPE, FACHE, *Integrated Delivery Systems: Ensuring Successful Physician-Hospital Partnerships*, 147 (Englewood, CO: Medical Group Management Association, 2010).

Randall S. Shulkin, MBA, FACMPE, "A Fix for Multiple Database Billing," *MGMA Connexion*, November–December 2009, www.mgma.com/WorkArea/mgma_download-asset.aspx?id=31871 (accessed January 7, 2011).

Case Study

St. John's Clinic, with 110 offices in southwest Missouri, uses a hybrid collection model. Each location is responsible for collecting patients' copays and self-pay balances at the time of service. The centralized business office (CBO) processes and collects payments from insurers. The CBO enables patients to discuss billing issues at any location. Collecting from patients at individual clinics increases collections as the number of self-pay and high-deductible plans increases.

Source: Donn Sorensen, MBA, FACMPE, and Henry Bird, MBA, "Up Front and Personal: How Front-End Collections Can Improve Your Revenue Cycle — and Patient Satisfaction," *MGMA Connexion*, February 2008, www. mgma.com/WorkArea/mgma_downloadasset.aspx?id=16442 (accessed January 7, 2011).

QUESTION 17

What is the best method of measuring the productivity of my billing office? Are there benchmarks for billing staff activities?

Comparative staff productivity data are difficult to locate and should be used wisely. Each practice is unique in terms of payer mix, staff mix, and business office functions. Therefore, staff productivity will vary. You should also benchmark your practice with MGMA survey data to compare the number of business office staff and expenses, gross charges, accounts receivable data, and other financial data. If you are within medical practice norms, your staff productivity may be acceptable.

Medical practice experts Deborah Walker Keegan, PhD, FACMPE, Elizabeth W. Woodcock, MBA, FACMPE, CPC, and Sara M. Larch, MSHA, FACMPE, provide the following figures for billing office staff workload ranges. They recommend that you review and emphasize the quality of the work, not just the quantity. The ranges are based on seven hours per day, assuming one hour for breaks and interruptions.

Staff activity	Per day	Per hour
Charge entry encounters (without registration)	375–525	55–75
Charge entry encounters (with registration)	280–395	40–55
Transactions posted manually	525–875	75–125
Account follow-up: • research correspondence and resolve by telephone • check status of claim and rebill	n/a n/a	6–12 12–60
Self-pay follow-up	70–90	10–13
Patient billing inquiries	56–84	8–12

© 2008 Walker Keegan, Woodcock, Larch. Reprinted with permission.

Note: Workload may depend on your information systems, Internet access, facility, flow of work (e.g., documentation required), additional tasks assigned, specialty(ies), and other variables.

Source: Deborah Walker Keegan, PhD, FACMPE, Elizabeth W. Woodcock, MBA, FACMPE, CPC, and Sara M. Larch, MSHA, FACMPE, *The Physician Billing Process: 12 Potholes to Avoid in the Road to Getting Paid, 2nd Edition,* 287 (Englewood, CO: Medical Group Management Association, 2008).

If the billing staff workload is below the above ranges, and your practice financial ratios are below MGMA benchmarks, you should investigate possible reasons and ways of correcting the issue:

➤ Are you using the practice management system to its full capabilities? Have staff members received adequate training, and are they using the program with maximum effectiveness? You may want to work with the system vendor to identify additional efficiencies.

➤ Ask the business office employees for ideas to improve the department's productivity. Can they identify issues that impede their work?

> ➤ Develop an incentive program based on increasing the group's billing efficiency and financial ratios. Make the employees vested in increased productivity, lowered accounts receivable, fewer patient complaints about bills, and so on.

QUESTION **I'd like to conduct a chart audit but don't know how to proceed. What advice can you offer me?**

18

Correct coding and complete documentation are important in many ways: It's the basis for ensuring the practice receives reimbursement for services performed, it reduces the number of denied claims, and it protects the practice against malpractice suits and investigations for fraud and abuse. A chart audit can also be used to identify whether physicians are following best practices and quality indicators that are becoming increasingly important as healthcare moves from quantity to quality reimbursement, including P4P. If the coding in your practice has never been audited, you may want to hire an experienced consultant or coding professional to conduct it.

When conducting a first-time audit, you will want to gather as many charts as possible to have a large representative sample of charts for different physicians, procedures, diagnoses, and service locations. Cindy Dunn, MGMA healthcare consultant, recommends 10 to 15 charts per chosen diagnosis per physician to evaluate for indicators of quality care.

Review the documentation and check for correct application of E&M level and use of procedure codes, modifiers, and diagnosis codes. You can also benchmark the coding levels among your practice's physicians or use the CMS data, especially for E&M coding. (MGMA.com has an online tool with E&M coding data by specialty available under Member Benefits Communities/Benefits and Tools: //www.mgma.com/WorkArea/DownloadAsset.aspx?id=40977). Keep in mind that CMS data are primarily populated by Medicare patient claims, which are for an older population. If coding discrepancies are found, correct the claims that haven't been submitted. For claims that were already submitted, you may want to discuss voluntary disclosure requirements with your legal counsel.

Physicians tend to undercode, often called "safe coding," especially the E&M codes. Although this may lessen their concerns about being investigated, it decreases the practice revenue and physician income. Develop training sessions on the proper use of E&M codes, discussing the factors for determining the codes and documentation to support it. Provide benchmarking data to show nationwide use of the codes.

EHRs can be utilized to provide computer-assisted coding. Providers should work with the EHR vendor's staff to ensure the templates and documentation fields will lead to accurate coding and supportive documentation. Auditors should conduct an initial review of EHR records for accuracy in coding and providers' utilization of the templates to document provided services.

After the initial audit, pull several records each month (consultants recommend 3 percent of each month's records) to monitor for any ongoing issues. Provide regular training on correct coding practices and new issues in coding. This will be especially important as the ICD-10 implementation date approaches. Accurate coding and documentation should be factors included in employee and physician performance reviews. As always, the key to continued success is communication: Ensure that physicians and coders are freely communicating so that correct coding is a team effort.

A CLOSER LOOK . . .

Who is responsible for setting the CPT and diagnosis codes?

Some coders believe they have the expertise and so should be held responsible for setting the codes, and physicians may relinquish the responsibility to them. However, it is the physician whose signature is at the bottom of the chart. Therefore, physicians are advised to work in direct concert with the coder or code the services keeping in mind the coder's advice and/or direction.

ADDITIONAL CODING RESOURCES

Centers for Medicare & Medicaid Services	www.cms.gov
Specialty societies	various Web sites
American Academy of Professional Coders	www.aapc.com
American Health Information Management Association	www.ahima.org
MGMA's books, articles, consultants	www.mgma.com
American Medical Association	www.ama-assn.org

Sources:

Cindy Dunn, "Podcast: Focus on Quality, Not Quantity, with Pay for Performance," MGMA Web site, www.mgma.com/article.aspx?id=29630 (accessed December 19, 2010).

Eric Lundin, FACMPE, "How to Convince Physicians to Stop Undercoding," *MGMA e-Source*, August 31, 2010, www.mgma.com/article.aspx?id=39246 (accessed December 19, 2010).

Jennifer Swindle, "Coding Audits Keep Physicians, Staff on Track," *MGMA e-Source*, May 13, 2008, www.mgma.com/article.aspx?id=18778 (accessed December 19, 2010).

Matthew Vuletich, "Follow the Code or Else . . . ," *MGMA e-Source*, November 24, 2009, www.mgma.com/article.aspx?id=31790 (accessed December 19, 2010).

Michael A. O'Connell, MHA, FACMPE, "Developing a Coding Department," ACMPE Fellowship Paper, August 2003.

QUESTION 19

I recently read about an accountant embezzling thousands out of a local medical practice. How can I make sure I have controls in place to prevent embezzlement or employee theft?

Unfortunately, embezzlement or theft in medical practices is not an unusual event. An MGMA survey found that nearly 83 percent of respondents had been affiliated with a practice that was a victim of employee theft or embezzlement.

Theft or embezzlement scheme
reported by MGMA survey respondents

	Count	Percent of respondents
Cash receipts (stealing cash either before or after it is recorded on the books)	335	44.7%
Cash on hand (stealing cash, such as petty cash, kept on hand at the books)	73	9.7%
Disbursements (forging a check, submitting false or personal invoices)	134	17.9%
Expense reimbursements (submitting fictitious or inflated business expenses)	27	3.6%
Payroll (creating a fictitious employee, unauthorized bonuses, or inflated pay rate or hours)	46	6.1%
Noncash (stealing cash assets such as supplies, equipment, or patient financial information)	56	7.5%
Other	78	10.4%

To find out if your practice is at risk for embezzlement or theft, ask the following questions from the MGMA Theft and Embezzlement Risk Assessment:

➤ Before hiring new employees, do you conduct extensive personal interviews or use any sort of employee integrity or background tests?

➤ Do you systematically assess the morale of your practice at least quarterly?

➤ Have you made it clear to every one of your employees or future hires that you believe honesty and integrity are essential for the success of your mutual interests in the practice?

➤ Do you have a written policy that explains the consequences of being found guilty of stealing?

➤ Is it practice policy to terminate employment immediately and prosecute for employee theft?

➤ Do you have safeguards built into your practice to protect you from embezzlement and theft that do not depend on the perpetrators themselves reporting the true state of transactions?

➤ Do you have an independent accountant/bookkeeper audit your business or your practice on a regular basis?

The questions address several keys related to preventing theft. Knowing your employees and their morale alerts you to any potential concerns. Cases often involved long-term employees who found temptation hard to pass up or had changes in personal financial situations.

The best protection is to remove temptation and opportunities by implementing internal controls that limit any one employee's opportunity. Controls should include

➤ Conduct financial background checks for all employees who have financial responsibilities.

➤ Ensure these employees are bonded. The bonding agency may require even more in-depth background checks.

➤ Segregate job responsibilities related to receipts, postings, and deposits. Consider cross-training and rotation of duties to spread the responsibilities. Conduct bank reconciliations yourself, and have someone else manage the general ledger.

➤ Check the charges daily to the sign-in or appointment schedule, and use direct deposit whenever possible.

➤ Occasionally review the checkbook and checks for possible illegitimate activities.

➤ Hire an outside accountant to frequently review the ledger and work of the practice's staff.

Segregation of responsibilities is probably the single most important control for limiting theft. Cash-receipts theft was reported most frequently in the MGMA survey and occurs when one person taking cash also can take payment, delete an appointment record, report a "no-show," write off an account, and/or take complaints. This is the reason receptionists were involved in 26 percent of the reported theft cases in the MGMA survey.

Cash-disbursement schemes were also fairly frequent and often involved paying personal bills with company funds by using business checks or credit cards. Internal controls should include limited access to company credit cards and checks and having an auditor or second person reviewing credit card statements, bank statements, and checks.

To decrease theft of supplies, particularly pharmaceutical supplies (discussed in more detail in Question 75), use locked cabinets and check-in/check-out logs with two employees monitoring the cabinet.

Your employees are your highest concern, but they can also be assets. Encourage employees to watch for warning signs or report if they have suspicions. You can set up an anonymous reporting structure but double-check whatever is reported.

Sources:

Denise McClure, CPA, CFE, "Case Studies: MGMA Employee Theft and Embezzlement Research," www.mgma.com/article.aspx?id=39259 (accessed January 8, 2011).

Elaine J. Beeble, FACMPE, "Trust Is Not an Internal Control: Understanding, Assessing, and Implementing Internal Controls in a Medical Practice," ACMPE Fellowship Paper, October 2007, www.mgma.com/WorkArea/mgma_downloadasset.aspx?id=16160 (accessed January 8, 2011).

Loretta E. Duncan, FACMPE, "Theft in the Medical Practice: Recognizing the Risks and Protecting Your Practice," ACMPE Fellowship Paper, October 2009, www.mgma.com/WorkArea/mgma_downloadasset.aspx?id=40370 (accessed January 8, 2011).

Marilyn Bromberg, "Size Matters: A Costly Affliction," *MGMA Connexion*, July 2007, www.mgma.com/WorkArea/mgma_downloadasset.aspx?id=13728 (accessed January 8, 2011).

Medical Group Management Association, "2009 Medical Practice Employee Theft & Embezzlement Study Findings," www.mgma.com/WorkArea/mgma_downloadasset.aspx?id=40054 (accessed January 8, 2011).

Medical Group Management Association, "Theft and Embezzlement Risk Assessment," www.mgma.com/WorkArea/mgma_downloadasset.aspx?id=8678 (accessed January 8, 2011).

CHAPTER 3

Human Resource Management

QUESTION
20
My board has decided it's time to recruit another physician. What are the steps I should take to ensure that we recruit a good match?

One key to a successful physician recruitment process is to plan ahead. MGMA members are reporting increasing challenges related to physician recruitment, as an impending physician shortage may already be affecting group practices. Planning ahead provides opportunities to be a step ahead of the process.

Practices should maintain a recruitment plan that incorporates awareness of the group's goals, current physicians' career and retirement goals, and the marketplace. You should be aware of what other practices and hospitals in your area are doing in terms of offers to recruited physicians and the specialties being recruited. If there is a medical school or residency program in your area, your physicians should take advantage of the opportunities to network with young physicians and introduce them to your practice. The recruitment plan should also be a retention plan: Keeping the physicians that you have is always a top priority.

Ensuring a successful recruitment process includes several steps and the patience to handle the process, which will probably take several months (five to eight months according to the MGMA *Recruiter Benchmarking Survey: 2009 Report Based on 2007 Data*).

Step 1. A first step is to visualize the ideal new physician for your practice. Physicians will immediately discuss the specialty and clinical qualifications of a new physician. Just as important are the personality and characteristics to match your practice's culture and goals. What type of work ethic is important? Will it be someone just out of residency or with experience? Are customer service and patient satisfaction important factors to consider?

Step 2. Commit the financial resources to recruitment and personnel time. Identify the budget for recruitment, including whether or not you will hire a physician recruitment firm. Determine which combination of methods will be used to recruit. Internet job boards and referrals are the methods most frequently used by MGMA members. Question 21 offers information on recruitment budgets.

Identify a recruitment team with a mix of positions and responsibilities to provide different viewpoints. Select a recruitment coordinator and someone with authority to negotiate and close the contract. Successful retention of the new physician will involve having someone mentor her initially, and the mentor should be part of the team.

Step 3. Determine the recruitment offer in terms of compensation range, benefits, and partnership opportunities. Depending on the competitive nature of your community and the specialty being recruited, you may have to offer a signing bonus and compensate for moving expenses or loan repayment. To stand out, you should also identify the professional opportunities you offer in terms of the practice culture, technological advances, and opportunities for practice leadership, research, or additional services.

Step 4. Begin initial screening of candidates through telephone interviews. The 30- to 60-minute interviews offer an inexpensive method to initiate the interview and selection process and reduce the number of candidates, if necessary. Describe what your practice and the community offer. Use the call to screen candidates by

➤ Geographic compatibility;

➤ Medical interests and strengths;

➤ Adequacy of your compensation package; and

➤ Agreement of your practice's and the candidate's goals.

Ask some open-ended questions to encourage the candidate to provide more information. Questions during the telephone interview include

➤ What led you to choose a career in medicine?

➤ What are you looking for in a practice?

> ➤   Are you willing to serve call coverage and hospital rounds (if appropriate)?

Step 5. Verify the candidate's credentials and background. After the applicant has signed a release of information, confirm his or her education, certification, licensure, work history, and hospital affiliations. The practice medical director or managing partner should conduct part of the reference check to confirm the applicant's clinical competence, issues affecting performance, and whether or not the reference recommends the candidate for the type of position being recruited.

Step 6. Bring the final selection of candidates in for an interview. This is the time to determine a match in personality, culture, goals, and skills between the candidate and your practice. MGMA healthcare consultant Kenneth T. Hertz, FACMPE, recommends that you develop clear goals for the site visit and interview and develop a specific agenda with the candidates and their spouses. Plans should provide the opportunity of seeing the candidates and their families in as many different situations as possible.

Develop a candidate assessment form to obtain standardized feedback from the interview committee for all candidates. Ask the candidates about difficult situations faced during their residencies and how they were handled, along with how they managed workload and time demands.

The mentor or other recruitment team members should take the candidate on a tour and offer opportunities to meet the physicians as well as many of the staff. You might want to offer a day when the candidate shadows a physician to understand a typical day. Discuss the workload and expectations, and judge the response. Understand that there may be generational differences.

Because of the importance of this step, the visit must be comprehensive and should involve the candidate's spouse or partner. This is when you sell your practice and the community. Introduce the candidate and partner to the community and what makes it unique. Include visits to critical sites and community services that will weigh on their decision. A casual dinner with the candidate and partner will provide additional time to learn about personalities and compatibilities.

Step 7. Once the choice is made, act fast to secure the candidate. Send the employment contract as soon as possible, and set a time frame for the offer to be accepted. Follow up with a telephone call to discuss any questions that may come up, and be prepared to offer additional incentives or compensation if the candidate is receiving other offers.

Successful physician recruitment requires an investment of time and resources. The process continues with a successful retention program (see Question 22). The results should be a long and successful relationship between physician and practice.

Sources:

Bhagwan Satiani, MD, MBA, FACS, FACHE, and Thomas E. Williams, MD, FACS, "Fill in the Blanks: 8 Steps to Make your Practice Competitive in the Physician Hiring Game," *MGMA Connexion*, August 2009, www.mgma.com/WorkArea/mgma_downloadasset. aspx?id=30048 (accessed December 30, 2010).

Jack Valancy, MBA, "Ask the Right Questions to Hire the Right Physician," *Medical Economics*, October 9, 2009, www.modernmedicine.com/modernmedicine/article/article-Detail.jsp?id=631643&sk=&date=&pageID=2 (accessed December 30, 2010).

Medical Group Management Association, "The State of Medical Practice: Physician Recruitment," *MGMA Connexion*, January 2010, www.mgma.com/WorkArea/mgma_downloadasset.aspx?id=32153 (accessed December 30, 2010).

Phillip Miller and Kurt Mosley, "The Physician Recruiting 'Iceberg,'" *MGMA Connexion*, April 2008, www.mgma.com/WorkArea/mgma_downloadasset.aspx?id=17574 (accessed December 30, 2010).

QUESTION 21 I would like to add another physician to meet our increasing patient demand, but the physicians are worried about the cost of bringing on another partner. How can I compare the cost versus the benefit of bringing on a new physician?

The decision of whether or not to hire a new physician is not an easy one and involves analysis of the options and consensus building among the practice's physicians and board. Begin by assessing the additional benefits of hiring another physician. Have patients complained about the wait time to make appointments within the practice? Have you experienced increased patient turnover that could be related to lengthy wait times? Are current physicians complaining about a high patient load or demands of call coverage? Do you refer out for services that a new physician could keep in-house? How many physicians within the practice are approaching retirement? Hiring now can be an opportunity to bring a new physician up to speed prior to another departing.

You should also consider at this time where the patients for the new physician will come from. Will they be patients currently seen by physicians in your practice, or will they be new patients bringing new revenue into the practice? Will a new service line be offered? This determination will also affect the marketing strategy once the physician is selected.

The next step in your assessment is to compare the potential investment required to bring a physician aboard with the objective benefits that the physician will offer. When calculating the additional expenses for your practice, include the following items:

Expenses	Estimated cost
Recruitment expenses (advertising, travel expenses, cost of recruiter, and so on)	
Physician's salary or compensation, including any sign-on bonus that is offered	
Benefits (health insurance, association dues, and so on)	
Physician's moving expenses covered by the practice	
Advertising and marketing expenses to promote the new physician to the public	
Malpractice insurance costs	
Additional staffing costs, if needed	
Cost of the new physician's office space and furnishings	
Cost of additional medical equipment and supplies for the physician	

If contracting with a physician-recruiting firm, negotiate the fee carefully and consider using a retained search versus a contingent search agreement. Recruiting firm charges may range from

$18,000 to $35,000 per search, depending on the location and specialty. Additional expenses for physician recruitment averaged $10,000 for relocation expenses and $22,900 for signing bonuses, according to a recent Merritt Hawkins & Associates survey.[1]

Revenue from new physicians is difficult to estimate and will depend on the market, the individual specialty, the physician, the time to complete licensing processes, and other factors. As a benchmark, MGMA has analyzed data related to the growth of new physicians' collections and compensation over time:

Physician collections by years in specialty (medians)

	1 year	2 years	3 years	4 years	5 years
Primary care	$203,352	$242,597	$260,727	$287,786	$344,245
Surgery specialists	$533,042	$602,888	$565,730	$514,970	$561,514
Medical specialists	$329,725	$412,372	$469,590	$546,942	$518,311

Note: Technical component and nonphysician provider component are excluded.

Physician compensation by years in specialty

	1 year	2 years	3 years	4 years	5 years
Primary care	$166,361	$182,293	$184,812	$195,000	$194,042
Surgery specialists	$322,801	$343,740	$375,002	$438,818	$418,989
Medical specialists	$225,633	$259,745	$277,375	$317,474	$289,790

Data are medians for full-time-equivalent physicians. Compensation includes salary, bonus and/or incentive, and distribution of profits.

Source: Medical Group Management Association, *Physician Compensation and Production Survey: 2010 Report Based on 2009 Data* (Englewood, CO: Medical Group Management Association, 2010).

Analysis of the MGMA survey data indicates that new physicians, particularly in primary care, may need initial support. You might consider financing options for the new physician, including an income guarantee through the hospital. Consider the impact that various options will have on the overall financial model prior to deciding. The initial support cost may be worthwhile when the long-term benefits are considered.

Reference:

1. Merritt Hawkins & Associates, "2010 Review of Physician Recruiting Incentives," MerrittHawkins.com, 2010, www.merritthawkins.com/uploadedFiles/MerrittHawkings/Surveys/mha2010incentivesurvPDF.pdf (accessed November 29, 2010).

Sources:

David N. Gans, "On the Edge: Pulling Their Own Weight," *MGMA Connexion*, V. 5, No. 9, October 2005.

Karen Minich-Pourshadi, "Recruiting from the Inside," *HealthLeaders Magazine*, V. 13 No. 3 (2010): 35–36.

Shelby D. Loggins, FACMPE, CPC, "Deciding How to Fund Bringing on a New Physician," ACMPE Fellowship Paper, March 2006.

QUESTION **22** Several of our practice's physicians recently resigned. What is the typical physician turnover rate? How can I be more proactive to retain physicians?

To find out your physicians' satisfaction and areas of concern, conduct a survey. This can be a formal questionnaire distributed to all physicians, an informal questioning of physicians, or discussions held during meetings. Gather what information you can on why the physicians left your practice. You may learn that they had personal reasons unrelated to your practice.

Medical group practices reported a 5.9 percent physician turnover rate in 2009, according to a survey conducted by the American Medical Group Association and Cejka Search. They also reported the top three strategies for physician retention: market-based compensation, productivity bonuses, and flexible schedules. In addition, the survey pointed out multigenerational differences. Physicians early in their careers were more interested in guaranteed compensation and advanced technology. Established physicians ranked productivity-based compensation and opportunities in partnership or leadership highest, while late-career physicians prioritized flexible schedules and greater quality of life.[1]

Other studies have found that compensation was not the most cited factor in physician departures. One project identified lower levels of physician career satisfaction with the perception that a lack of insurance has increased among Americans, the physician workload is greater, and that autonomy is limited. Satisfaction was noted as increasing when the physicians perceived improvement in access to resources and the quality of care they could provide.

Key factors for physician satisfaction included

- ➤ Meaningful work that makes a difference;

- ➤ A sense of community;

- ➤ Affirmation of physicians' value by regular, reliable, positive feedback;

- ➤ Regular communication between physician and healthcare leaders; and

- ➤ Being supported with practice leaders asking, "Is there anything you need?" or "What can I do to help?"

Ideas that other organizations put in place to increase physician retention include

- ➤ Assessing the recruitment process to ensure new physicians are a match for the organization in terms of culture, vision, values, and mission, and clearly stating expectations on compensation, schedules, professional growth, and participation in governance and ownership;

- ➤ Developing or expanding a physician orientation program;

- ➤ Increasing the social events and interactions to create a sense of community;

- ➤ Promoting new physicians and introducing them to the practice and the community;

- ➤ Evaluating compensation and benefits to ensure they are competitive; and

- ➤ Investigating job sharing, part-time, and other options to match the lifestyle objectives of new and current physicians.

A physician orientation program is vital to physician retention. An experienced physician should be assigned to each newly recruited physician to serve as a mentor and support and guide the new recruit on patient care issues. The mentor should also explain professional expectations, personal conduct, ethical behavior, organizational goals and mission, and relationships with staff members and other medical groups. Develop an orientation checklist to ensure all items are covered. An orientation manual should include supporting documents, telephone numbers and e-mail addresses, hospital contact information, an organizational chart, and relevant policies and procedures. The physician's spouse should be invited to group events and matched with another spouse for introductions into the community.

A CLOSER LOOK . . .

Sample New Physician Orientation Checklist

Use this sample as a starting point to developing your own checklist. It should be used to assign the person responsible for sharing the information and to note at what point during the orientation period it should be discussed.

Topic	Who (administrator, mentor, HR, medical director)	When
Organization — history, mission, organizational structure, customers, facilities, etc.		
Compensation — pay schedule, salary reviews		
Benefits — insurance, pension, savings plans, incentive programs		
Leave and holidays		
Security — security procedures, passwords, after-hours		
Internal communications — employee handbook, voice mail, e-mail, reporting structure		
Performance — physician expectations, quality, code of conduct, disciplinary process, and so on		

The first three years of the physician's stay in your practice will be important. If they stay that long, they're more likely to remain with the practice. Ensure the physicians receive regular encouragement and positive feedback. Physician leadership should meet with new physicians on a weekly basis in the first six months and then monthly for the next two years to ensure the new physicians feel welcome to the practice and to address any issues that arise. One of the most critical factors will be two-way communication — that is, listening to the new physician — and what is being said and inferred — not just talking at the new physician. Questions to ask during these meetings might include

➤ Have your expectations regarding this practice been met? If not, why not?

➤ What are the top three issues you believe the group faces in the next year?

➤ Describe your involvement in decision-making.

➤ Describe your level of clinical satisfaction.

Reference:

1. Cejka Search, "Medical Groups Are Adjusting to Meet Economic Challenges Reports Cejka Search and AMGA Survey," March 30, 2010, http://cejkasearch.com/media/news/2010/MAR/cejka-search-amga-survey-announcement.htm (accessed January 14, 2011).

Sources:

Bruce A. Harrison and Amri B. Johnson, "A Generation of Difference," *Healthcare Executive*, V. 23, No. 5 (September/October 2008): 76–80.

Kenneth H. Colin, "The Lifelong Iterative Process of Physician Retention," *Journal of Healthcare Management*, V. 54, No. 4 (July/August 2009): 220–26.

Kenneth T. Hertz, FACMPE, "The Ties that Bind," *MGMA Connexion*, V. 7, No. 9 (October 2007): 50–53, www.mgma.com/WorkArea/DownloadAsset.aspx?id=14770 (accessed January 14, 2011).

Mary-Ellen Just, RN, MBA, FACMPE, "Practice Overhauls Physician-Orientation Program to Help New Providers," *MGMA e-Source*, May 27, 2008, www.mgma.com/article.aspx?id=19068 (accessed January 14, 2011).

QUESTION Some new issues have developed in the practice related to physicians' benefits and policies. What information do you have on part-time physicians and maternity leave for physicians?

Practices are increasingly dealing with these issues for several reasons: The number of female physicians is increasing, younger physicians need time to care for children or aging parents, and experienced physicians want to transition toward retirement. Some practices may choose to deny these requests because of the increased workload and resentment that affect the remaining physicians. Of course, the size of your practice will affect the ability of the practice to accept a part-time schedule, but choosing to ignore the requests could be a dangerous move today. It is estimated that 20 percent of physicians in the United States work at some part-time schedule. In a survey on physician retention, 22 percent of part-time physicians were males aged 55 and older and 34 percent were females aged 44 or younger.[1] Accommodating part-time schedules and accepting maternity leave could help you retain and recruit productive physicians.

Several practices have already developed part-time and maternity-leave policies for their physicians, and you may be able to learn from your peers. The MGMA Member Community discussion groups frequently bring up these topics.

Method used to accommodate part-time physicians	Better-performing practices	Other practices
Paid less and provided fewer benefits	37.43%	38.10%
Changed the overhead rate	10.78%	9.80%
Encouraged job sharing rather than part-time employment	5.69%	5.04%
Part-time physicians were not employed at the practice	29.64%	22.69%
Other accommodations for part-time physicians	10.48%	10.36%

Source: Medical Management Association, *Performance and Practices of Successful Medical Groups: 2010 Report Based on 2009 Data* (Englewood, CO: Medical Group Management Association, 2010).

The first priority is to develop a policy, so the practice deals with this and other requests in a fair and equitable manner. The physicians within the practice should approve the policy. Approval may not be easy, but most physicians will recognize that someday they may need to make the request themselves.

Policies for part-time physicians should include

➤ Reasons for which changes in schedules or call coverage will be allowed, including childbirth, health issues, caring for aging parents, and transition to retirement.

➤ The amount of notice required to prepare the practice for the change and to recruit an additional physician or locum tenens. One year warning might be appropriate for a physician transitioning toward retirement, but less time may be acceptable for family reasons.

➤ Changes in physicians' status regarding partnership status and participation in governance. For example, the physician cannot be a partner if the number of hours or productivity measure drops below a set level. The physician may then be considered an employed physician. Buy-out options must then be considered.

➤ How the call schedule can be changed. Options in call changes include no nights but weekends, reduced number of days on call, or no changes allowed. Options for changing compensation for reduced call coverage include setting a dollar amount per day or per on-call period or developing a pool of call-coverage money and distributing that among physicians based on the percentage of calls taken.

➤ Method by which compensation will be affected. If compensation is productivity based, then compensation will decrease with reduction in hours, encounters, and procedures. Expense allocation should also be reduced, but you should consider that actual practice costs may not shrink proportionately to the reduction in hours. Other compensation models will have to be modified in other ways. A salary can be lessened equal to the change in hours or productivity.

➤ The required number of years in the practice prior to allowing transition toward retirement or other schedule changes.

➤ Options for the new, reduced schedule: more time off per year, fewer days per week, fewer hours per day, or just changes in call coverage, hospital duties, or surgery.

➤ The length of time that a reduced schedule will be allowed. For physicians transitioning to retirement, the time is often set at two to five years.

Maternity leave policies are more dependent on federal and state regulations. The Family and Medical Leave Act (FMLA) specifies who is eligible. The size of your practice is the determining factor. If your practice has 50 or more employees, you are required to provide eligible employees with up to 12 weeks of unpaid leave each year for any of the following reasons:

➤ Birth and care of the newborn child of an employee;

➤ Placement of a child for adoption or foster care with the employee;

➤ Care for an immediate family member (spouse, child, or parent) with a serious health condition; or

➤ Medical leave when the employee has a serious health condition.

More information can be found at the United States Department of Labor Web site: www.dol.gov.

State laws may require businesses with fewer than 50 employees to offer maternity leave but for a different time period (6 weeks or 16 weeks, as in California). Check your state labor department or similar department for more information.

Postings on the MGMA online Member Community offer insights on how practices deal with family and medical leave. If a physician is compensated by productivity, then compensation is usually reduced while on leave. If physicians are salaried, then leave is unpaid after using personal leave time (vacation and sick leave). FMLA requires that health benefits be continued by businesses through allowed leave time. After personal leave is used, the practice may require physicians (and staff) to pay for their benefits. To handle the reduction in call coverage during leave, physicians in some practices offer to take extra call coverage prior to or after returning from family leave.

Sources:

1. Cejka Search, "Medical Groups Are Adjusting to Meet Economic Challenges Reports Cejka Search and AMGA Survey," http://cejkasearch.com/media/news/2010/MAR/cejka-search-amga-survey-announcement.htm (accessed January 14, 2011).

Bruce A. Johnson, JD, MPA, and Deborah Walker Keegan, PhD, FACMPE, *Physician Compensation Plans: State-of-the-Art Strategies* (Englewood, CO: Medical Group Management Association, 2006).

Medical Group Management Association, "Party Line: Compensating a Physician Who Wants to Drop Call," *MGMA Connexion*, March 2009, www.mgma.com/WorkArea/mgma_downloadasset.aspx?id=26756 (accessed December 26, 2010).

United States Department of Labor, The Family and Medical Leave Act, www.dol.gov/compliance/laws/comp-fmla.htm (accessed December 26, 2010).

QUESTION 24 How should I deal with a physician who displays inappropriate behavior?

Physicians may behave inappropriately for a variety of reasons. Your first action should be to identify and document the objectionable behavior. Make sure that the behavior is disruptive to the practice and not just a case of an employee having a personal conflict with the physician. It is important to separate personal issues from those that are not. If the behavior is truly inappropriate or goes against the practice's culture, you should approach the medical director or other physician leader to present the gathered information and discuss how to proceed. The medical director should approach the physician with clearly documented events or actions that have raised concern. Sensitivity and tact should be used to identify the cause of the behavior, and the cause will determine the appropriate action.

As with most issues, prevention is the best method for handling a situation. Practices can implement strategies to ensure inappropriate behavior is not tolerated and to specify the consequences. Although the emphasis here is physician behavior, much of it is applicable to clinical and administrative employees. Strategies for preventing disruptive behaviors include

➤ Define inappropriate or disruptive behavior. Many individuals may feel that they are behaving appropriately in a situation, but the behavior has an impact on the people around them. Known inappropriate behaviors include drug or alcohol use, physical and sexual abuse, yelling, or abusive anger. Also included are condescending attitudes, showing disrespect, and insulting or berating individuals.

➤ Implement policies and procedures to specify standards of appropriate behavior. Formal policies ensure a standard approach and minimize the interference of personal bias. Employment agreements or handbooks and codes of conduct should be developed that define inappropriate behavior and specify consequences. Both should emphasize prevention over punishment.

➤ Create awareness of the issue and expectations for appropriate behavior during the recruitment process, new physician orientation, organizational meetings, and performance assessments.

➤ Develop the organizational culture of behavioral expectations with commitment from organizational leadership. The board and clinical and administrative leadership must show support for the code of conduct with personal compliance, frequent reiteration of the statements, and appropriate response with policy violations.

➤ Provide education on the performance expectations and code of conduct. Discuss personality, gender, and generational differences, and provide training on diversity and sensitivity issues.

➤ Develop procedures on reporting and follow-up by specifying whom staff should communicate with if inappropriate behavior is observed, whether directed toward them or others. Include how the practice will respond if an incident is reported and who will be in charge.

The physician leadership or medical director must take the lead when the behavior of a physician becomes an issue. Large practices may have a committee of physicians to evaluate the situation and recommend the response. Administrators should be aware of the situation and involved if the situation affects employees.

When a situation arises, medical directors can use a three-step approach (see the following "A Closer Look" sidebar) to address the issue, understand the physician's side, and discuss resolutions. Use the policies, physician's employment agreement, code of ethics, or other practice documents to support the practice's position. Discuss the behavior that needs to be changed and which disciplinary action may be taken if no changes occur. Disciplinary action can include mandatory counseling, treatment programs, written reprimands, and, eventually, termination. Offer options such as counseling prior to discipline, if possible.

A CLOSER LOOK . . .

The following is a three-step approach toward data gathering and conflict resolution:

1. Ask questions to learn each party's viewpoint and listen. Don't interject your own view; just clarify each side.

2. Ask, "Is there anything else I should know about this?" Let the person know you've heard and understand. State that you want some time to think about the issue, and suggest another time to meet.

3. At the next meeting, reiterate what you understand to be the issue and suggest a solution. In the following discussion, use mostly questions, rather than statements, to respond to objections.

Source: Marshall Colt, "Know-How: Managing the Difficult Doc," *MGMA Connexion*, V. 5, No. 9, October 2005.

If the inappropriate behavior is caused by substance abuse, a quicker, stronger response may be necessary to protect patient safety. Administrators and supervisors should learn to recognize the indications of impairment as described by Christopher J. Ramos, FACMPE:

➤ Late to appointments;

➤ Increased absences;

➤ Unknown whereabouts;

➤ Unusual rounding times, either very early or very late;

➤ Increase in patient complaints;

➤ Increased secrecy;

➤ Decreased quality of care;

➤ Careless medical decisions;

➤ Incorrect charting or writing of prescriptions;

➤ Decreased productivity or efficiency;

➤ Increased conflicts with colleagues;

➤ Increased irritability and aggression; and

➤ Erratic job history.

It is important to recognize that these symptoms can present for various reasons and do not alone imply impairment. It is the accumulation of several indicative behaviors and the consideration of whether the physician is "unable to practice medicine with reasonable skill and safety to patients."

An impaired physician should be advised to enter a treatment program or face termination. With issues related to substance abuse, you should seek the advice of your legal counsel or a human resources attorney to ensure that proper procedures are followed. Commit to seeing the issue through to the end to ensure the physician completes the treatment program or is terminated; following the path only part way will lead to future problems.

Sources:

Alan H. Rosenstein, "Disruptive Behaviour and Its Impact on Communication Efficiency and Patient Care," *Journal of Communication in Healthcare*, V. 2, No. 4 (2009): 328–40.

Christopher J. Ramos, FACMPE, "The Impaired Physician — Difficult Decisions Facing Administrators," ACMPE Fellowship Paper, October 2010.

Karen Sandrick, "Disruptive Physicians," *Trustee*, V. 62, No. 10 (2009): 8–12.

Will Latham, MBA, CPA, "Take the 'Dys' out of Function: Moving to a Culture That Values Team Effectiveness," *MGMA e-Source*, September 23, 2008, www.mgma.com/article.aspx?id=22082 (accessed January 14, 2011).

QUESTION 25

I am interviewing for a group practice administrator position and would like some advice on evaluating the employment agreement they have offered. What should I look for in the agreement?

There have been several cases of promises made during interviews for administrator positions that were not fulfilled, leading to later confusion or even termination. Signing an employment agreement commits both you and the practice to responsibilities, compensation, benefits, and other items discussed during interviews, thus limiting the possibility of discord or unhappiness with unmatched expectations.

There are many benefits for both the practice and the administrator in having an employment agreement. The benefits you will appreciate in having an agreement include

➤ Delineating the role and responsibilities of your position compared to the governing board, physician leadership, and other management figures;

➤ Clarifying physician expectations and commitment to the administrator;

➤ Financial protection by specifying the compensation amount or methodology and in the event of termination; and

➤ A basis for performance management and review expectations.

The organization benefits by having

➤ Clear delineation of responsibilities for decision-making and governance that are recognized throughout the organization;

➤ Protection with the clauses addressing termination of employment; and

➤ Opportunity for organizational strategic thinking and direction for both the practice and the administrator.

With so much importance tied to the agreement, you are wise to review it carefully prior to accepting an offer and signing the employment contract. The major elements in the agreement should include

➤ **Terms of employment.** Confirms the position title, starting date, period covered by the agreement, location, hours of employment, and reporting structure. Employment agreements typically cover one to three years but may be rolling or evergreen contracts that continue until a reason for change or termination.

➤ **Duties/Responsibilities.** Review the list to ensure alignment between the agreement and job description. Watch for items discussed during the interview that aren't included or duties included that weren't discussed and could become an issue. You may want to discuss adding responsibilities based on your knowledge or experience.

    ➤ The responsibilities may specify a business expense, which the administrator must confer with the physicians. This will clarify the spending authority and dollar limit of the administrator.

➤ **Compensation.** Specifies the starting or base salary and pay schedule (monthly, bimonthly, or weekly). Make sure that all promises agreed upon during the interview and negotiations are included, especially if the practice committed to a specific compensation increase at a certain time. Salary increases are usually left open-ended ("subject to review") in the agreement, since they will be based on performance reviews, performance of the organization, or other factors, although there may be some information on how increases or bonuses will be determined.

➤ **Benefits.** The agreement should include the benefits and perquisites for the administrator or executive position.

Typical benefits that might be included are

- Annual days off, including vacation, sick, holiday, and professional development days;
- Insurance coverage, including life, medical, dental, and vision care and whether or not your family is covered;
- Disability benefits;
- Professional association dues;
- Continuing education, including tuition assistance; and
- Employee assistance programs.

➤ **Termination of employment.** Specifies the financial protections between the administrator and the practice and reasons for termination.

- Lists the notification requirements for the administrator to end the contract.
- Termination "with cause" stipulates that you will be fired for significant misconduct including committing a crime, failure or refusal to perform duties or comply with policies or procedures, or other breach of contract. Termination for poor performance is difficult to legally specify within the agreement.
- Termination "without cause" provides an opportunity to fire the administrator for any reason and is frequently used in cases of poor performance or insurmountable differences between executives and board. Organizations are usually protected by state "employment at will" laws that allow termination at any time for no specific reason.

➤ **Severance plan.** Severance plans can take several forms and may be dependent on the termination being without cause. Voluntary termination on the part of the administrator or termination with cause may not include any severance compensation. The number of months of severance pay is dependent on the organization and the length of service. Hospitals may offer severance pay for 12 to

24 months, but smaller group practices may offer only a few months to 12 months. The agreement should also specify if any insurance benefits would be continued after termination and for how long and whether the practice will fund outplacement services.

➤ **Change of control and termination.** Discusses termination arrangements in case the practice merges or is bought by a hospital and the administrator's position is eliminated. Should also specify severance payment and continuation of benefits.

➤ **Noncompete and nondisclosure clauses.** These clauses will specify if you are allowed to consult or work in additional positions while working for the practice and if you'll be limited by where you can work after you leave the practice. Nondisclosure or confidentiality statements are fairly standard but should be reviewed closely. Noncompete clauses can be too restrictive for the administrator position and should be negotiated out of the contract.

➤ **Death during employment.** This states that the practice will pay the compensation to the estate or survivors of the administrator for the remainder of the month or a set period if the administrator dies during the contract period.

Several of the elements are standard and don't need to be negotiated. Others are negotiable. Part of the negotiation process is to remind the physicians why they selected you and the value that you will bring to the organization. They may not know much about business and practice management and should be informed of the benefits you will bring. You will have to determine which terms are acceptable to you and which must be changed, or you will not accept the offer.

Sources:

Employment Contracts for Healthcare Executives: Rationale, Trends and Samples, 5th Edition (Chicago: Health Administration Press, 2009).

Hal Patterson, *Take Charge of Your Employment Agreement: A Win-Win Communication Tool for Medical Practice Executives* (Englewood, CO: Medical Group Management Association, 2002).

Medical Group Management Association, "Group Practice Administrator — Employment Contracts," *Information Exchange* #4455 (Englewood, CO: Medical Group Management Association, 2004).

QUESTION I've just been hired as a practice administrator for a new practice. The physicians want me to develop my own compensation plan. What's the best way to include an incentive system and to develop my performance expectations?

Including a bonus or incentive system in practice administrators' compensation plans provides the same message as incentive systems for physicians or employees: dedication to the practice's success will be rewarded. The difficulty in all incentive systems is to develop the program that produces the desired behavior and results without generating resentment or manipulating the system.

Incentive systems should be clearly stated, based on measurable factors, and tied closely to the performance management and review process. The easiest system for physicians to manage is to base the incentive on practice revenue or profit. Based on an informal MGMA survey, that is the most common incentive system:

Type of incentive	Percent of respondents
Based on practice profit	56%
Discretionary cash award based on exemplary performance	47%
Raise based on merit	41%
Profit sharing	34%
Discretionary noncash award based on performance	2%

Source: Medical Group Management Association, "Administrator Incentive Plans," *Information Exchange* #6530 (Englewood, CO: Medical Group Management Association, December 2008).

Discussions regarding administrator incentive systems in the MGMA Member Community discussion groups provided several ideas currently used by group practices:

➤ "My bonus was tied to total collections and total owner compensation. We took a set percentage of each number and averaged out the two. This forces you to seek new business and do everything possible to get paid for the work you do; you also have the incentive to keep costs down, as this has a direct effect on owners' compensation. If you have a guaranteed amount, the difference would be your bonus. In my case, we opted for no guarantee."

➤ "Here's one model: As additional compensation, a maximum incentive bonus, based on performance and the attainment of goals, equal to as much as 20 percent of the base salary, shall be awarded at the discretion of the board of directors and in accordance with the incentive bonus plan for each of the following criteria:

   ➤ Budget target for physician compensation (0 percent to 25 percent);

   ➤ Accounts receivable days below XX (0 percent to 25 percent);

   ➤ Budget target for cost of practice/operations (0 percent to 25 percent); and

   ➤ Board discretion/leadership (0 percent to 25 percent)."

➤ "I like mine: quick, immediate and easy to figure. Base salary, constant. My bonus is paid monthly — 5 percent of profits. In this profit number I exclude the doctors' salaries and expenses, as I have no control over that. My bonus annually is usually greater than or equal to my base salary."

➤ "I have a bonus structure that pays quarterly based on a number of categories and performance within those categories. While the financial success of a practice is a huge deal, there are lots of other components that conspire to make a practice successful — or not."

➤ "We break these into broad categories of service, quality, people, financial and growth. As practice administrators, we attempt to balance the needs/demands of our providers, patients and employees. That's our job. However, to say that we are successful based solely on the changes to physicians' annual income marginalizes the other contributions we make to the growth and stability of the practice."

The final response addresses an interesting point that total net revenue or physicians' income doesn't incorporate all of the administrator's contributions to the practice. Incentive compensation programs that address more of the responsibilities can be developed if they are tied to the employment agreement or job description's list of responsibilities and specific goals developed in the performance management process.

Physicians in the practice may prefer to limit the performance review and incentive on a few easy-to-track financial goals, such as increasing revenue, reducing costs, or reducing A/R. Limiting the review to these factors doesn't allow you to demonstrate your contribution in other areas, such as patient satisfaction, employee satisfaction and retention, implementation and management of new information technology tools, monitoring of compliance plans and procedures, and innovative ideas for operations or revenue. Developing performance expectations helps align your goals with the organizational objectives and defines priorities in your list of responsibilities.

In developing a performance management plan, follow these recommended steps:

➤ Meet with the physicians to

➢ Review the organizational strategy and objectives, both long and short term;

➢ Establish five to six personal objectives to achieve organizational objectives;

➢ Discuss personal professional development plans;

➢ Identify means of measuring and evaluating progress toward meeting objectives; and

➢ Establish timetable for meeting goals and managing expectations.

➤ Schedule meetings with the board or physician leadership during the year to discuss progress in meeting organizational and personal objectives and ensure that any changes in either are addressed.

➤ Schedule an annual performance review meeting. Present information on accomplishments during the full year and success in completing the objectives (using visual aids where possible). Begin the discussion on next year's goals and objectives.

Effective performance reviews are

➤ A shared discussion between you and the physician(s). It starts with an honest self-assessment of your accomplishments based on facts, not opinions.

➤ Forward-looking with an emphasis on plans and ideas for improvement in the next year.

➤ Open discussions of what can be changed to help you do your job better.

➤ Don't include surprises, since meetings during the year kept the physicians informed of your progress and performance as well as their sharing information on changing priorities or goals.

The performance management and review process is an opportunity for you to educate the physicians regarding your complete set of responsibilities, accomplishments that occurred during the

A LOOK AT THE NUMBERS . . .

According to an MGMA informal survey, administrator performance reviews are conducted by

Board of directors	31%
President of the board	25%
Senior physician	14%
Medical director	6%

Performance appraisals were a factor in determining merit raises for 75 percent of respondents and influencing bonuses for 48 percent.

year, and your success in meeting organizational goals. It may be easier to go without a review, but the process ensures you and the physicians are in agreement on the priorities and that you are emphasizing those priorities. Incentive or bonus compensation based on achieving your performance expectations aligns your and the practice's goals and commitments.

Sources:

Employment Contracts for Healthcare Executives: Rationale, Trends and Samples, 5th Edition (Chicago: Health Administration Press, 2009).

Hal Patterson, *Take Charge of Your Employment Agreement: A Win-Win Communication Tool for Medical Practice Executives* (Englewood, CO: Medical Group Management Association, 2002).

Medical Group Management Association, "Administrator Performance Appraisals," *Information Exchange* #6530 (Englewood, CO: Medical Group Management Association, July 2008).

Medical Group Management Association, "Party Line: Do You Have an Administrator Bonus Plan?" *MGMA Connexion*, January 2008, www.mgma.com/WorkArea/mgma_downloadasset.aspx?id=15818 (accessed December 29, 2011).

QUESTION 27 I'm looking for information on the staffing ratios in a medical practice. How do I know if I have the right number of staff for my practice?

If your staffing numbers are a little high compared to other practices around you, your first instinct may be to make some staff reductions. However, MGMA member practices that are identified as better-performing practices consistently have higher staff ratios than other practices responding to MGMA's annual Cost Survey. Since the first edition of this book, staffing ratios for better-performing groups increased slightly, while the ratios for other practices decreased compared to 2007 data. Better-performing groups are accomplishing the goal of determining the right staffing model to maximize their productivity and revenues related to staff expenses.

The number of staff per physician in group practices is tracked in the annual MGMA *Cost Survey Report* and the *Performance and Practices of Successful Medical Groups Report:*

Total FTE support staff per FTE physician

Specialty	Better-performing groups	Others
Primary care single specialty	4.65	3.51
Medicine single specialty	5.63	3.65
Surgical single specialty	6.41	3.83

Note: FTE = full-time equivalent

Source: Medical Group Management Association, *Performance and Practices of Successful Medical Groups: 2010 Report Based on 2009 Data* (Englewood, CO: Medical Group Management Association, 2010).

Analysis of MGMA data on staffing numbers and financial ratios shows that medical practices have poorer financial performance at the lowest and often the highest staffing levels. If a practice has too few employees, it isn't maximizing provider productivity and revenue is reduced. If there are too many employees, their salary and benefit expenses outweigh the benefits of increased productivity.

The concept of rightsizing to determine staffing levels for your practice has been around for several years. Rightsizing is the systematic process of reviewing employee numbers, tasks, and work processes to determine the appropriate number and mix of staff needed to meet medical practice goals. Rightsizing involves quantitative and qualitative analyses to answer two key questions: "Do you have the right staff?" and "Are they doing the right things?"

As medical practices and the healthcare system evolve, practice administrators have grown to realize that it's more about the right staffing numbers. The key is also to recognize the specifics of your practice and ensure that you have the best staffing model and the best employees for your practice. Innovations in medical practice management, health information technology, and healthcare reimbursement may affect the types and number of employees. Examples include

➤ Implementing EHRs will shift staff from medical records to information technology;

➤ Integrating nonphysician providers requires analysis of
  their roles and the need for additional staff to support their
  activities;

➤ Participating in patient-centered medical homes or quality
  reimbursement incentives may require different nursing
  and nonphysician provider staff;

➤ Introducing Web-based patient portals, virtual visits, and
  social media, which are changing the physician-patient
  interaction, will require personnel with new information
  technology skills; and

➤ Understanding that physicians and employees from
  Generations X and Y expect flexible and less-demanding
  schedules.

Deborah Walker Keegan, PhD, FACMPE, author of *Innovative
Staffing for the Medical Practice*, recommends addressing these
themes when analyzing staffing numbers for your practice:

➤ Implement flexible staffing models and schedules to have
  the staff available to support specific functions at specific
  times.

➤ Organize around a patient-centric approach, so the patient
  and work flow concentrate on providing value to the
  customer rather than the convenience of physicians and
  nurses.

➤ Emphasize teamwork and staff for a "well-coordinated care
  team that is professional and empathetic."

➤ Recruit staff for their ability to contribute new ideas and
  skills to the practice.

Deborah Walker Keegan recommends you begin by reviewing
your current staffing levels and your current staff deployment
model. Review the work functions, who completes these functions, and how the tasks are completed. Ask why you have the
current model, when was it last changed, where are there work
backlogs in key functions, and what is the quality and quantity
of the work performed? Are the right employees performing
the right work, or are personnel working below or above their

licensure and skill level? Practice inefficiencies can develop when employees are expected to multitask or physicians are performing tasks that others should be doing.

Deborah Walker Keegan identifies four steps to analyze and optimize your staffing model:

➤ Benchmark current staffing ratios and costs using MGMA survey data and other research.

➤ Compare your staffing numbers with expected workload ranges. MGMA resources such as *Innovative Staffing* and *The Physician Billing Process* provide benchmark data on expected workload by staff function.

➤ Identify ways to redesign work flow to reduce waste and streamline and standardize processes. Develop staff teams that create efficient work flows and a sense of ownership in team functions. Use lean theory to evaluate work processes (see Question 81).

➤ "Innovate your model" using the staffing numbers and redesigned work flow to implement a new staffing model.

For example, analyze your current telephone management strategies and evaluate who is assigned telephone operations and the number and type of calls they handle. Then identify ways to separate tasks related to patient flow (check-in, check-out, and so on) from telephone operations, analyze call volume to identify busier and quieter times, and look for information technology or other ideas to limit the number of calls. Finally, adjust the staffing model to accommodate the increased efficiencies and shift in tasks.

Another key in successful staffing is "talent management." As Deborah Walker Keegan states, "The key to talent management is holding individuals accountable for performance and results." This means modifying the recruitment process to hire the individuals who will contribute the most, expecting the most out of the staff and supporting them in education and development plans, soliciting feedback on what is needed to best accomplish their work, and implementing performance review and incentive programs to accomplish these goals.

Having the right staff with the right work flow, support, and incentives is key to an efficient and profitable practice.

Sources:

Deborah Walker Keegan, PhD, FACMPE, *Innovative Staffing for the Medical Practice* (Englewood, CO: Medical Group Management Association, 2011).

Nick A. Fabrizio, PhD, FACMPE, "More than Staffing Ratios: What to Consider When Evaluating the Need for Information Technology Employees," *MGMA Connexion*, V. 6, No. 4, May/June 2006.

QUESTION I think we are experiencing high staff turnover. Does MGMA track turnover ratios in medical practices that I can use to benchmark?

MGMA does track employee turnover rates for better-performing groups in the annual *Performance and Practices of Successful Medical Groups Report*:

Position	% turnover
Receptionists and medical records staff	16.2%
Nursing and clinical support staff	12.5%
Billing/collections and data entry staff	8.1%
Administrative staff	0.0%

Source: Medical Group Management Association, *Performance and Practices of Successful Medical Groups: 2010 Report Based on 2009 Data* (Englewood, CO: Medical Group Management Association, 2010).

Some turnover is to be expected, and new employees bring new ideas to a practice. However, if your turnover ratios are higher than these averages, you should determine the reasons for the turnover, the degree of employee satisfaction in general, and the steps you can take to reduce turnover. If you are challenged on the amount of effort you spend to reduce turnover, remind the challenger of the costs related to employee turnover and its impact on patient satisfaction.

The total cost for replacing an employee is estimated to be 50 percent to 150 percent of the annual salary of the position, with the higher percentages for managerial staff. That means it can cost an organization up to $75,000 to replace a $50,000-a-year employee. These percentages include all related costs, such as recruiting, hiring and training, using temporary employees during transitions, and lost productivity during the first six months of employment.

Employee satisfaction is the key to retention, and it begins with the hiring process. Ensure that your recruitment process leads to hiring individuals who have the skills and personality to match the job and the practice culture. Both the hiring manager and the job candidate need to have a clear understanding of the position and expectations, and the selection process should be lengthy enough to assess a match. Each new employee should go through an orientation program that includes a thorough description of the position's responsibilities, the goals of the practice, and the communication channels for questions and issues.

Conducting regular employee satisfaction surveys will help you address any issues before they become turnover issues. Sample satisfaction surveys can be obtained from the MGMA Information Center, various print resources, and the online MGMA Member Community.

Studies have found common factors in employee satisfaction and morale. Employees are more apt to remain in a practice that

➤   Offers attractive salaries and benefits;

➤   Accepts flexible scheduling;

A CLOSER LOOK . . .

Employee satisfaction and retention can be related to patient satisfaction

Patient satisfaction surveys consistently indicate that the Murray (Kentucky) Woman's Clinic exceeds its patients' expectations. Gary P. Houck, practice administrator, says one explanation for the practice's success is the low employee turnover, which provides a familiar, professional atmosphere for patients. The practice provides a sense of ownership and encourages employee suggestions.

➤ Supports continuing education and training to improve job capabilities and encourage advancement opportunities;

➤ Encourages open communication, including regular meetings and appearances by practice leadership;

➤ Has effective relationships among supervisors and physicians, including showing appreciation and providing positive feedback;

➤ Listens to employees' suggestions and ideas; and

➤ Offers a sense of community or family and employee ownership in the success of the practice.

To help determine why employees are leaving your practice, conduct an exit interview. Asking a few questions will provide insight on issues within the practice that may be affecting employee satisfaction and retention. The MGMA Member Community discussion groups frequently share sample exit interviews in their libraries. The questions asked include

➤ What influenced your decision to leave?

➤ How could the group have made your job more manageable or rewarding?

➤ Were the employee orientation and on-the-job training adequate, or could these have been improved?

➤ How has management responded to your concerns?

➤ Were the salary and benefits adequate for the responsibilities assigned?

➤ What did you like and dislike about this practice, its work processes, and your interpersonal relationships?

Employee retention is a factor in the practice's financial well-being and employee morale. Therefore, it is worth the effort of ensuring an effective recruitment process and a commitment toward employee satisfaction.

EMPLOYEE SALARY SURVEYS

These sources conduct employee salary surveys that can help determine if you offer competitive salaries:

MGMA Management Compensation Survey	mgma.com/store
MGMA State Associations	mgma.com/states
The Healthcare Group, Staff Salary Survey	thehealthcaregroup.com
Professional Association of Healthcare Office Managers, Annual Salary Survey	pahcom.com
U.S. Bureau of Labor Statistics, Wages by Area and Occupation	bls.gov/bls/blswage.htm
Professional associations by position (state and national nursing associations, American Academy of Procedural Coders, and so on)	Too many to list.

Sources:

Karen S. Schechter, "Staying Attuned to Employee Needs Can Lower Turnover," *American Medical News*, September 22/29, 2008, www.ama-assn.org/amednews/2008/09/22/bica0922.htm (accessed December 30, 2010).

Medical Group Management Association, "Rewarding Staff. Snapshot of Success: Low Staff Turnover Boosts Patient Satisfaction," *MGMA e-Connexion*, Issue 114, January 2007.

Ruth Gaulke, "Turnover Costs: Eliminate Your Practice's Employee Turnstile," *MGMA e-Source*, July 2007, www.mgma.com/article.aspx?id=13924 (accessed December 30, 2010).

Shirley Cress Dudley, MA, LPC, FACMPE, "Improving Employee Morale in High Stress Medical Practices," ACMPE Fellowship Paper, October 2008.

QUESTION 29 I'm struggling to develop an effective employee performance review process. What is the best approach to take?

Employee performance reviews or appraisals are a necessary part of human resource management. They play a role in achieving organizational goals, providing customer satisfaction, and maintaining employee productivity and morale; however, they are never easy and can even be painful. Constant research is conducted and new ideas proposed to improve the process and do away with the pain.

A summary of research on effective performance reviews provides us with keys to successful programs:

- ➤ Separate meetings should be used to identify annual goals, provide feedback, and address changes in compensation.

- ➤ Goals and objectives should be understandable and closely tied to organizational goals, vision, and culture.

- ➤ Goals, objectives, and measurement standards should be developed prior to the performance review.

- ➤ Managers should use the appraisal to share honest feedback, both praise and constructive criticism.

- ➤ The review should be seen by the employee as an opportunity to discuss and commit to future improvement. Allow time for discussion.

- ➤ Supervisors should minimize actions that cause employees to become defensive or complacent.

- ➤ Supervisors can benefit from coaching on how to provide effective feedback and constructive criticism.

- ➤ Supervisors should be aware of factors affecting bias and not let personality traits or issues interfere.

- ➤ Employees respond better to processes that encourage their input.

- ➤ Managers need to have personal knowledge and understanding of the employee's performance and not base reviews on hearsay.

Confusion about goals and how the employee can reach them impact the job performance and an employee's morale. Goals should be tied to the purpose of the employee's job and the significant or positive contribution it has on the customer, his or her team of coworkers, and the organization. The goals should not allow status quo performance or operations but link to the improvement of the business as a whole. The employee and supervisor should agree upon the actions to achieve the goals and how to determine when the results are achieved. Performance appraisals are based on those actions and results.

Several keys for effective performance management are related to feedback. When done properly, feedback will inspire employees to maintain or improve to achieve great performance. When done poorly, employee morale suffers. Feedback is often most effective if it's shared close to the time of an action. For this reason, personnel managers should consider regular feedback rather than waiting for an annual review. Prior to providing feedback, supervisors should ask themselves,

- Do I have all the facts related to the topic?

- What is the purpose of my feedback — to provide positive comments or encourage improvements?

- What are the specific behaviors or actions that I want to encourage or correct?

- What suggestions or support can I offer?

The Society of Human Resource Managers has identified several frequent blunders in performance appraisals:

- **Over-evaluation.** Not considering the total performance of an employee over the time period and concentrating on recent weeks or months. Evaluating the performance based on the employee's total performance can help overcome this issue.

- **Overkill.** Letting performance issues with an employee build until the supervisor is overcome with frustration. Waiting until an annual performance meeting may delay issues that need to be dealt with as they occur. Encourage supervisors to provide more regular feedback.

- **General labels.** Don't allow general performance comments such as "employee has a bad attitude" or "needs to improve customer relations." The labels should be converted to specific behaviors and what makes them inappropriate or what needs to be improved.

- **Potential disability claims.** Changes in behavior or performance should not lead a supervisor to ask about disability, depression, or other physical or mental causes. The supervisor should concentrate on performance and report

A CLOSER LOOK . . .

Social Media and Performance Evaluations

Employers are using social media programs as new tools in providing performance feedback. The goals are to make performance reviews more real-time, flexible, fun, useful, and dynamic. They could even make the dreaded annual appraisal a thing of the past.

One Twitter-like program encourages employees to post questions such as, "What did you think of my presentation?" or "How could I have run that meeting better?" The e-mails go to managers, peers, and others. The short anonymous replies are compiled and forwarded to the employee. Another Facebook-like program has employees post on their profile pages their goals for the week, month, or year. Supervisors can quickly review the pages for goals, or lack thereof, and the employee's success in meeting the goals.

Source: Jena McGregor, "Job Review in 140 Keystrokes," *BusinessWeek*, March 23, 2009, Issue 4124, 58.

---

to a human resource professional if an employee claims a physical or mental condition is affecting performance.

A new performance review idea is the negotiated performance appraisal model. It uses a dialogue between supervisor and subordinate to agree on how performance can be improved with specific measurements tied to the organizational needs. Prior to the appraisal meeting, both the supervisor and employee complete three lists related to the performance:

➤ Performance areas in which the employee has done well.

➤ Performance areas in which the employee has improved since the last review.

➤ Performance areas in which the employee has not met expectations and still needs improvement.

By starting the discussion with where the employee has done well, the review begins in a positive manner and encourages an honest exchange or dialogue. The positive feedback received during the first two items should open the employee to a sincere exchange related to self-identified areas of improvement. The negotiation occurs when there are differences in opinion on accomplishments and improvement areas and should be an open discussion. The final step is review of a fourth list developed by the subordinate answering the question, "What can the supervisor do differently to help the employee excel?"

MGMA RESOURCES

The Maximizing Performance Management Series by Susan A. Murphy, MBA, PhD, (Item #PK7097) includes the following titles:

➤ *Aligning the Team with Practice Goals*, Item #7092

➤ *Leading, Coaching, and Mentoring the Team*, Item #7094

➤ *Building and Rewarding Your Team*, Item #7093

➤ *Relationship Management and the New Workforce*, Item #7095

Sources:

Gregorio Billikopf, "The Negotiated Performance Appraisal Model: Enhancing Supervisor-Subordinate Communication and Conflict Resolution," *Group Facilitation: A Research & Applications Journal*, V. 10 (2010): 32–42.

Jeffrey Russell and Linda Russell, "Talk Me through It: The Next Level of Performance Management," *T+D*, V. 64, No. 4 (2010): 42–48.

Jonathan A. Segal, "Performance Management Blunders," *HR Magazine*, November 2010, 75–78.

QUESTION 30 What types of employee incentive plans do medical group practices have in place?

A 2010 informal survey of MGMA member practices found that 65 percent of respondents offer incentive pay plans for their employees. The reasons for the plans were to improve morale, influence productivity and performance, build a sense of ownership and loyalty to the practice, and increase the sense of inclusion within the practice.

Respondents to the Information Exchange used the following types of incentives:

Raise based on merit	54.7%
Profit sharing	44.2%
Bonus based on practice profit	43.2%
Discretionary cash awards for exemplary performance	37.9%
Bonus based on collection percentage	22.1%
Bonus based on production	16.8%
Discretionary noncash award for exemplary performance	15.8%

Source: Medical Group Management Association, "Employee Incentive Plans," *Information Exchange* #6567 (Englewood, CO: Medical Group Management Association, 2010).

It's interesting to note that factors related to employee morale and commitment to the practice were frequently cited as reasons for incentive programs. Properly developed incentive systems demonstrate the employee's role in the success of the organization and enable employees to share when the practice does well. These issues increase employee morale and sense of loyalty.

Incentive programs should be aligned to organizational mission, vision, and objectives. Examples include increasing patient satisfaction, collections, or revenue; reducing errors; and improving the quality of care provided. Incentives should reward the behaviors or actions that you want repeated and recognize when actions are done well. They also serve the intrinsic need in everyone to receive positive feedback and personal recognition and to feel part of a community. They can be used to recognize individual, team, or organization-wide successes or a combination of all three. Employees can participate in incentive-program development by identifying individual or team goals or participating in planning committees. Rewards and recognition should be provided in public formats wherever possible.

There are two categories of reward and incentive systems: formal and informal. Formal programs are typically long-term programs linked to organizational goals and objectives. They objectively measure and reward behavior and have a dedicated budget.

Rewards are formal and rewarded at specific times. The most frequent example is merit increases tied to performance reviews. Other examples include employee anniversaries, completion of education plans, or being assigned additional responsibilities.

Case Studies

A hospital-owned family practice implemented a comprehensive program to increase collections that included an employee incentive program. Monetary rewards were earned by employee collection teams and paid at quarterly intervals. The program included five goals:

➤ High patient satisfaction;

➤ Denial percentage below 4 percent;

➤ Charge entry completed within 24 hours;

➤ A net practice revenue increase by 5 percent over the previous quarter; and

➤ A $20 increase in average collection per patient.

It was decided to pay a partial monetary reward for meeting some of the goals. The incentive pay ranged from $50 to $250 per employee per quarter. Managers identified tools and training needed to help obtain goals, including scripts for speaking with patients regarding payments. After implementation, the program increased employee and patient satisfaction and revenue for the practice.[1]

Murray Woman's Clinic in Kentucky has a successful employee suggestion program. An annual survey asks employees for their suggestions on how to increase practice productivity and profitability. Another form is used to collect comments and suggestions that employees hear from patients. The physicians review the suggestions on a regular basis. The employees with the winning suggestions are rewarded with two extra vacation days. All employees also receive an annual bonus based on practice profitability.[2]

May Grant Associates, a 25-provider OB/GYN practice in Lancaster, Pa., eliminated the annual discretionary bonus and implemented a performance-based bonus. At the annual performance review, staff members earn a low, average, or excellent rating on job performance and work attitudes. Each rating is assigned a point value along with points for tenure. Monetary values are assigned to point levels, and bonuses are distributed based on those levels.[3]

To be successful, formal programs must directly connect to the organizational goals, specified desired results, and objective measurement standards.

Informal incentive programs celebrate successes, promotions, and examples of good behavior and include rewards that can be offered at any time. Rewards include cash, gift cards, flowers, merchandise, food, additional time off, plaques or trophies, parties, or employee-of-the-month parking spots. Recognition can also be in the form of congratulations for a good job or a good employee suggestion during a staff meeting, notes or other contact from practice leadership, or just a thank-you when good behavior is observed. Informal recognition programs are effective when there's a limited budget, when they have an immediate impact, and when they can be customized to individual employees. They can incorporate peer-to-peer recognition.

References:

1. Carla D. Johnson, FACMPE, "Improving Collections," ACMPE Fellowship Paper, October 2009, www.mgma.com/WorkArea/mgma_downloadasset.aspx?id=40373 (accessed January 23, 2011).

2. Sue Zipf and Mona Engle, RN, "Motivate Staff to Work for the Good of the Whole," *MGMA Connexion*, October 2008, www.mgma.com/WorkArea/DownloadAsset. aspx?id=22184 (accessed January 23, 2011).

3. Ruth Gaulke, MPW, "Snapshot of Success: Low Staff Turnover Boosts Patient Satisfaction," *MGMA e-Connexion*, Issue 114, January 2007, www.mgma.com/article. aspx?id=1100 (accessed January 23, 2011).

Source:

Kimberly Wishon-Powell, MBA, FACMPE, "Intrinsic vs. Extrinsic Motivation: How Much Does Money Really Matter?" ACMPE Fellowship Paper, April 2006.

QUESTION 31 We're about ready to have a generational battle. What advice do you have to help us deal with some generational differences?

There have always been differences between generations, but the current generation gap may be greater than previously experienced. In a Health Leaders survey, two-thirds of responding physicians felt that generational differences affected practice operations and one-fourth felt they impacted recruitment, productivity, and culture. However, the generations are here to stay and must be accepted. The key is to learn about the contributions that all generations can provide, understand their values and priorities, and adjust methods of communication and HR practices to accommodate the differences.

The three generations in the workforce now have been given different names and breakouts, but basically they are known as Baby Boomers, Generation X, and Generation Y or Millennials. At the risk of over-generalizing, here are the values and characteristics frequently associated with the generations:

➤ **Baby Boomers,** born between 1943 and 1960, are optimistic, team-oriented, and looking for personal gratification and growth. They value involvement, personal relationships, good management, and signs of respect. They respond to public recognition, chances to demonstrate their worth and contributions, solicitation of their opinions, and rewards for their work ethic and commitment.

➤ **Generation X-ers,** born between 1960 and 1980, value diversity, technology, informality, flexibility, fun, and self-reliance. They are more difficult to retain, since they expect to change positions and careers several times, and need more variety and challenges. They will ask "Why?" more and need to know the implications and contributions of their work.

To obtain the most from Generation X-ers, provide lots of projects, access to the latest technology, regular positive and constructive feedback, and opportunities for participation and advancement. They don't appreciate being shown how to accomplish a task; they want to be given the goal and the tools and allowed to complete the task in their way. Social media and texting may be the best communication tools.

➤ **Millennials or Generation Y-ers,** born between 1980 and 2000, tend to be optimistic, confident, and team-oriented. They accept diversity and are tech savvy. Similar to Generation X-ers, they want projects to learn from, flexibility, fun, regular feedback, and quick responses via e-mail or telephone messages. Since they're new to the workforce, they need more guidance but do well under mentoring programs. Managers should learn Generation Y employees' personal goals and how to link them to organizational goals, as well as provide opportunities for education and skill-building and opportunities to share their ideas and knowledge.

There are several ways for you to adapt to and incorporate the generational differences into your practice. To accommodate the characteristics of the younger generations, consider the following actions:

➤ Modify the compensation and benefit packages to emphasize skills and task completion, and move away from dependence on length of service.

➤ Recognize differences in motivation in performance management and incentive systems. Meeting organizational goals and profit sharing will be less appealing than additional time off, gift cards, cash rewards, and participation in new projects. Learn the priorities of younger employees to customize rewards for their interests. Public recognition of good work or accomplishing difficult tasks is also important.

➤ Increase the frequency of feedback, including some real-time feedback, rather than relying on annual performance reviews. Consider using social media and e-mails to provide feedback.

➤ Incorporate flexible schedules. Concentrate on getting the tasks done and meeting goals, not the hours in which they're done.

➤ Use technology to increase the number of communication methods to match different styles. Baby Boomers still appreciate employee newsletters, memos, and formal meetings, but younger generations communicate electronically.

➤ Develop mentoring programs to train younger workers and increase their commitment to the organization, and provide opportunities for older employees to learn from and about the younger generations.

➤ Provide opportunities for continuing education, skill development, and taking on new challenges.

➤ Adjust meeting styles toward shorter and less frequent meetings, with opportunities for engagement and delegating tasks.

A real concern is the development of conflict brought on by the differences in generational values and styles. The key is to obtain a commitment from everyone to listen to and learn from each other. Commitment should come from the practice leadership team to accept generational differences and embrace them.

Provide opportunities for members of the younger generation to describe who they are and what they want out of life. Mentoring should be seen as an opportunity for individuals to get acquainted with the other and recognize that both have something to contribute. Gen X-ers and Millennials can learn from the Boomers' experience and corporate knowledge, while Boomers can learn about technology and new research or ideas from the younger employees. Their career and job changes can bring unique experiences to the workplace. Boomers should recognize that Gen X-ers lifestyle values aren't signs of laziness or lack of commitment. Boomers might learn about balancing work and life to reduce stress and enjoy life more. Younger employees can learn that occasional short-term sacrifices, like working overtime to complete a specific project, may be needed for long-term gains and don't interfere with life's goals.

Younger generations expect to work in teams and on team projects with their shared goals, joint responsibilities, and open communication. These can be opportunities for learning about each other and accepting differences. Their frequent questions or suggestions shouldn't be seen as challenges but part of their personalities. Learn to acknowledge the suggestions and share ideas on how to question without seeming to challenge. Provide the team goal and let the generations contribute their positive characteristics to reach the goal. If conflict develops, work toward collaboration rather than letting one side win or gain dominance.

PHYSICIANS

Physicians have the same generational differences and potential conflicts as other people in the workforce. Physician leaders need to accept these differences and find ways to capitalize on the positive values that younger physicians bring to the practice. Although younger physicians are less willing to accept long hours and call coverage, their efficiency and use of technology can increase their productivity. The younger generation brings skills and values that are very important in the changing healthcare industry, including an acceptance of technology, emphasis on teamwork, and experience in accessing information, analyzing data, and problem-solving to address clinical issues. These skills are necessary with the expansion of EHRs, development of collaborative care teams, and use of clinical tools and databases for deciphering medical conditions and evidence-based care. Younger physicians are passionate about their careers, even if they believe in lifestyle management, and bring an understanding of public health and whole-person care that matches the growing emphasis on patient outcomes and quality care.

Sources:

Elyas Bakhtiari, "Time for Dr. Next?" *HealthLeaders Magazine*, V. 12, No. 7 (2009): 14–22.

David Boyd, "Ethical Determinants for Generations X and Y," *Journal of Business Ethics*, V. 93, No. 3 (2010): 465–69.

Keven Haeberle, Jami Herzber, and Terry Hobbs, "Leading the Multigenerational Work Force," *Healthcare Executive*, V. 24, No. 5 (2009): 62–67.

Ronald Finnan, "Encouraging Collaboration to Avoid Collision: Managing the Intergenerational Workforce in Healthcare," ACMPE Fellowship Paper, October 2007, www.mgma.com/WorkArea/mgma_downloadasset.aspx?id=25858 (accessed January 25, 2011).

 QUESTION 32 An ex-employee has recently filed suit against the practice, making me realize we need an employee grievance policy. Do you have a sample policy?

The most difficult aspect of a practice administrator or supervisor's job is dealing with employee issues that arise. It is normal for interpersonal conflicts or disagreements with management policies to occur, but managers must learn to recognize issues that could lead to more serious complaints and potentially legal issues.

Kenneth T. Hertz, FACMPE, principal consultant with the MGMA Health Care Consulting Group, offers the following advice for creating the right practice culture to limit reasons for employee grievances:

➤ Create an atmosphere that encourages employees to speak up without fear of retaliation;

➤ Provide educational opportunities on interpersonal communication, workplace diversity, and hostile environment or harassment issues;

➤ Include employee grievance and workplace harassment policies in the employee handbook, including lines of communication to address issues as they arise; and

➤ Enforce policies and procedures in a fair and consistent manner.

The following sample employee grievance policy (Policy 11.05) is from MGMA's *HR Policies & Procedures Manual for Medical Practices*, by Courtney Price, PhD, and Alys Novak, MBA (2007). The authors advise that practices make appropriate adaptations to the sample according to the group's management philosophy, organizational needs, staff size, and state requirements.

The policy of the Practice is to encourage employees to bring concerns or complaints about work-related conditions or problems to the attention of management. Employees have the opportunity to present these complaints through a formal grievance/dispute procedure.

➤ All employee complaints should be resolved fairly and promptly.

➤ A grievance is defined as employee dissatisfaction with conditions of employment or treatment by supervisory employees.

➤ Employees are encouraged to use the grievance procedure and are not penalized for doing so.

➤ Whenever an employee wishes to file a formal grievance, he or she completes the employee grievance form and submits

it to the immediate supervisor within seven days of the occurrence. (This is Step 1.)

➤ The supervisor considers the grievance and gives written
notice of a decision within seven days. The immediate
supervisor is given the first opportunity to resolve the employee's dissatisfaction.

➤ If not satisfied with the supervisor's response, the employee
may then submit the grievance to the department director
for review within seven days of the supervisor's response.
(This is Step 2.) If the employee's grievance is with the immediate supervisor, the employee is permitted to submit the
grievance to the department director to avoid an awkward
situation, thus skipping Step 1.

➤ If the supervisor fails to respond to the grievance, the employee may proceed to Step 2.

➤ The department director considers the grievance and
renders a decision within seven days after receiving the
grievance.

➤ If the aggrieved employee is not satisfied with the department director's decision, he or she can proceed to Step
3 within seven days from receiving an answer from the
department director.

➤ In Step 3, a representative for top management investigates
the grievance and renders a final decision. This representative is selected by the administration.

➤ In situations involving severe penalties, dismissals, or
alleged discrimination, an aggrieved employee who is dissatisfied with top management's decision is permitted to
present the grievance to a hearing officer selected by the
Practice. In these cases, the hearing officer's decision is final
and binding on both parties.

➤ Information concerning an employee grievance is received
in confidence, and the grievance is discussed only with
those involved in its processing.

➤ Time spent processing grievances in discussions with management during working hours is considered hours worked.

➤ If two or more employees have a common or similar grievance, management selects one of them to represent all employees concerned and management's decision is binding
on all members.

➤ Grievances not filed within the specified time limit are considered untimely. Untimely grievances at any step in the grievance process are denied and the employee forfeits his or her appeal rights.

➤ Only regular status employees may file a grievance.

Employee grievances related to sexual or other workplace harassment require extra precaution in handling. MGMA's *HR Policies & Procedures Manual for Medical Practices* includes a separate policy (Policy 2.04) specific to harassment in the office:

WORKPLACE HARASSMENT POLICY

The Practice is committed to providing a working environment in which its employees are treated with courtesy, respect, and dignity. The Practice does not tolerate nor condone any actions by any individuals that constitute any kind of harassment, particularly sexual harassment of an employee.

➤ The Human Resources manager shall educate, in various ways, including through seminars and the employee handbook, all managers, supervisors, and employees on the medical practice's workplace harassment policy.

➤ This education shall define sexual harassment as unwelcome sexual advances, requests for sexual favors, and other verbal, nonverbal, written, or physical conduct of a sexual nature by employees, supervisors, clients, or contractors where such conduct is either made an explicit or implicit term or condition of employment, is used as the basis for employment decisions, or has the purpose or effect of substantially interfering with the employee's work by creating an intimidating, hostile, or offensive working environment.

➤ Deliberate, repeated, and unsolicited comments with sexual overtones, sexual jokes or ridicule, physical gestures or actions of a sexual nature, and solicitations for sexual favors, offensive comments about one's race, age, disability, or sexual orientation are violations of this policy and subject the offender to discipline, which may include discharge.

➤ A complaint of a hostile work environment/harassment situation should be directed to the HR manager, who shall promptly and fully investigate the complaint to ensure compliance with this policy. Confidentiality shall be maintained to the maximum extent possible, consistent with the need to investigate the complaint.

When a supervisor or HR personnel discuss a grievance or harassment complaint with an employee, the following information should be documented:

➤ Name of employee and date of the incident(s);

➤ Name of supervisor or HR manager and date of interview;

➤ Allegation of the grievance or harassment; and

➤ Corrective action requested by the complainant.

The HR manager or supervisor should also meet with the individual or individuals accused of having committed the harassment or reason for the grievance. The interviewer should record the alleged harasser's description of the situation and if there were any witnesses or other pertinent information. The supervisor or manager should document his or her plan of action to correct the situation, when it was implemented, and the results.

Sources:

Courtney Price, PhD, and Alys Novak, MBA, *HR Policies & Procedures Manual for Medical Practices, 4th Edition*, 55, 324–25 (Englewood, CO: Medical Group Management Association, 2007).

Kenneth T. Hertz, FACMPE, "The Seat of Solomon: How You Handle Employee Grievances Affects Practice Morale, Staffing and Patient Care," *MGMA Connexion*, October 2008, www.mgma.com/WorkArea/mgma_downloadasset.aspx?id=22170 (accessed February 11, 2011).

QUESTION **33** I'm thinking of converting our practice to paid time off rather than vacation and sick leave. Do you have any advice in handling the conversion?

Many group practices and other businesses have considered the switch to paid time off (PTO). The question often arises when managers become frustrated by employees who frequently take sick leave on short notice, leaving the practice short-staffed.

PTO combines vacation, sick, and personal leave so that each employee can decide to use the time when he or she wants and, usually, with more advanced notice. Employees may be concerned about the change in policy, thinking they will be cheated out of time off. For this reason, it is best to maintain the total PTO time per year at the same number of hours or days as the current total of vacation and sick leave. Eventually, employees will appreciate the idea of having the total leave time available to use as they wish. As an administrator, you will appreciate not worrying about reasons for absences and having only one leave bank to manage.

A LOOK AT THE NUMBERS . . .

1
2
3

A recent survey among human resource professionals (conducted by IOMA Corp.) found that 44.9 percent have implemented PTO versus 38 percent that separate vacation and sick leave. The majority of respondents (60 percent) saw a decline in unscheduled absenteeism. Carrying over PTO was allowed by 80 percent of the respondents' organizations.

Prior to converting to PTO, several issues must be addressed. Develop a policy specifying

➤ How many hours of PTO can be carried over from year to year.

➤ Total number of hours that can be accrued if you allow carryover.

➤ Whether or not to pay accrued time to departing employees.

➤ How much notice is required before PTO time is taken.

➤ If the PTO time is given at the beginning of the year or earned per pay period. Having it accrued during the year eliminates the possibility of an employee running out of PTO or resigning after using a year's worth of PTO.

➤ What increments of PTO time can be used: full day, half day, or hourly.

Share the policy with employees. Answer any questions or issues that arise. When making the conversion, decide how to deal with the vacation and sick time each employee has accrued: roll it all over into the new plan, or wait until the beginning of the year and start each employee with just the PTO? One medical practice chose to convert each employee's vacation time into PTO but left the sick leave separate until it was used up.

It will take clear communication to explain the new system and ensure that it is used appropriately. Most practices that have made the conversion experience less frequent short-notice absences and less concern about violation of sick- or vacation-leave policy.

The following policy is from MGMA's *HR Policies & Procedures Manual for Medical Practices*. It is meant only as an example. The specific numbers should be determined by your practice.

Paid-Time-Off Policy

1. Paid time off may be used for holidays, vacations, short-term illnesses, or personal needs. Employees cannot borrow or lend PTO, but can donate PTO using an approved process.

2. Employees must request PTO at least two weeks in advance by requesting such leave in writing. Before approving PTO requests, supervisors consider medical practice workload needs.

3. PTO is accumulated by full- and part-time employees from the day they are hired. With the exception of agency-recognized holidays, employees may not use PTO until they complete the 90-day provisionary period.

4. Full-time employees may accrue 12 hours of PTO every month their first year; then 16 hours monthly through the fifth year; 20 hours monthly through the tenth year; and 24 hours monthly every year starting with the 11th year of service.

5. Earned, unused PTO is paid when an employee leaves the company. Employee may accumulate a maximum of 240 hours.

Source: Courtney Price, PhD, and Alys Novak, MBA, *HR Policies & Procedures Manual for Medical Practices, 4th Edition*, 124 (Englewood, CO: Medical Group Management Association, 2007).

Sources:

Cecilia M. Bowden, FACMPE, "Moving a Practice to a Paid-Time-Off Leave Structure," *MGMA e-Source*, July 2007.

"How Does Your PTO Bank Measure Up?" *HR Focus*, V. 86, No. 5 (May 2009): 3–5.

QUESTION 34

I need to update our employee handbook to include some issues that I increasingly have to deal with. How can I limit cell phone and smart phone usage in the practice?

Younger generations of employees are bringing new issues into the practice as the Baby Boomer generation did to the previous generation. Some of these issues aren't limited to younger generations but involve all generations in the workforce. The best manner to deal with employee issues is to evaluate their impact on quality of care, patient and coworker relationships, and employee productivity. Then develop clear and fair policies to limit the disruptive impacts.

Defining appropriate use of cell phones and smart phones is an issue that many practice administrators have dealt with. Cell phones are becoming ubiquitous; however, frequent use of cell phones, including texting, can interrupt employees' commitment to their responsibilities and to patient care. For this reason, many medical practices and other healthcare organizations are restricting the use of phones at the workplace.

Some organizations are relying on employee discretion to self-manage cell phone use so that it doesn't impact job responsibilities or interfere with patient relations or other employees. Employee discretion is also expected in terms of the use of downloaded ring tones rather than vibrate or normal ring tones. Other practices have developed strict policies limiting the use of cell phones and text messaging. An example of the latter cell-phone use policy is

> The Practice is committed to providing service and attention to the patients. Therefore cell phone use during patient care hours is not allowed. Texting and calling is permitted during morning, afternoon, and lunch breaks in designated break areas. The office phone

number should be used as your contact number for emergencies. Excessive cell phone usage or text messaging will lead to employee disciplinary action, including termination.

There may be some employees who must use their cell phones to conduct practice business. The policy may specify the employees that are exempted from the policy for business purposes. These individuals should not be excluded from cell phone limits for personal business, or resentment among other employees will develop. Respectful use of cell phones should still be expected, limiting their use during patient encounters, meetings, or when they interfere with employee interaction.

Medical practices frequently issue cell phones or other portable electronic devices to physicians, administrators, and managers. Practice policies should limit the use of these devices for business reasons to separate personal and practice time and information. Users should fully understand the potential implications for the release of sensitive information if messages are intercepted or the devices are misplaced.

The increasing use of cell phone cameras and other small cameras to post videos or pictures on the Internet is a concern in medical practices, as it relates to patient privacy and HIPAA regulations. The use of cell phone cameras to take pictures of patients without patient permission should be expressly prohibited. The use of cameras should also be limited to protect business information and practice security.

All employees should be reminded of HIPAA privacy regulations and patient confidentiality related to any information they share with others via texting, Tweeting, or Facebook postings. Many individuals understand the privacy issues related to the communication of patient and business information when talking with others but don't think of the same concerns via e-mail or social media. HIPAA compliance training should remind employees that patient information is confidential in all forms of communication. The same should be true for confidential organization information.

Sources:

Courtney Price, PhD, and Alys Novak, MBA, *HR Policies & Procedures Manual for Medical Practices, 4th Edition* (Englewood, CO: Medical Group Management Association, 2007).

Dom Nicastor, "Technology: Opportunities, Challenges," *Health Leaders*, February 2010, 12–13.

Matthew Vuletich, "Hang up and Work!" *MGMA e-Source*, January 26, 2010, www.mgma.com/article.aspx?id=32442 (accessed February 12, 2011).

"Should Cell Phones Be Banned?" *H&HN (Hospitals & Health Networks)*, November 2008, 19.

CHAPTER 4

Information Management

QUESTION 35

What resources are available for helping me select a new practice management system? Should I add a business intelligence program?

Selecting a new practice management system (PMS) involves several steps and can be applied to selecting any information system. The trend is the merging of PMS and EHR functions into one system, and this option should be considered. It guarantees integration of medical records, clinical information, appointments and scheduling, and billing functions for comprehensive practice management. The details of identifying the desired criteria and functions, developing a request for proposal (RFP), viewing demonstrations, and making the final decision are described in Question 37 on selecting an EHR.

> ## KEY POINT
>
> *Integration of PMS and EHR functions into one system provides many advantages. According to a 2010 MGMA survey, 65 percent of responding group practices have a fully integrated EHR and PMS from a single vendor.*
>
> *Source: Medical Group Management Association, "Electronic Health Records: Status, Needs and Lessons — 2011 Report Based on 2010 Data," www.mgma.com/ehr.*

There are several tools related to PMS selection or analyzing the PMS functions of integrated systems. MGMA and the American Medical Association (AMA) developed the *Selecting a Practice Management System Toolkit* available at MGMA.com under Member Benefits and Communities (www.mgma.com/mc/default.aspx?id=34210). It includes the step-by-step process for selecting a PMS vendor, a PMS vendor directory, PMS criteria checklist, and a sample RFP. The basic PMS functions listed in the toolkit are the administrative and billing functions, including

> ➤ Capturing patient demographics;

> ➤ Scheduling appointments;

> ➤ Pre-registering patients including verifying insurance;

> ➤ Maintaining contact information for payers;

> ➤ Performing billing processes; and

> ➤ Generating administrative reports.

Since you currently have a system, list the likes and dislikes of that system and changes that staff would want in a new system. Consider whether you will be using the current hardware or the type of hardware you would use, or if you are willing to shift to a new system.

Ensure that the PMS will be compliant with the HIPAA version 5010 standards for electronic transactions and how the system incorporates or will upgrade to ICD-10-CM (see Question 44 for more information). The vendors will state that they are or will be compliant, but check the details to determine whether the current software is compliant or if it will require a download or upgrade and if there will be additional cost involved.

Benchmarking practice financial and operations data are key to understanding your practice's financial status and trends over time. The PMS should produce data in areas important to benchmarking your activities. Frank Trew (www.mydataplus.com) recommends that you evaluate the system capabilities for tracking and reporting the following areas:

> ➤ Gross and net collection rates;

> ➤ Denials by payer, payer group, CPT codes, and origin or reason;

> ➤ Evaluation and management bell curves;

> ➤ Bad debt;

> ➤ Accounts receivable days;

> ➤ Encounter numbers by office or procedure, payer, and location;

> ➤ Referral sources and type;

> ➤ Payer mix to track number of patients and total revenue;

> ➤ Underpayments; and

> ➤ Comparing fee schedules by payer.

Evaluate the types and formats of reports that the PMS includes. Have the representative demonstrate them and the abilities to create custom reports. What are the capabilities for developing electronic dashboards to present information to physicians and practice personnel?

A final factor to consider in PMS selection is interface with other systems, interoperability, and the use of standard vocabulary. Increasing efficiencies can be gained as more functions are electronically connected internally with your EHR and externally with hospitals, payers, and other providers. Many payers have instituted real-time claim adjudication that increases time-of-service collections. Practices are using systems to interface with hospitals' systems for point-of-service information and claims capture and automated claims posting. The results include reduction in A/R days and reduced denials.

BUSINESS INTELLIGENCE TOOLS

Technology and systems are so complex and advanced that they generate mountains of information. The problem is examining the massive amounts of data to sift out the facts that are crucial to help manage the practice. You should assess the PMS capabilities, but usually separate business intelligence (BI) tools are the key. Examples of BI tools specific for healthcare management are InfoDive and Anodyne Health Partners.

BI tools and systems allow operational leaders to gather, store, access, and analyze data to aid in the strategic decision-making process. The ability to visualize across payer detail, practice management, and clinical lines provides a different dynamic. Strong healthcare business intelligence allows the practice to

> ➤ Use hard facts to negotiate and assess payer fee schedules;

> ➤ Analyze reimbursement trends across payers;

> ➤ Evaluate and benchmark provider coding patterns;

➤ Track fee-for-service payer performance; and

➤ Manage targeted marketing campaigns.

BENCHMARKING AND KEY PERFORMANCE INDICATORS

Efficiency and accuracy are of the utmost importance within the revenue cycle process at all healthcare organizations. Most medical practices already apply some internal benchmarking to their operations. Financial key performance indicators (KPIs) such as gross collection percentage, adjusted net collection percentage, and days in A/R are monitored monthly. In today's environment, operational leadership must keep a closer eye on all facets of the practice, and enhanced benchmarking is required.

BI systems are utilized by practices for financial reporting, understanding profit centers, and identifying opportunities for potential growth. By consolidating this information down to a single system, analysis and reporting time are reduced to seconds as opposed to the many hours operational leaders can spend massaging and manipulating data in disparate systems. BI provides the ability to drill down into financial information in order to quickly get the desired answer, providing real-time access to data in a meaningful way without interrupting the flow of a practice.

BI analysis should be combined with patient quality, outcomes, and satisfaction analysis to track and report the cost and quality measures important under pay-for-performance and accountable-care environments.

Sources:

Frank Trew, "Ten Ways to Improve Your Bottom Line by Analyzing the Data from Your Practice Management System," www.mgma.com/WorkArea/DownloadAsset.aspx?id=39366 (accessed January 28, 2011).

John R. Thomas, "Automation Improves Revenue Cycle," *MGMA e-Source*, May 26, 2009, www.mgma.com/article.aspx?id=28716 (accessed January 28, 2011).

Lisa H. Schneck, MSJ, "Real-Time Claims Adjudication Turns Weeks into Seconds," *MGMA e-Source*, June 2007, www.mgma.com/article.aspx?id=13436 (accessed January 28, 2011).

Medical Group Management Association and American Medical Association, "How to Select a PMS Vendor," www.mgma.com/WorkArea/mgma_downloadasset.aspx?id=34212 (accessed January 28, 2011).

QUESTION **I need to champion the value of an EHR to some of my physicians. What data are out there to support the return on investment (ROI) for EHRs?**

MGMA analyzed data from practices that have implemented EHRs compared to those that haven't in the *Electronic Health Records Impacts on Revenue, Costs, and Staffing: 2010 Report Based on 2009 Data.* Data from this report show that multi-specialty groups with EHRs have higher median total medical revenue, total operating costs, and total medical revenue after operating costs per FTE than similar practices with paper medical records. For nonhospital-owned multispecialty groups, the median total revenue was 16.6 percent higher after operating costs than for practices without EHRs. EHR-owning practices did have higher operating costs, often due to increased information technology staff costs, but they overcame those costs with much higher revenue.

MGMA's 2011 *Electronic Health Records: Status, Needs and Lessons* report found that the median costs per physician were $30,000 for the EHR system (including hardware, software, and training) and the median annual operating costs were $550.[1] Researchers from a 2005 study of small practices concluded that the initial costs were covered in less than three years, and the practices showed increased profits greater than $30,000 in the following years. After the initial difficulties related to implementation, the physicians reported increased efficiencies, improved billing, improved quality of life, and the ability to access records from different locations.[2]

The focus on pay-for-performance and quality reimbursement programs will require medical practices to have EHRs to improve internal patient wellness programs, track their own quality data, and use the data to negotiate with payers. The passage of the American Recovery and Reimbursement Act (ARRA) has resulted in mandated measurement and reporting as a condition for receiving federally funded EHR payments. The goal is to keep patients healthy and develop new, more cost-effective approaches to treating and managing the total care of patients, especially those with chronic diseases. ARRA also requires health plans to ensure quality of care and improve patient outcomes, further driving the need for medical practices to purchase and implement EHRs.

With the increasing data on the benefits of EHRs, you should still conduct an ROI for an EHR within your own practice. This will show the benefits of the system to your specific operations compared to the initial costs of the purchase and the costs of your current medical records operations. During the ROI analysis, you should include operational efficiencies and improvements in quality of care as well as financial benefits. The analysis will be more effective if the benefits are quantified. Benefits include reduction in medical errors, increased patient and employee satisfaction, improved knowledge for negotiating with health plans, and patient care tracking for quality reimbursement initiatives. Another benefit of EHR implementation is the Medicare and Medicaid incentive payments for the "meaningful use" of EHRs (see Question 39).

Develop a template for tabulating the benefit categories, the quantifiable benefits, and the time frame to realize the benefits. Examples of quantifiable benefits include

➤ The charts are available in the exam rooms 100 percent of the time compared to the current X percent; or

➤ It currently takes X minutes to pull a paper chart that is accessible within Y seconds electronically.

Margret Amatayakul, author of *Electronic Health Records: Transforming your Medical Practice, Second Edition*, recommends the following categories for EHR benefits:

➤ Enhanced patient safety through drug-interaction checks, chronic-disease management, and drug- or device-alert notices;

➤ Improved patient wellness practices with automated reminders, customized instructions and education materials, and tracking through referrals;

➤ Increased provider productivity with easy data capture, reporting functions, and ready access to records and additional data and knowledge;

➤ Increased organizational productivity with automated scheduling, lab or imaging test ordering and tracking, prescription writing, and patient recall;

➤ Improved employee satisfaction with automation and improved work flows;

➤ Increased patient satisfaction with automated scheduling and other functions, plus provider's increased access to information; and

➤ Increased revenue with eased insurance verification, benefit determination, and coding assistance, along with incentive payments for meeting meaningful use requirements.

To track the costs of your current system, itemize all the costs related to the management of paper records. MGMA's Web site includes an "ROI for IT Purchases" spreadsheet for calculating the costs (MGMA.com, under Member Benefits and Communities/ Benefits and Tools). Record the current costs, expected changes in those costs with EHR implementation, and the reasons for those assumptions. Current costs should include

➤ Paper chart supplies (folders, paper, tabs, file drawers);

➤ Transcription costs;

➤ Storage expenses for onsite records and offsite nonactive records;

➤ Staff salaries and benefits for records department (Note: Potential reduction in medical records staff may be offset by increased personnel for information system management.);

➤ Malpractice premium if reductions are offered by insurance carrier; and

➤ Uncaptured charges due to inefficiencies of current system.

CREATE A BUDGET

To determine the total costs related to purchasing and implementing the EHR, obtain detailed information from the EHR vendors and talk with other administrators who have implemented EHRs to identify unexpected or hidden costs. The calculations should span a five-year period and include hardware (factoring in replacing computer work stations every three years), software, costs of consultants or conferences to support the selection process, implementation and training, and ongoing maintenance, including hardware service, software licenses, and staff expenses. Training costs are usually under-calculated; include ongoing costs to train all new employees and providers and for all future software upgrades. Additional factors to include are the costs of data conversion from the current system and the costs of reduced productivity during the implementation and learning phase. You will also have to decide how to fund the purchase of the EHR and determine the potential costs related to financing it.

After investigating practices and their successes post-EHR implementation, Dave Gans, MGMA vice president of innovation and research, discovered that "while most practices say the pain and difficulty of converting to EHRs is something they wish never to repeat, they agree that physicians and staff would never return to using paper medical records."[3]

Case Study

Summit Medical Associates (Tennessee) saved $175,000 per year in transcription costs after implementing an EHR. Medical records staff were reduced from three full-time and two part-time staff to two full-time people. Patsy Brown, practice administrator, says, "Our nurses love EHRs. I think it makes them feel more like nurses than paper pushers."

Source: Rosemarie Nelson, MS, and Derek Kosiorek, CPEHR, CPHIT, "When It Comes to EHR, Paperless Practices Can Be Green in More Ways than One," *MGMA Connexion*, July 2010.

References:

1. Medical Group Management Association, "Electronic Health Records: Status, Needs and Lessons — 2011 Report Based on 2010 Data," www.mgma.com/ehr.

2. Robert H. Miller, PhD, "The Value of Electronic Health Records in Solo or Small Group Practices," *Health Affairs*, V. 24, No. 5 (2005): 1127–37.

3. Dave N. Gans, MSHPA, FACMPE, "Going Electronic Pays Off," *MGMA Connexion*, October 2010, www.mgma.com/WorkArea/DownloadAsset.aspx?id=39576 (accessed January 26, 2011).

Source:

Margret Amatayakul, *Electronic Health Records: Transforming Your Medical Practice, Second Edition* (Englewood, CO: Medical Group Management Association, 2010).

QUESTION 37 We've decided to implement an EHR system. How should we go about selecting one?

There are several steps related to selecting an EHR system for your practice. Make sure you allow plenty of time for the process to involve all personnel and correctly identify the system that provides the best interface and functions to ensure that the physicians, nurses, and other employees use the new system to its full potential.

Identify an EHR selection team with representatives from all departments that will interface with the EHR. It's important to get participation and buy-in from everyone who will be using the system, so make sure department representatives or the selection team meets with all staff to discuss functional requirements and human-computer interface preferences. Physicians and employees should recognize that the EHR will change how they operate but will offer tremendous opportunities for improvement in operations and patient care. Make sure physicians participate in developing selection criteria and product demonstrations so they aren't surprised by the selected system and refuse to use it. Physicians and nurses should pay particular attention to the documentation and note systems in the EHRs.

Current work flow should be analyzed and flow-charted. Discuss how automated systems would help in streamlining these processes. Consider a patient portal function for patient requests and communications that currently are received via telephone calls, including appointment requests, prescription refills, and test results. The analysis can identify opportunities for cost savings that can be quantified and compared with the potential cost of the system.

Determine the budget for the EHR purchase and how it will be funded. (Financing options are discussed in Question 38.) You should also decide if a consultant will be hired to aid in the selection process. Consultant knowledge can bring valuable insights and can help with staff time constraints.

The selection committee, with staff input, will develop a list of the desired features and functions and the requirements based on the current and desired information-system structure and interface. These should be included in the RFP.

RFPs should be sent to no more than four vendors. While waiting for vendors to reply, the selection committee should determine the criteria for selection. These should be the key items in the functional and technical requirements to compare in the RFPs. Based on the selection criteria, the committee will select no more than three vendors to demonstrate their products.

A CLOSER LOOK . . .

Contents of RFP

➤ Purpose of RFP

➤ Instructions for vendor response, including contact information and due date

➤ Practice information, including current internal and external systems that the EHR must communicate with

➤ Functional requirements, including patient demographics, histories, medications, allergies, care plans, guidelines, and formularies. The ability to write prescriptions, diagnostic tests, referrals, and patient reminders. Support for claims processing, research projects, health maintenance, task scheduling, communication with medical devices, and hand-held communication tools.

➤ Technical requirements, including the current information structure that should be interfaced with, replaced, or supplemented for EHR implementation, preferred human-system interface, and security requirements

➤ Request for information on vendor's involvement in testing, staff training, and implementation

➤ Support and maintenance costs and plans

➤ Request for vendor's capabilities specific to RFP, company information (financial resources, number of customers, background, references, and so on)

➤ Price quote

Frequency of EHR system vendors	
Allscripts	17.6%
NextGen Healthcare	11.4%
GE Healthcare	8.6%
Epic	8.0%
eClinicalworks	7.8%
Sage Software	3.8%
Greenway Medical Technologies	3.2%
E-MDs, Inc.	2.6%
Practice Partner/McKesson Corporation	2.3%
Cerner Corporation	2.2%
Other vendor	32.5%

Source: Medical Group Management Association, "*Electronic Health Records: Status, Needs, and Lessons Study, 2011 Report Based on 2010 Data*," www.mgma. com/WorkArea/DownloadAsset.aspx?id=1248503.

The product demonstrations are key to understanding the functions that are vital to practice operations and patient care. Ensure all physicians and key personnel participate. The demo should cover standard features, optional requested modules, demonstration based on a scenario from the practice, and hands-on opportunities for physicians, nurses, and other key personnel to test their interaction. Physicians should test data-entry methods used during a patient visit and inquire about data-entry tools (voice recognition, tablets, laptops). Allow a full day for each product, and use a scoring sheet for employees and providers to document their scores for the different functions to compare different products. Ensure practice issues are addressed, notice and question any gaps in the presentation, and make sure there is plenty of time for physicians and staff to test modules. Create a demonstration "script" for the vendor to follow, one that mirrors your typical work flow from patient arrival, encounter with physician, and order entry to charge capture.

Include time for information technology (IT) staff to meet independently and for the CFO or administrator to discuss contractual issues. The EHR team should meet immediately following to talk about the demonstration while it is fresh. Demonstrations should be scheduled relatively close together to improve comparisons.

The vendor's references should be checked, and site visits to actually view the functionality and work flow should be mandatory before a final purchase decision is made. Physicians should speak with other physicians, and IT staff members should speak with other IT staff members. Ask about strengths and weaknesses, and likes and dislikes of the system.

Request a copy of a contract prior to the demonstration, and bring up issues or concerns during the meetings with the vendor's representative. Remember that contracts are always negotiable, especially the payment plans. Partial payment should be sent at milestones in implementation.

The secret to successful EHR purchase is allowing enough time to develop the functional and technical requirements, evaluate the RFP responses, ensure staff and physician buy-in, and verify that the system offers opportunities for operational improvement beyond just converting from paper to digital medical records.

RESOURCES TO AID IN FUNCTIONAL REQUIREMENTS

➤ Institute of Medicine (IOM), *Key Capabilities of an Electronic Health Record System* (www.iom.edu/?id=19374);

➤ Health Level Seven (HL7) functional models and standards (www.hl7.org/ehr);

➤ Certification Commission for Healthcare Information Technology (www.cchit.org);

➤ Vendor Web sites;

➤ Trade shows;

➤ Specialty societies; and

➤ Recommendations from peers and colleagues.

RESOURCES FOR EHR PROGRAM SELECTION

Annual MGMA Buyer's Guide and EHR Selector Tool list	www.mgma.com
American EHR Vendor Directory	www.americanehr.com
Capterra	www.capterra.com/software_buyers
EHR Buyers' Guide	www.ehrbuyersguide.com
Health Management Technology, Resource Guide and articles	www.healthmgttech.com
Klas Research, vendor and product performance ratings	www.klasresearch.com
Medical and specialty societies	Too many to list.

Sources:

Derek Kosiorek, CPEHR, CPHIT, "Podcast: Top Tips for Selecting an EHR," www.mgma.com/article.aspx?id=21338 (accessed January 26, 2011).

Gregory J. Mertz, FACMPE, "8 Steps for Evaluating an EHR," *MGMA e-Source*, June 24, 2008, www.mgma.com/article.aspx?id=20070 (accessed January 26, 2011).

Karen Coloraft, MBA, CPHIT, "10 Tips for Hosting a Successful EHR Vendor Demonstration," *MGMA Connexion*, April 2009, www.mgma.com/WorkArea/mgma_downloadasset.aspx?id=28014 (accessed January 26, 2011).

Margret Amatayakul, MBA, CHPS, FHIMSS, *Electronic Health Records: Transforming Your Medical Practice, 2nd Edition* (Englewood, CO: Medical Group Management Association, 2010).

Matthew Vuletich, "Focus on EHR: Lessons from Worst-Case EHR Scenarios," *MGMA e-Connexion*, February 2007, www.mgma.com/article.aspx?id=11516 (accessed January 26, 2011).

QUESTION **What are the best options for funding an EHR?**

There are several financing options for practices to fund the purchase of an EHR:

➤ Borrow the money from a bank or other lender;

➤ Obtain funding from a hospital or other organization;

➤ Lease the system with operating leases that include software and/or hardware; or

➤ Use an application service provider or hosting service with regular payments.

A LOOK AT THE NUMBERS . . .

Primary means of paying for EHRs	
From the business' cash reserves	32%
Business or personal loan	29%
Subsidized by hospital, integrated delivery system, or other parent organization	22%
Business or personal lease	7%
From providers' personal cash reserves	2%

Source: Medical Group Management Association, "*Electronic Health Records: Status, Needs and Lessons — 2011 Report Based on 2010 Data*," www.mgma. com/ehr.

Seeking purchase assistance from hospitals or other healthcare organizations became an option when the U.S. Department of Health and Human Services (HHS) announced an exemption for EHR purchases. The August 2006 rule exempts hospitals, health plans, and other entities from Stark law and anti-kickback statutes in providing EHR and e-prescribing software to physicians. The physician must still fund 15 percent of the total value of the program, but the hospital may donate the remaining 85 percent. Physicians must pay for the 15 percent without assistance from the hospital and by cash, not via services or referrals. The only requirement is that the EHR system be interoperable and include an e-prescribing function.

Loans may be obtained from local banks or other lending organizations. Your practice may qualify for small business loans and incentives. Bank loans are often at lower interest rates and with easy payments, but the application process may be lengthy. The bank may also require a down payment. Start with the entity that is currently handling most of your banking arrangements. They will use your A/R as collateral and will ask for information to support your financial status and patient population. Review the terms of the loan carefully prior to signing and your patient privacy requirements under HIPAA prior to releasing any information.

Vendors are offering financing deals to make their systems more appealing. Prior to considering their financing offers, ensure they have the right product for your practice. Select the system based on your requirements and not on the financial deal. EHR vendors frequently use third parties for financing, so investigate the arrangements and the lending party thoroughly.

Many of the financing deals are delayed payments or loans until the practice receives its "meaningful use" incentive payment from the federal government. Remember that it is up to you to prove meaningful use. Ensure that the software is a certified product and that you'll be able to implement the meaningful use requirements in time to participate in the incentive program.

Leasing the hardware, software, or both may be an option for some practices, especially if you envision upgrading to another system in a few years. The initial costs are lower, and the lease may qualify as a tax-oriented or capitalized lease according to IRS guidelines. There are at least three types of leases available for EHR funding:

➤ **Operating or service lease offered by EHR vendors.** This usually includes financing and maintenance of the EHR software and hardware, and the agreement includes a cancellation clause;

➤ **Financing lease for the hardware.** This option is appropriate for small practices with few or no IT staff. The lease agreement doesn't include a cancellation clause and may include language related to regular replacement of the hardware; and

➤ **Hybrid leases.** These are variations of operating and financing leases and may include maintenance and service promises as well as a cancellation clause.

Many EHR vendors operate as application hosting services or application service providers (ASPs), using the Internet to provide access to their program at a remote location. Medical practices pay a monthly payment to cover the software and hardware costs and maintenance. An increasing number of vendors are offering cloud computing services, shifting more of the EHR system onto remote servers and decreasing the in-practice hardware requirements. Advantages of ASPs and cloud computing include

➤ Reduced initial costs;

➤ Reduced staffing requirements;

➤ System upgrades handled seamlessly by contractor;

➤ System expertise of vendor's tech support and maintenance staff; and

➤ Payments spread out over the life of the product.

Possible disadvantages include

➤ System must still interface with other IT functions within the practice;

➤ Practice must have or purchase hardware for onsite functions;

➤ Concerns over ability to customize program and receive onsite support;

➤ Contractor controls price increases at end of contract;

➤ Practice data are located offsite; and

➤ The total cost of the system may be more than if purchased or leased.

A LOOK AT THE NUMBERS . . .

What best describes your practice's current EHR system design?

	Fewer than 3 FTE physicians	3 to 5 FTE physicians	6 to 20 FTE physicians	21 or more FTE physicians
Self-contained system operating on computers integral to the practice	66.7 %	72.1%	77.5%	75.7%
ASP system where vendor operates server and practice accesses EHR through Internet	31.4%	25.1%	19.8%	20.6%

Source: Medical Group Management Association, "*Electronic Health Records: Status, Needs and Lessons – 2011 Report Based on 2010 Data*," unpublished data, www.mgma.com/ehr.

Prior to contracting with an ASP, investigate their security and backup systems, connectivity capabilities, and privacy measures. Review the contract for data ownership clauses to ensure that you maintain ownership of your practice's data.

Prior to signing a lease, vendor's loan, or ASP contract, consider several questions carefully:

➤ What are the financial terms, and what will be the total cost to the practice?

➤ Will the vendor be around for the life of the agreement? Look at its history and financial status.

➤ Does the contract clearly state that your practice owns its data and will continue to have access to it if there is a missed payment, if the vendor goes bankrupt, or if the vendor is bought out?

➤ Where will the backup data be stored? If at a vendor's off-site location, how will you access data in case of emergency or vendor's default?

➤ What happens if you miss a payment? Will they be willing to work with you? Will they confiscate your equipment or cut off access to your data?

➤ How are payments tied to service expectations? If payments are made to a third party, how do you enforce service if an issue develops?

Sources:

Gregg Blesch and Joe Carlson, "Zero Tolerance," *Modern Healthcare*, V. 40, No. 9, March 1, 2010.

Margret Amatayakul, MBA, CHPS, FHIMSS, *Electronic Health Records: Transforming Your Medical Practice, 2nd Edition*, 184–86 (Englewood, CO: Medical Group Management Association, 2010).

Michael Deyett, MHA, "How to Pay for that EHR," *MGMA Connexion*, April 2007, www.mgma.com/WorkArea/mgma_downloadasset.aspx?id=12134 (accessed January 27, 2011).

U.S. Department of Health and Human Services, "New Regulations to Facilitate Adoption of Health Information Technology," August 1, 2006, www.hhs.gov/news/press/2006.html.

QUESTION **What are the meaningful use requirements for EHRs, and how do we qualify?**

39

The EHR incentive program, mandated as part of the ARRA, provides payments to providers who meet the "meaningful use" definition. "Meaningful use" is intended to show that the EHR, meeting specific criteria, is implemented and used within a provider's location. The act described "meaningful use" as

➤ The use of a "certified" EHR with e-prescribing capability as determined appropriate by the secretary of HHS;

➤ The ability to report on clinical quality measures as specified by the secretary; and

➤ The use of EHR technology that allows for the electronic exchange of patient health information.

The incentive payments are available to eligible professionals who are enrolled in Medicare or Medicaid, have a national provider identifier (NPI), and are enrolled in the Provider Enrollment, Chain, and Ownership System (PECOS). To qualify as "meaningful use," eligible professionals must meet all of the following core objectives and select five of the menu objectives, one of which must be menu objective 9 or 10.

CORE objectives (all required)	Menu objectives (must select five) *One of the menu objectives must be a public health objective
1. Computerized provider order entry (CPOE)	1. Drug formulary checks
2. E-prescribing	2. Incorporate clinical lab test results as structured data
3. Report ambulatory clinical quality measures to CMS/states	3. Generate lists of patients by specific conditions
4. Implement one clinical decision-support rule	4. Send reminders to patients per patient preference for preventive/follow-up care
5. Provide patients with an electronic copy of their health information, upon request	5. Provide patients with timely electronic access to their health information

6. Provide clinical summaries for patients for each office visit	6. Use certified EHR technology to identify patient-specific education resources and provide to patient, if appropriate
7. Drug-drug and drug-allergy interaction checks	7. Medication reconciliation
8. Record demographics	8. Summary of care record for each transition of care/referrals
9. Maintain an up-to-date problem list of current and active diagnoses	9. Capability to submit electronic data to immunization registries/ systems*
10. Maintain active medication list	10. Capability to provide electronic syndromic surveillance data to public health agencies*
11. Maintain active medication allergy list	
12. Record and chart changes in vital signs	
13. Record smoking status for patients 13 years or older	
14. Capability to exchange key clinical information among providers of care and patient-authorized entities electronically	
15. Protect electronic health information	

Source: Centers for Medicare & Medicaid Services,"Eligible Professional Meaningful Use Table of Contents," www.cms.gov/EHRIncentivePrograms/Downloads/EP-MU-TOC.pdf (accessed January 28, 2011).

The payment program begins after a provider has shown meaningful use of a certified EHR technology and is serving Medicare patients. The payment may equal 75 percent of a physician's total Medicare allowable with annual caps. Payments can begin in 2011 and continue until 2016. Physicians eligible for the incentives beginning in 2011 or 2012 may receive a total incentive of up to $44,000 over five years. Medicaid has a separate incentive program for up to $63,750 over six years for providers who have more than 30 percent Medicaid patients or 20 percent for pediatricians. Beginning in 2015, professionals not demonstrating meaningful use of an EHR will face reductions in their Medicare fee schedule reimbursement rates. The penalty will equal 1 percent in 2015, 2 percent in 2016, and 3 percent in 2017 and each subsequent year.

To be eligible for the incentive payments, physicians must use a certified EHR system as determined by the Office of the National Coordinator for Health Information Technology (ONC) and its "authorized testing and certification bodies" (ATCB). The list of certified EHRs and ATCBs is available at http://healthit.hhs.gov.

Eligible providers must also electronically submit aggregate clinical quality measures (CQM) numerator, denominator, and exclusion data to CMS or the states. Physicians will have to report on three core CQM and three additional CQM. The quality core criteria are

➤ Hypertension/blood pressure management;

➤ Tobacco use assessment and cessation; and

➤ Adult weight screening and follow-up.

Alternative core criteria include

➤ Influenza immunization for patients 50 years of age or older;

➤ Weight assessment and counseling for children and adolescents; and

➤ Childhood immunization status.

For current information on "meaningful use," go to the MGMA Government Affairs Web pages at mgma.com/policy or the HHS Health IT Web site at www.healthit.hhs.gov.

Sources:

MGMA Government Affairs, "FAQs: EHR Incentives," www.mgma.com/meaningfulusefaq (accessed January 28, 2011).

MGMA Government Affairs, "The Federal EHR Incentive Program: Achieving 'Meaningful Use," *MGMA Connexion*, September 2010, www.mgma.com/WorkArea/mgma_downloadasset.aspx?id=39288 (access January 28, 2011).

QUESTION 40

What are the keys to a successful EHR implementation? Should we scan our current medical records or use another method to populate the EHR?

Once you've selected the EHR system that is right for your practice, you'll need to develop a careful implementation plan to ensure success while minimizing disruption. Implementation is a very involved process affecting all the work flows within the practice. It is important to devote plenty of time and attention to it, including developing a comprehensive project management plan.

> ## KEY POINT
>
> *Cindy Dunn, RN, MGMA healthcare consultant, reminds practice administrators of the importance of adhering to project management principles due to the complexity and scope of EHR implementation. The project management plan should include the following steps:*
>
> - *Define scope of project and set budget;*
> - *Create shared project plan and timeline with vendor;*
> - *Identify tasks office needs to do;*
> - *Assign responsibilities to staff and physicians;*
> - *Track progress on all tasks and milestones;*
> - *Develop risk assessments and mitigation plans;*
> - *Track issues and resolution plans; and*
> - *Prioritize project time for staff and physicians.*

You'll work closely with the vendor, but you and your staff must handle much of the planning. The amount and quality of help the vendor provides will depend on your contract, the vendor, and the type of system; a comprehensive product and contract will include more support than an application hosted off site.

The vendors typically handle hardware and software installation, building the system and its interfaces, converting data from your current information systems, and training. You may need to coordinate efforts with more than one vendor, including the hardware vendor and lab or imaging system vendors.

During project planning, develop a timeline for the necessary steps in implementation and coordinate this with the vendor. Use a communications plan to keep physicians and employees informed of the reasons for the change, implementation plans, and status, and to identify how patients will be informed. Post the communication tool in areas where it can be easily accessed and read such as the break room and Web site. Ensure that physicians and others have the necessary skills (including typing) to be comfortable with the system. Don't implement other major changes during this period.

It is important that you dedicate staff time for managing the implementation, including the EHR project manager, champion physician(s), and other key staff. You may want to hire a consultant or temporary staff to assist in the process.

The steps in implementing an EHR are

> **Work flow redesign or process mapping.** Chart your current processes and identify the ideal process that will increase efficiency and provide needed information. Use flow chart tools to map the start and end point for each process, each step in between, what information is needed, decision points, and results. Learn what the selected EHR product can do, and validate the desired future work-flow descriptions.
>
> Develop detailed process maps for the future work flows, and create transition plans from current to future work flows. Use work-flow redesign and staff preferences to determine input-device selections. If possible, accommodate position and personnel preferences for PDAs, PCs, tablets, and other devices. Review current policies and procedures and update to incorporate the new processes.

➤ **Testing.** There are several tests that should be planned and conducted. The project timeline should identify when they will be conducted, who will participate, and what will be tested. Successful tests are often key points for paying the vendor an agreed-upon amount. Typical tests during implementation include:

➤ The unit and function test ensures major functions work as promised, identifies the need for design changes, and checks various screens, note fields, and clinical alerts and reminders. Review system reports for accuracy, contents, and customization capabilities. Physician involvement is vital in this stage, especially related to documentation templates, order sets, medication order strings, and decision-support tools.

➤ The system test checks the interface between the EHR and PMS and between separate modules. Look for data availability, flow and integrity, accuracy of outputs and reports, and function of clinical decision-support tools.

➤ The performance and stress test assesses the response time during a peak demand period.

➤ Acceptance testing continues for a specified amount of time after the "go-live" date to address issues and errors that have developed and the need for further customization.

If testing does not go as planned, reassess and adjust the work-flow design, parameters, configurations, and training as needed. Do not "go live" until testing goes well.

➤ **Contingency downtime plans.** Determine mechanisms to limit down time and the response if it occurs. Test the contingency and backup plans and include them in training.

➤ **Training.** Training should be comprehensive and conducted with specific groups or functions in mind. According to a recent MGMA survey, 53 percent of respondents felt they had underestimated the amount of time needed for training. Several of the respondents' comments related to the difficulty of obtaining enough physician time dedicated to training.

Physicians and nonphysician providers typically prefer separate, one-on-one training. IT staff, medical records, clinical staff, receptionists, and other office staff will use different functions of the system and will benefit from separate training. Training should cover as many functions as possible to acquaint all users with the full capabilities of the system. Trainers and super users should be trained first, and others will receive training just prior to the date of startup. You can use train-the-trainer techniques or have the vendor provide all training.

Ensure that proper resources are dedicated to training, including staff time and a separate location with the same equipment. Use your own practice's data and input devices for training to test the data conversion and ensure the functionality for your practice.

➤ **Data conversion.** The options for transferring data from the current medical records into the EHR include scanning the entire chart, scanning key parts of the chart, abstracting information to enter, a combination of scanning and abstracting, or no preload of information. You and your physicians will have to decide which is most appropriate for your practice and specialty. Some practices have found scanning selected parts of the chart or abstracting data to be time consuming in identifying what should be added. Scanning all of the record transfers can be more expensive and means key information may be less accessible. Many practices have chosen to scan one to two years' worth of paper charts and key in discrete data in only a few circumstances.

Data backup methods should be determined prior to the conversion process. Determine the frequency, media, person responsible, and storage location for frequent backups.

➤ **Transition.** The old system can run parallel to the new system to reassure everyone that the new system is functioning, or a clean cutoff can be accomplished to switch to the new system. You may choose to have every function go live at once or phase in specific functions or departments. If the latter is chosen, start with the department or functions that have the most interested or technologically accomplished participants. During the startup day, ensure the practice is operating at full staff levels and that vendor support is on hand, and schedule a reduced patient load. Gradually increase the number of patients over several weeks.

➤ After the "go live" date there will still be many issues to take care of, among them:

   ➤ Prioritizing outstanding issues;

   ➤ Working with users struggling with the system;

   ➤ Maintaining regular contact with vendors and vendor user groups;

   ➤ Assigning someone to approve all requested EHR changes and maintain a "change log"; and

   ➤ Revisiting and testing contingency plans.

A CLOSER LOOK . . .

Practice administrators who have implemented EHRs provide the following advice:

➤ Obtain physician leadership commitment to the implementation plan, training, and the use of the new system. Practice leaders may be called on to work with physicians who don't want to use the EHR.

➤ Involve physicians in work-flow redesign and planning. Encourage them to visit another practice that has your vendor's system.

➤ Physicians must agree to a reduced patient schedule during the training, roll over, and adjustment period.

➤ Choose the "go live" date based on practice readiness. It may be better to delay the date rather than stick to a date that employees aren't ready for.

➤ Accept that problems will come up during implementation. Be patient and help others overcome the challenges.

Sources:

James Margolis, MPA, FACMPE, "The Great, the Awful and the Scary: What Adopters Have to Say about Implementing an EHR," *MGMA Connexion*, July 2008, www.mgma. com/WorkArea/DownloadAsset.aspx?id=20182 (accessed January 28, 2010).

Margret Amatayakul, MBA, FHIMSS, *Electronic Health Records: Transforming Your Medical Practice, Second Edition* (Englewood, CO: Medical Group Management Association, 2010).

Margret Amatayakul, MBA, FHIMSS, and Steve Lazarus, "Implementing an EHR to Qualify for the ARRA Incentives and Improve Medical Group Performance," presentation, Medical Group Management Association Webinar, February 23, 2010.

Morgan Lewis Jr., "10 EHR Lessons from 10 Practices," *Medical Economics*, February 5, 2010, www.modernmedicine.com/modernmedicine/Modern+Medicine+Now/10-EHR-lessons-from-10-practices/ArticleStandard/Article/detail/655757 (accessed January 28, 2010).

QUESTION 41 Now that we've implemented an EHR, how do we optimize its use?

The important thing to remember about EHRs is they are not just automated paper charts. They are information systems that can generate knowledge, improve patient care, and create greater efficiencies, but to accomplish these goals, they must be fully utilized. As you found out during implementation, current paper processes do not make good electronic processes. New work flow is needed to optimize the benefits of EHRs.

A few months after the "go live" date, begin an evaluation and review of the EHR and practice operations. Practices typically zero in on the technical functions at this point, but evaluation of the people and their acceptance and use of the EHR are more important. Cynthia Dunn, RN, MGMA healthcare consultant, advises, "Successful practices succeed with change management; embrace the skeptics and manage the disruptive." Achieving optimization will depend on good communication, positive attitudes, transparency, and patience.

During the post-implementation period, ask the following questions:

➤ Is the EHR meeting the goals set during the selection and planning phases?

➤ Are physicians and staff using it as envisioned, or is more training needed? Are they following the new work flow or stuck in the old ways?

➤ Are physicians doing what they should be doing, or are they doing clerical work or using a work-around?

➤ Is the work flow reaching the ideal as it was mapped, or do changes need to be made?

➤ Are employees still writing down or printing information unnecessarily?

➤ Is after-hours time needed to catch up on work? What efficiencies are needed to accomplish it during the day?

➤ How are the interfaces with labs, pharmacies, hospitals, and billing companies working? Measure this by determining the percentage of lab orders, prescriptions, and hospital interactions handled electronically.

➤ Are charges captured and posted correctly?

One of the greatest complaints post-implementation is reduced physician productivity because of added time in recording the patient visit. As one practice medical director commented, "There's nothing quicker than scrawling an illegible note." Productivity frequently recovers with increased practice and use of the EHR system. However, data-entry methods should be reviewed to identify means of increasing efficiency or the use of alternative methods (voice recognition, scribes, touch screens) to decrease delays. Patient satisfaction should also be monitored to ensure the technology doesn't create a barrier in provider-patient relations.

The greatest benefit in EHR will be the improved care management and clinical data management. Physicians will find it easier to track patient follow-up, compliance, progress, medications, and continuity of care. The timeliness of diagnosis, treatment, and patient education should also improve. The practice will be able to identify patients by disease to send reminders and develop care plans. Practice guidelines can be integrated providing point of care decision support for chronic disease management.

Full optimization of the EHR in this area will take time. Criteria for the meaningful use of EHRs (see Question 39) provide a framework to get started. Conduct a gap analysis to determine which criteria are not currently in place in your practice.

Prescription management is an easy area with which to begin. The EHR vendor may have populated the system with basic medication information, including drug interactions and alerts. Determine how the formularies for your payers can be entered. Contact your major health plans regarding obtaining electronic formats for their formularies. Some practices choose to enter medication lists and allergies for specific patients, while others use the scanned paper records and populate the data fields over time. Test the EHR alert system related to prescription errors, interactions, and interface with pharmacies.

Other types of CPOE can be implemented after prescription management. They will require testing the interoperability of your EHR system with the system used at the laboratory or other facility. The interface and communication between the two systems needs to be carefully planned out and tested prior to going live to ensure that no physician orders or returning results are lost or misdirected.

The use of EHRs in care management is more involved. The first step requires physicians in the practice to agree on practice guidelines and chronic disease management standards/protocols. You might want to start with one disease and expand to others. There are many sources for practice guidelines and quality care standards (see Question 77). Once the physicians select the tools, they should be entered in your EHR. Work with the system vendor to ensure accuracy of entry and utilization of the care guidelines. Test how the decision-support tools operate including the reminders and alerts. Enter your practice's patient education materials and develop links to other resources. Review how the EHR operates to identify and track outcomes. Effectiveness of EHR systems' decision-support tools varies widely, and some organizations have purchased or developed separate systems.

After integration of practice guidelines and protocols into the EHR, review the processes related to work flow and care management. Meetings should be held to identify means and share ideas for expanding the use of EHRs to improve patient care and outcomes management. Some of the issues that should be addressed include

➤ Does the EHR support the data gathering and documenting needs of providers during patient visits? Are medication and problem lists easy to use?

➤ Does it provide appropriate alerts (not too many or too few) related to prescriptions, allergies, needed tests, test results, and other concerns? Do the providers respond appropriately to the alerts, or do they ignore them? Are there additional alerts or reminders that could be added?

➤ Are interfaces with hospitals, labs, pharmacies, and insurance and billing companies working smoothly? How can data exchanges with these organizations and referring physicians be improved?

➤ Are any employees or physicians using a work-around rather than using the EHR as agreed upon? What changes are needed to eliminate this?

➤ Have there been improvements in continuity of care? What additional changes need to be made?

➤ How does the system track outcomes and assist in the analysis of outcomes data? Are there ways of improving on this function in the practice? Are the data being used to improve care and report practice successes to payers, patients, and the public?

➤ Do providers have access to patient education materials via the EHR that are appropriate for various levels of patients' health-literacy status?

Patient interface becomes just as important as providers' use of EHRs. If your practice doesn't already have one, it's time to develop a patient portal. Most patients are interested in taking an active role in their care. Providing remote access to their information and patient education materials can be a big step in improving their compliance and well-being. See Question 42 for more information.

To continue optimizing the use of the EHR, meet regularly with the vendor and user groups to obtain ideas. Use your practice's super users to identify opportunities to maximize the use of EHR functions. As new ideas develop, include them in the ongoing training programs. Identify ways to modify processes to obtain improved data and efficiencies.

Sources:

Carrie Vaughan, "Unlock Value," *HealthLeaders Magazine*, V. 12, No. 10 (2009): 51–53.

Cynthia Dunn and Derek Kosiorek, "Implementing and Operating Your EMR: Ensuring Efficiencies and Earning Incentives," Medical Group Management Association Webinar presentation, February 24, 2011.

Margret Amatayakul, MBA, CHPS, FHIMSS, *Electronic Health Records: Transforming Your Medical Practice, 2nd Edition* (Englewood, CO: Medical Group Management Association, 2010).

QUESTION 42 What are patient portals, and how are group practices using them?

Patient portals are tools for increasing communications and access to a medical practice via a Web site. In today's society, patients are expecting to reach your practice outside of normal business hours and in more interactive ways. Besides increasing patient satisfaction, patient portals can include tools that increase practice efficiency and reduce costs. They provide a secured means for communicating and accessing information.

Patient portals can be designed with a variety of functional tools:

➤ **Request an appointment.** Online portals are open 24 hours a day seven days a week (24/7), enabling patients to submit requests at their convenience. Appointment request forms can include information on the best time to contact to decrease phone tag. Referring physicians should also be provided this convenience. Some practices may expand to include online scheduling with the option to require staff review and approval of each patient-scheduled appointment.

➤ **Form completion.** Patients can access registration and medical history forms and complete them prior to a visit. Patients can then be asked to bring them into the office, eliminating the time and awkwardness of completing forms in the reception area, or even submit them online. If submitted prior to a visit, practice personnel can review the information, including reason for visit, and conduct insurance verification prior to the visit.

➤ **Prescription renewals.** This option offers the convenience and time savings of 24/7 functionality and electronic submission. Digital requests can be submitted directly to appropriate personnel, reviewed, and accepted or denied based on practice policies and patients' records and then forwarded to pharmacies. Time-consuming tasks are eliminated, security is confirmed, and chances of errors from misunderstanding voice messages or handwriting are decreased.

➤ **Test results.** Technology can be used to e-mail patients when results are available and include a link to a secure, private location for viewing the results. Positive results should still be delivered via a telephone call or patient visit.

➤ **Visit reminders.** E-mails can include requests to follow a link to view a personalized message on the portal. Messages can include reminders for scheduling annual exams, chronic care follow-up, diabetes testing, or other reasons and include a link to request or schedule an appointment.

➤ **Online medical visits.** Patient portals are designed with the security to maintain privacy of a patient-provider interaction. If physicians are comfortable with electronic visits, check with your payers on their reimbursement policies for online medical evaluations.

➤ **Surveys and screening.** In one demonstration project, medical practices posted surveys to screen patients in advance of their scheduled primary care visit to aid in identifying those dealing with chronic conditions. The results enable providers to prepare for the visit and spend more time discussing the condition.

➤ **Online bill paying.** With connectivity to the practice's billing system, medical practices can join other businesses in providing this convenient service.

As EHRs and patient portals become more sophisticated, they can be linked to enable patients to access their medical information. Patient health records (PHR) can be purchased turnkey products or developed in-house to provide access to certain information such as vitals, allergies, immunizations, prescriptions, living wills, and advance directives. Patients would be encouraged to monitor trends in their healthcare and participate in their care planning by submitting additional information. Eventually, the PHR will become the single source for information from all healthcare providers and facilities that have seen an individual. Currently, different providers seen over time at different hospitals hold an individual's health history. This is a real issue when a patient arrives at another facility or in an emergency situation.

Primary care practices in one integrated health system use a patient gateway with a medications module. It enables patients to view their complete list of medications; update their record with comments on allergies, side effects, and other medication-related concerns; and share this information with providers. Patients using the module liked having the additional opportunity to share important information with their physicians prior to visits.

Kaiser Permanente found that use of its member Web site tripled in the first three years of its offering. Areas used by members in order of their use were viewing test results, scheduling appointments, prescription refills, and e-mailing physicians. The Kaiser Permanente Web site also includes information on previous office visits and patient education materials and tools. Use studies found that patients visiting the Web site represented a diverse patient population, although the highest use was seen in patients from the 51- to 60 age group and patients with higher education and income levels.

ROI determinations prior to building a patient portal should not concentrate specifically on financial benefits. Other considerations include increased quality of care and outcomes and satisfaction for physicians, staff, and patients.

When preparing to implement patient portals, remember that not all patients are ready to access online tools and share information electronically. However, the percentage of patients participating in it will increase over time.

Case Study

Yolanda Raffert, MHA, CPC, practice administrator of About Women OB/GYN in Woodbridge, Va., developed the patient portal with the assistance of a planning team of one member from each department and one physician. Team members provided feedback from their scheduling, registration, billing, and nursing departments. A vendor was selected to assist in design and development. The portal includes tools for submitting questions, requesting prescription renewals, and confirming information prior to visits.

The catchy slogan, "Why call when you can click?" was used to promote the portal on banners in the practice, on the Web site, in e-mails, and on buttons worn by staff. Patients arriving for appointments were told about the portal at the front desk, where time-saving measures were promoted; by physicians during the visit; and at checkout, where they were handed information on how to use the portal.

Physicians are impressed with the reduction in phone tag and options for responding to questions after hours. Yolanda Raffert is pleased with the savings: "What we soon discovered is the postage we save in one week literally pays for the portal for one month."

Source: Medical Group Management Association, "Executives' Corner: Why Call When You Can Click?" *MGMA e-Source*, January 11, 2010, www.mgma.com/article.aspx?id=40606 (accessed January 20, 2011).

Sources:

Anna-Lisa Silvestre, Valerie M. Sue, and Jill Y. Allen, "If You Build It, Will They Come? The Kaiser Permanente Model of Online Healthcare," *Health Affairs*, V. 28, Issue 2 (2009): 334–44.

Elizabeth W. Woodcock, MBA, FACMPE, CPC, "Online Patient Portals Improve Work Flow, Handle Multiple Functions," *Dermatology Times*, April 1, 2010, www.modernmedicine.com/modernmedicine/Modern+Medicine+Now/Online-patient-portals-improve-work-flow-handle-mu/ArticleStandard/Article/detail/665032 (accessed January 27, 2011).

Marianne Aiello, "Patient Portals Pay Off," *HealthLeaders Magazine*, V. 13, Issue 7 (2010): 52.

Susan L. Zickmund, Rachel Hess, Cindy L. Bryce, Kathleen McTigue, Ellen Olshansky, Katharine Fitzgerald, and Gary S. Fischer, "Interest in the Use of Computerized Patient Portals: Role of the Provider–Patient Relationship," *JGIM: Journal of General Internal Medicine*, Supplement 1, V. 23, Issue S1 (2008): 20–26.

Suzanne G. Leveille, PhD, RN, Annong Huang, MD, Stephanie B. Tsai, MA, Saul N. Weingart, MD, PhD, and Lisa I. Iezzoni, MD, MSC, "Screening for Chronic Conditions Using a Patient Internet Portal: Recruitment for an Internet-based Primary Care Intervention," *JGIM: Journal of General Internal Medicine*, V. 23, Issue 4 (2008): 472–75.

QUESTION How do we implement e-prescribing in the practice?

Electronic prescribing is another means of gaining efficiencies by automating a practice function but with the added benefits of reducing errors and increasing patient safety. MGMA defines e-prescribing as

➤ Electronically accessing information regarding a patient's drug benefit coverage and medication history, with a patient's consent;

➤ Electronically transmitting the prescription to the patient's choice of pharmacy;

➤ Electronically sending renewal requests between the physician's office and pharmacist for approval; and

➤ The means to support the entire medication management process — prescribe, transmit, dispense, administer, and monitor.

The benefits of e-prescribing include real-time access to formularies and pharmacy benefit-eligibility information for patients' insurance. The programs should include functions to alert for potential drug interactions and drug allergies, and suggest alternative medications. Reduction of errors related to handwriting or incorrect data entries are additional benefits.

E-prescribing programs can be used to maintain medication lists for each patient. The lists will track the date prescriptions are written and the duration and number of refills allowed. This saves pulling a patient chart to review prescriptions and determine refill eligibility. The practice can also notify patients when refills are due or it's time for a visit. The system can alert the practice if a patient is late in requesting a refill (and not complying with their care plan) or requesting refills too frequently. The automation results in significant time savings by reducing the number of telephone calls and faxes. One MGMA study, "Analyzing the Cost of Administrative Complexity" (2004), put the latter savings at up to $10,000 per physician per year.

The potential benefits of e-prescribing are large enough that incentives for its implementation were included in the ARRA of 2009. Medicare also began a four-year incentive payment program in 2009. To qualify for the Medicare incentive program, providers must use a "qualified e-prescribing system," either a standalone software system or a system integrated into an EHR. Incentive payments are a percentage increase in the amount of total estimated allowed charges for covered professional services (Part B charges). The increase is 1.0 percent for 2011 and 2012 and 0.5 percent for 2013. In addition, Medicare providers that did not successfully adopt e-prescribing by June 2011 will be fined 1.0 percent of professional service charges in 2012. The penalty increases to 1.5 percent in 2013 and to 2.0 percent for 2014 and beyond.

There was initial concern regarding limitations on using e-prescribing for controlled substances. In March 2010, the Drug Enforcement Administration (DEA) issued a final rule providing clinicians with the option of electronically writing prescriptions for controlled substances and also permitting pharmacies to receive, dispense, and archive these electronic prescriptions.

Monitor the MGMA (www.mgma.com/policy), DEA (www.justice.gov/dea), and CMS Web sites (cms.gov) for changes on the penalty rulings and other e-prescribing issues.

Sources:

Kate Berry and Robert Tennant, MA, "Tech Talk: The Latest on E-prescribing," *MGMA Connexion*, May/June 2008, www.mgma.com/WorkArea/mgma_downloadasset. aspx?id=19226 (accessed January 28, 2011).

Medical Group Management Association, "Analyzing Cost of Administrative Complexity in Group Practice," 2004, www.mgma.com/about/default.aspx?id=280 (accessed March 27, 2008).

Medical Group Management Association, "DEA Regulation on E-prescribing of Controlled Substances Now in Effect," *MGMA Washington Connexion*, June 23, 2010, www.mgma.com/article.aspx?id=33979 (accessed January 28, 2011).

MGMA E-Prescribing Resource Center, www.mgma.com/policy/default.aspx?id=27064 (accessed January 28, 2011).

MGMA Government Affairs, "Final 2011 Medicare Physician Fee Schedule Analysis," www.mgma.com/WorkArea/DownloadAsset.aspx?id=40300 (accessed January 28, 2011).

Rosemarie Nelson, MS, "Are the Phones Ringing Off the Hook?" *MGMA Connexion*, May/June 2010, www.mgma.com/WorkArea/mgma_downloadasset.aspx?id=33803 (accessed January 28, 2011).

QUESTION 44 What steps can I take to prepare my group practice for HIPAA 5010 and ICD-10-CM? And why do we have to convert?

Although it will be expensive and time consuming to convert to the new electronic transmission standards for HIPAA 5010 and ICD-10, the result should be improved operations, communications, and recording of clinical data for quality management. It is a good idea to prepare for the implementation deadlines well in advance. All electronic claims must use Version 5010 starting January 1, 2012, and the conversion to ICD-10 will be required starting October 1, 2013.

Several technical issues were quickly identified in the original HIPAA standards for electronic transactions, Version 4010, after they were implemented in 2003. The new Version 5010 includes improvements to address the issues and eliminate the need for specific adoptions that each insurance payer developed. The new standards will also accommodate ICD-10.

HHS will issue a final rule establishing a transaction standard and a single set of associated rules for health claims attachments that will be consistent with the X12 Version 5010 transaction standards. The use of standardized electronic claims attachments will significantly accelerate the claims adjudication process and eliminate costs associated with the copying and mailing of supporting documentation. The rule should be released by January 2014, and the date of implementation is expected to be January 1, 2016.

The World Health Organization (WHO) created ICD-10 to provide increased detail compared to ICD-9. It will be in two coding sets to replace the three volumes of ICD-9: ICD-10-PCS for procedures performed in hospitals and ICD-10-CM for diagnosis codes used by providers.

There are several reasons for the creation and adoption of ICD-10-CM:

> Adding codes for preventive services and new procedures and diagnoses;

> Incorporating the detail needed for research and clinical outcome studies;

> Providing information for pay-for-performance and other quality management programs;

> Improving data for reimbursement and payment systems;

> Reducing the need for attachments for specific conditions; and

> Allowing the comparison of international data for tracking diseases and treatment outcomes.

Because of the significant differences between ICD-9-CM and ICD-10-CM, the CMS and CDC's National Center for Health Statistics have developed General Equivalence Mappings (GEMs). They can be used as translational or crosswalk tools to assist in identifying the new codes from knowledge of the ICD-9. Since the ICD-10 is not a direct conversion from ICD-9, the GEMs will not show a one-to-one translation but the new, related codes.

The significant differences in ICD-10-CM also mean that implementation will be complicated and require extensive training and a lengthy learning period. There are several steps you must take to prepare your practice for HIPAA Version 5010 and ICD-10-CM:

> Determine all of the current systems and processes that use ICD-9 codes, including practice management systems, EHRs, clinical documentation, superbills, contracts, and

quality management reports. The sooner you start this list, the more locations and processes you and your staff will be able to identify.

➤ Ask your information system vendors (PMS, EHR, and so on) about their plans to accommodate the upcoming changes. Ask how and when your software will be updated, including whether the upgrade will require the purchase of new versions. Find out if the upgrades will require faster processors or increased memory than that provided by your current hardware.

➤ Talk with your payers and any clearinghouses or billing services you use about their implementation plans. Discuss how you can work together to ensure a smooth transition.

➤ Identify with your payer if the increased detail of ICD-10 offers opportunities for modifying reimbursement methods and quality reporting.

➤ Look at your current work flow and processes to locate needed changes during the transition, including encounter forms and clinical documentation.

➤ List the clinical and administrative staff that will require training on ICD-10. Physicians and clinical staff should be trained approximately six months in advance of the October 2013 implementation deadline. Many administrative staff members also need to be aware of the changes and their impacts.

➤ Determine the budgetary needs for the time and costs related to implementation. Expenses include training, resource materials, costs for system changes or upgrades, developing and printing new superbills, and related expenses. Some experts are predicting this will cost approximately $27,000 per physician.

➤ Conduct tests with your payers, clearinghouses, and system vendors prior to implementation. Ask well ahead of time when they will be ready for testing and set a timeline.

The following resources are available to help in training and implementation:

CMS ICD-10 Web page, includes links to the GEMs	www.cms.gov/ICD10/
CDC National Center for Health Statistics, includes the GEMS	www.cdc.gov/nchs/icd/icd10cm.htm
World Health Organization ICD-10 information	www.who.int/whosis/icd10/index.html
MGMA Web site resources	www.mgma.com (search "ICD-10")

Sources:

Jeanetta I. Lawrence, MBA, CPC, FACMPE, "The Canadian Experience with the Implementation of Version 10 of the International Classification of Diseases (ICD 10)," ACMPE Fellowship Paper, October 2008.

MGMA Government Affairs, "Checklists: Transition to ICD-10/5010," www.mgma.com/policy/default.aspx?id=39682 (accessed January 9, 2011).

MGMA Government Affairs, "Washington Link: Preparing for Change: HIPAA Version 5010 and ICD-10," *MGMA Connexion*, November/December 2010, www.mgma.com/WorkArea/mgma_downloadasset.aspx?id=40209 (accessed January 9, 2011).

Robert M. Tennant, "Managing Change Effectively: Preparing Your Practice for HIPAA 5010 and ICD-10-CM," in *Performance and Practices of Successful Medical Groups: 2010 Report Based on 2009 Data*, 3–11 (Englewood, CO: Medical Group Management Association, 2010).

QUESTION 45 How long do I need to retain medical records, especially if we convert to EHR?

Medical records should be retained for the length of the statute of limitations for malpractice actions. Because the statute of limitations varies from state to state, ask your state medical board, state health department, or your practice's attorney for this information.

Inactive records on adult patients should be kept for at least seven years. Keep pediatric records for at least seven years past the patients' age of majority. The American Health Information Management Association (AHIMA) recommends that adult-patient records be retained for 10 years beyond the most recent encounter and pediatric records retained up to the age of majority plus the statute of limitations. Their Web site (AHIMA.org) also provides information on state-specific retention requirements.

You should also check your physicians' malpractice coverage. How long is the coverage in force? This information may guide you in determining the length of time to keep medical records. Medical records related to a patient who initiates a malpractice or wrongful suit against your practice should be retained for the length of the litigation.

CMS has online information about records retention for specific documents at www.cms.gov. CMS requires that providers submitting cost reports retain all patient records for at least five years after the closure of the cost report.

Keep X-rays and other imaging records, raw psychological testing data, fetal monitoring tracings, electroencephalograms, electrocardiograms, and other records for at least five years. AHIMA advises that master patient/person indexes, birth and death registries, and registries of surgical procedures should be kept permanently.

If you are short of space for records within your facility, you may want to store inactive patients' charts in an off-site facility. Make sure that the facility is HIPAA compliant and protected from natural or human-caused disasters. You can also investigate converting your records to an EHR system. Once medical records are entered into an EHR, usually by scanning, the paper record may be destroyed. The EHR record should be retained for the length of time specified for paper records. Cloud computing vendors are worth investigating for storing digital records, especially those with high memory demand, including scanned or digital images. Costs for cloud storage vendors may be less than your storage costs, and they will absorb the costs of upgrading to new storage media as it develops.

When the retention period has passed and you destroy the records, make sure you are compliant with applicable state regulations and the HIPAA Standards for Electronic Security for disposing of medical records. Destroy paper documents by shredding them to ensure they cannot be read or recovered. Delete electronic documents and database records by wiping them from local, network, and backup drives and/or disks. Erasing information from storage media may not be sufficient because hackers may have means of accessing the information. Electronic media such as CDs, DVDs, and electronic tapes should be physically destroyed or have their data-bearing layers removed. You may want to hire a professional service to shred the paper documents and destroy the electronic media.

To ensure your practice complies with the recommendations and regulations, you need to develop a retention schedule and policy. The policy should incorporate state, federal, malpractice insurer, and specialty-specific requirements. Specify which storage medium will be used. List the types of documents and their specific retention schedules, including business records, claims forms, and compliance documentation.

Explanation of benefits (EOBs) are classified as business or financial records, along with superbills and encounter forms, and don't fall under the same retention requirements as medical records. Retention periods should depend on the use of EOBs in following up and challenging denied or rejected claims; at least one year is recommended.

Sources:

American Health Information Management Association, "Practice Brief: Retaining Healthcare Business Records," www.library.ahima.org/xpedio/groups/public/documents/ahima/bok1_010766.hcsp?dDocName=bok1_010766 (accessed January 21, 2011).

American Health Information Management Association, "Practice Brief: Retention of Health Information (Updated)," www.library.ahima.org/xpedio/groups/public/docu-ments/ahima/bok1_012545.hcsp?dDocName=bok1_012545#t3 (accessed January 21, 2011).

"The Basic Advantages of Cloud Computing," *Health Data Management*, January 10, 2011, www.healthdatamanagement.com/news/HIMSS_cloud_computing-41710-1.html (accessed May 9, 2011).

Centers for Medicare & Medicaid Services, "Medical Record Retention and Media Format for Medical Records," www1.cms.gov/MLNProducts/Downloads/MLN_Podcast_Medical_Record_Retention_and_Media_Format.pdf (accessed January 21, 2011).

David A. Kelch, FACMPE, "Medical Records: Perpetual Storage or Scheduled Destruction," ACMPE Fellowship Paper, September 17, 2007, www.mgma.com/WorkArea/mgma_downloadasset.aspx?id=16254 (accessed January 21, 2011).

Robert C. Scroggins, "Q&A: How Long to Keep Explanation of Benefits Statements?" *Medical Economics*, September 4, 2009, www.modernmedicine.com/modernmedicine/Modern+Medicine+Now/QampA-How-long-to-keep-explanation-of-benefits-sta/ArticleStandard/Article/detail/621953 (accessed January 21, 2011).

QUESTION **I'm having issues with one physician who frequently fails to complete his charts. What ideas do you have to help me?**

46

Unfortunately, this issue is an all too common concern for medical practice administrators. Physicians often do not realize the potential consequences for not completing documentation and signing charts. You or physician leadership should discuss the consequences in meetings with all physicians. Chart completion is necessary because incomplete documentation can lead to downcoding by payers or no reimbursement at all, raises malpractice liability concerns due to the lack of complete information, and can violate state and Medicare regulations. Emphasize that accurate and complete documentation translates into diagnosis codes that result in full reimbursement.

Requirements for completing charts in a timely manner should be included in documents related to behavioral expectations of physicians within your practice. Examples of these documents are new-physician orientation materials, policies in the physician handbook, employment agreements, performance reviews, codes of conduct, and/or other documents signed by physicians. Support for enforcing the policy must be obtained from practice leadership, and compliance and consequences must be clear and carried out equitably.

There are a variety of ideas that practices and hospitals have implemented to obtain physician cooperation in completing documentation. Peer pressure can be used by pointing out the number of incomplete charts per physician at regular meetings. Compensation can be impacted if bonuses or compensation are related to completion of all duties.

Lack of signature is a frequent cause of noncompliance, especially with charts dictated by nurse practitioners and physician assistants acting under a physician's direction or charts dictated by nurses or other staff. In these instances, the physician must still sign the chart. Some medical records or billing staff members schedule a time with the physician for chart completion, eliminating the excuse that the physician didn't have time or forgot.

If there is an issue in the practice, the physician is probably not completing or signing charts in the hospital either. Find out how the hospital enforces its documentation requirements. Some hospitals will suspend physicians who violate hospital policies. Suspensions may be in stages or all at once and can include no admissions or discharges of patients, no elective surgeries, or no performance of any inpatient or outpatient duties in the hospital. A few hospitals even restrict the privileges of other physicians within the same group practice.

To manage incomplete records until the physician finishes them, the following procedures are recommended:

➤ File incomplete records separately. If filed within a patient's chart, incomplete records are more difficult to access and will likely be forgotten. This will make them more accessible when the physician comes to complete the records.

➤ Notify physicians regularly (at least weekly) of incomplete records.

➤ Review state, Medicare, and other requirements for chart completion to impress upon physicians the seriousness of the situation. Joint Commission on Accreditation of Healthcare Organizations (JCAHO) standards are 30 days after discharge, but California and Alaska have 14-day requirements.

Another advantage of EHRs is their automated systems for monitoring chart completion and sending notices when charts are not complete. However, EHRs won't eliminate all issues related to physician compliance with chart completion.

Sources:

Christopher Clarke, "Practical Approaches to Improving Physician Workflow & Chart Completion," March 3, 2010, HIMSS presentation available at www.himss.org/content/files/proceedings/2010/168.pdf (accessed January 28, 2011).

Cindy Doyon, "How Does Your Facility Maintain and Process Incomplete Records? Tips for Filing, Obtaining Signatures, and Managing Records," *Journal of Healthcare Compliance*, V. 6, Issue 3 (May/June 2004): 50–53 (accessed January 28, 2011).

CHAPTER 5

Organizational Governance

QUESTION **How can I develop a physician compensation model that physicians will be happy with and that will maintain our productivity and revenue?**

47

Physician compensation models are frequently reviewed and modified. Changes in the practice, in the group's income, in physicians' attitudes about its fairness, and a variety of other reasons lead to doubts that the current plan is the best plan. Because of the personal impact of the plan, physicians will be concerned about changes and should be involved in any revisions.

Compensation plans have two facets: (1) the strictly financial aspect of the distribution of the group's income and expenses and (2) the cultural aspect. The latter is often not considered, but how revenue is distributed affects and reflects the organizational culture (for example, its individual competitive, cooperative, or team-oriented nature), and so the plan should reflect the desired culture in the organization.

Because of the importance of the compensation plan in physician satisfaction and practice success, development of a new plan should go through a several-step process and evolve through a concession-building process. The exact order and number of steps may vary depending on the approach.

Step 1. Identify who will develop the new plan. The options include practice leadership or board, a committee, a consultant, or a combination of these options. Because of the importance of the plan and the diversity of factors to be considered, the recommended approach is a compensation plan committee with a membership representing the diversity of physicians in the practice. A consultant or practice administrator may be used as a facilitator to the committee or to bring in an outsider's perspective.

Step 2. Review the practice's mission statements, core values, and vision. How does the practice see itself, how is the environment changing, and how do you position for the future? Without understanding these issues, it will be impossible to develop a plan that supports the organizational culture, mission, and plans for the future. In addition, the compensation plan should have its own "mission" or stated objectives against which the current and future plan can be measured. For example, plan objectives could include improving individual productivity and encouraging clinical quality.

Step 3. Assess what is wrong with the current compensation plan. Why are you revising it? Have there been changes in the practice (more physicians), practice financials (declining revenue), or demographics? Is the push for health reform changing reimbursement or incentives (trend toward pay-for-performance plans)? Do physicians feel that the plan is unfair or causing behavior counter to the organizational vision and culture? To get at the real issues, you may need to conduct individual interviews as well as group discussions.

Step 4. Learn about options in compensation plan design. Review the literature, listen to what your peers are doing, or bring in a consultant. There are a few basic models: (1) fixed salary with minimum production goals, (2) fixed base salary with production bonus, (3) a split between salary and productivity, and (4) 100 percent productivity. Typically, practices prefer productivity-based plans to provide the incentives to maximize practice revenues. Changing reimbursement options may soon require practices to include factors such as patient satisfaction, clinical quality, and utilization in compensation plans.

Step 5. Decide what to include in the plan. Which option is best for your practice? Combine the information gathered in Steps 3 and 4 to identify which plan options match the reason for changing your current system. Identify productivity or quality indicators that need to be changed with the new plan and how you will benchmark them. For instance, productivity can be measured by net collections, work RVUs, or number of encounters. Plans should also consider compensation for nonclinical activities and starting physicians. Determine the method for allocating practice expenses. Part-time physicians and physicians at different stages of their careers should also be addressed.

Work RVUs (wRVUs) are frequently used in calculating productivity and distributing income because they are a standardized measurement to compare work effort and aren't biased by payer mix, specialty, variations in fee schedule, or other factors. Compensation using wRVUs can be based on a calculated net practice income per RVU, a share of the total RVUs in the practice, or by an incentive system (increase in RVUs over previous year, percentage above a benchmark, and so on).

Productivity measures preferred in compensation methodology by MGMA member practices include

Compensation methodology	Percentage of physicians using method
Number of RVUs	60%
Collections for professional charges	39%
Gross charges	21%
Adjusted charges	13%

Preferred basis for incentive or bonus payments in compensation plans:

Quality indicators	62%
Patient satisfaction	61%
Peer review	18%
Community outreach	9%

Note: Respondents could select more than one option, so percentages total more than 100.

Source: Medical Group Management Association, *Physician Compensation and Production Survey: 2010 Report Based on 2009 Data* (Englewood, CO: Medical Group Management Association, 2010).

Step 6. Develop and present a draft compensation plan. The committee may choose to develop more than one plan. Provide actual examples on how the plan will work. Solicit feedback among all of the practice's physicians and leadership. Measure the plan against the original goals and objectives. It may be impossible to satisfy every physician in the group, but work toward a general consensus. Physicians may be worried about the change, so present a plan to transition to it from the current plan.

Everyone should recognize that it will take time to adjust to the implemented plan; indeed, you might want to have a lengthy transition period, and some adjustments may be required even after it is implemented. Compensation plans should be reactive to potential payer reimbursement changes, such as accountable care organizations (ACOs) and bundled payments.

A CLOSER LOOK . . .

Pay for Performance and Quality Incentives

The changing healthcare environment is pushing practices to consider alternatives in straight productivity. Participating in pay-for-performance (P4P) or other reimbursement programs that emphasize patient wellness and quality indicators will require a shift in compensation plan incentives. Plans will have to factor in the use of best practices, the percentage of chronic patients receiving regular exams, prescription management, participation in quality indicator programs, and other measures.

Practice physicians will also have to determine how to distribute revenue from P4P and similar programs, dependent on the incentive program itself, how the practice has implemented it, and the amount of revenue involved. One option is to pass the revenue directly to individual physicians specified in the payer's incentive program. The other is to allocate the revenue among all the physicians that participate in the practice's patient wellness and quality efforts as a way to recognize specific physicians' efforts even if they aren't part of the initial P4P program. You will have to monitor the incentive programs to see if they maintain, increase, or decrease the practice's total revenue.

Source: Bruce A. Johnson, JD, MPA, and Deborah Walker Keegan, PhD, FACMPE, *Physician Compensation Plans: State-of-the-Art Strategies* (Englewood, CO: Medical Group Management Association, 2006).

MGMA RESOURCES

"A Compensation System Self-Assessment Tool: 12 Questions for Better Results," MGMA Member Benefits and Tools, MGMA.com

Bruce A. Johnson, JD, MPA, and Deborah Walker Keegan, PhD, FACMPE, *Physician Compensation Plans: State-of-the-*

Art Strategies (Englewood, CO: Medical Group Management Association, 2006)

Kathryn Glass, MBA, MSHA, PMP, *RVUs: Applications for Medical Practice Success, 2nd Edition* (Englewood, CO: Medical Group Management Association, 2008)

Information Exchanges (informal surveys) on Income Distribution

Physician Compensation and Production Survey Report (current year's report)

Sources:

Bruce A. Johnson, JD, MPA, and Deborah Walker Keegan, PhD, FACMPE, *Physician Compensation Plans: State-of-the-Art Strategies* (Englewood, CO: Medical Group Management Association, 2006).

David N. Gans, MSHA, FACMPE, "Data Mine: What You Reward, You Get — and Lots of It," *MGMA Connexion*, February 2009, www.mgma.com/WorkArea/mgma_downloadas-set.aspx?id=26358 (accessed December 20, 2010).

Jeffrey B. Milburn, MBA, CMPE, "Ease New Physicians into Productivity-Based Compensation Plans," *MGMA e-Source*, November 9, 2010, www.mgma.com/article.aspx?id=39957 (accessed December 20, 2010).

Will N. Ginn III, FACMPE, "10 Tips for Designing or Redesigning a Physician Compensation Plan," *MGMA e-Source*, May 27, 2008, www.mgma.com/article.aspx?id=19060 (accessed December 20, 2010).

QUESTION 48

We are starting to recruit for a new physician, and I would like to review our buy-in structure ahead of time. What are new trends and issues that the practice should consider in the buy/sell agreement?

Buy/sell agreements are one of several documents that should be reviewed regularly to ensure they are current with your practice's goals and the marketplace. Some of the keys to effective and long-lasting buy/sell agreements, according to Hobart Collins, MA, CMPE, of MGMA's Health Care Consulting Group, are

➤ The buy/sell agreement is consistent with the group's mission, goals, and objectives;

➤ The terms of the buy/sell agreement welcome new members and ease the transition of departing members with financial terms that are manageable for the physicians and the group;

➤ The terms of the buy/sell agreement are integrated with other economic components, such as the income-distribution system, profit-sharing strategy, retirement plans, and other benefit program;

➤ The group has reasonable sensitivity to the marketplace, recognizing that young physicians completing their training are generally averse to large buy-ins; and

➤ The group has a fairly objective awareness of its attractiveness as a long-term professional home for new physicians.

Bruce Johnson, JD, of MGMA's Health Care Consulting Group, recommends that the buy/sell agreement specify:

➤ The methodology for determining the practice value, including what percentage interest the physician will be purchasing;

➤ How the physician will be allowed to pay (cash or payments over a period of time);

➤ The handling of current and future accounts receivable; and

➤ The details of the buy-in. Is it

➤ A mandatory buy-in to a practice corporation or partnership;

➤ A buy-in to related businesses, such as real estate or equipment entities; or

➤ A mandatory buy-in to the practice entity and optional buy-in to real estate or equipment entities?

The buy-out portion of the agreement will cover

➤ What events can cause a buy-out to occur (retirement, death, termination of employment, disability, and so on);

➤ How the purchase price will be determined and how it will be paid;

➤ How A/R will be handled; and

➤ The handling of ongoing issues after the buy-out, including noncompete clauses, malpractice "tail coverage," and confidentiality.

The environment has changed, and a new generation of physicians has new attitudes compared with previous generations. They have a heavy debt load from the costs of medical school and their training, they are in a competitive recruiting environment, and many physicians now consider the practice as a workplace rather than an equity and retirement investment. All of these factors make a low buy-in threshold appealing.

It is also important to understand how the buy-in payments will be allocated within the practice. Will funds be distributed to owners or remain in the practice? How will funds be generated to fund the buy-out?

When making an offer to a recruited physician, you will want to inform the physician of expectations regarding partnership, including the time period after which ownership may be offered, and what factors are considered in offering partnership. The practice should consider cultural fit, patient satisfaction, practice contributions, and initiative as well as professional and clinical skills. Explain the additional responsibilities of partnership and the average time commitment along with information on how compensation will be affected. The physician may ask if ownership is mandatory or if there is an option to remain as an employed physician and the consequences of that choice. Be prepared to show the physician documents to demonstrate the financial well-being of the practice and reasons for the determined value.

A LOOK AT THE NUMBERS . . .

How Many Years Must a Physician Work in the Practice before He or She Can Buy In?

Years	Percentage of respondents
One year	27%
Two years	41%
Three years	13%
Four years or more	4%

(continued)

Valuating method for practice buy-in and buy-out	Percentage of respondents
Value of net assets	47%
Goodwill	14%
Discounted cash flow	12%
Capitalization of earnings income	11%
Excess earnings capitalization	6%

Source: Medical Group Management Association, "Buy-in and Buy-out Agreements," *Information Exchange* #6529 (Englewood, CO: Medical Group Management Association, February 2009).

Sources:

Bruce A. Johnson, JD, "Clean Dealing: Legal Considerations for Buy/Sell Agreements," *MGMA Connexion*, special article reprint, updated 2008, www.mgma.com/WorkArea/DownloadAsset.aspx?id=16348 (accessed December 29, 2010).

Hobart Collins, MA, CMPE, "Grabbing or Releasing the Brass Ring: Strategic Buy/Sell Agreement Considerations," *MGMA Connexion*, special article reprint, updated 2008, www.mgma.com/WorkArea/DownloadAsset.aspx?id=16348 (accessed December 29, 2010).

Keith Borglum, CHBC, "What You Need to Know about Buying and Selling a Practice," *Medical Economics*, October 9, 2009, www.modernmedicine.com/modernmedicine/Modern+Medicine+Now/What-you-need-to-know-about-buying-and-selling-a-p/ArticleStandard/Article/detail/631650 (accessed December 29, 2010).

QUESTION 49   One of our partners has announced that he will retire soon. What resources are there to help us plan the transition for the physician and the practice?

There are many details to take care of related to the departure of a physician for any reason. Strategic plans, physician recruitment plans, and other internal documents will help the practice with the transition, but there are also resources specific to physician retirement and "closing" a physician's practice. MGMA's "Physician Retirement and Practice Transition Self-Assessment Tool" will help in the preparation for physician retirement (visit MGMA.com and select Member Benefits and Communities/Benefits and Tools/Human Resources Tools).

One of the first issues to address is whether another physician will be hired. Your physician recruitment plan (see Question 20) will have created awareness of the group's goals, physicians' career and retirement goals, and the marketplace to help in this stage. If the decision is made to hire a physician of similar specialties and skills as the current physician, you should begin the process immediately due to the length of time involved in the recruitment process. You may want to have the departing physician serve as a mentor for the incoming physician.

The next difficult question is the contractual agreements with the retiring physician, particularly the buy-out agreement. The physician may have been hired during another time; what seemed like reasonable buy-out terms then may be more difficult in today's financial times and given new physicians' goals. Even if there isn't a written buy-out agreement, the departing physician might have expectations that need to be addressed. You may want to consult with the practice legal counsel on this and other contractual agreements with the physician. Buy-in and buy-out agreements are addressed in Question 48.

The buy-out and employment agreements should specify issues such as

➤ Notification requirements prior to physician retirement or departure;

➤ Ownership of A/R after the physician leaves;

➤ Whether the practice will cover the ongoing malpractice insurance (tail coverage);

➤ Benefits promised to retiring physicians and staff;

➤ The presence of noncompete covenants;

➤ Maintenance and storage of the medical records; and

➤ Malpractice insurance requirements and who pays.

The medical records should stay with the practice, but state regulations will determine this. If the physician is moving to another practice, patients who choose to also change practices can request copies of their records. The practice should determine if it has or wants to require a noncompete agreement.

A CLOSER LOOK . . .

Checklist for Physician's Retirement

Task	Timeline	Person responsible
Notify legal counsel.		
Review relevant corporate documents.		
Agree on the actual retirement date.		
Settle all buy-out issues.		
Notify staff of the retirement and the transition plan.		
Have physician resign from leadership position.		
Send notice to the physician's patients, and provide them with names of other physicians. Check state laws for notification requirements.		
Determine how the physician's patient charts will be managed (typically retained in the practice).		
Notify Medicare, Medicaid, and third-party payers.		
Contact hospitals where physician has staff privileges.		
Notify referring physicians.		
Notify DEA and relevant state agencies.		
Contact your malpractice insurer and set up tail coverage.		
Determine ownership of A/R after the physician's departure. Is it specified in the contract?		
Ensure physician's charts are completed with full documentation.		
Remove the physician's name from the answering service, telephone system, marketing materials, and so on.		

The practice must also plan for ongoing care of the departing physician's patients. The plan may determine whether to hire a new physician. Notify patients well in advance (60 to 90 days if possible), and provide them with the option of which physician they can see. Introduce patients to the new physician or the current physicians who will be taking over the cases. Check if there are state regulations affecting patient notification.

If the physician served in a leadership position within your practice, you will need to implement the succession plan and identify physicians to serve in that role. Question 52 includes information on physician-leadership training and succession planning.

You should also be prepared for the impact of the physician's departure on the staff and others in the practice. The departure of any member of the practice's team, especially if it's the departure of a leader, can affect the morale and stability of the practice. Discuss the transition plans with staff members, and encourage them to ask questions and share their feelings. Prepare them for handling questions from patients.

There is a lengthy list of contacts to notify, and the practice administrator and departing physician should develop and coordinate that list well ahead of time. The checklist on the preceding page includes some of the contacts to notify and other items to address to ensure a smooth transition.

MGMA RESOURCES

MGMA Member Community discussion groups (MGMA.com) frequently share sample checklists, policies, and letters.

An ACMPE fellowship paper by Laurie W. Mays, FACMPE, CPC, includes a sample patient notification letter and physician departure policy. See link in the following Sources section.

Sources:

Bruce A. Johnson, JD, MPA, "Physician Retirement and Practice Transition Self-Assessment Tool," www.mgma.com/WorkArea/mgma_downloadasset.aspx?id=5564 (accessed January 10, 2011).

Laurie W. Mays, FACMPE, CPC, "Group Practice Considerations in Dealing with a Physician's Departure," ACMPE Fellowship Paper, August 2006, www.mgma.com/WorkArea/mgma_downloadasset.aspx?id=10976 (accessed January 10, 2011).

Medical Group Management Association, "Old-School Physician-Retirement Plans Often Flunk Today's Practice Viability Tests," *MGMA e-Source*, July 2007, www.mgma.com/article.aspx?id=13922 (accessed January 10, 2011).

QUESTION 50 Our board of directors wants some resources for self-assessment and evaluating its effectiveness. What resources do you have to assist us?

The starting point to determine board effectiveness is to clarify the board's role, individual responsibilities, and structure. The duties of board members should reflect the role of the governing board and the structure provided in the practice bylaws. The board serves to provide direction and guidance for the organization, letting the administrative positions handle the strategies and day-to-day operations. The roles of the board include

➤ Developing the organization's mission and vision;

➤ Identifying organizational goals;

➤ Participating in strategic planning;

➤ Ensuring executive performance by hiring, setting expectations, and evaluating the organization's chief executive officer or administrator;

➤ Supporting the executive in executing practice operations and implementing board decisions;

➤ Overseeing the provision of quality of care;

➤ Monitoring the financial health of the organization and ensuring financial support to carry out the mission;

➤ Managing external relations with the media, the community, and government; and

➤ Conducting self-assessments on board effectiveness.

Boards typically consist of a chair or president, several officers, and several board members. The president's responsibilities typically include

➤ Presiding over the board and, if applicable, the executive committee;

➤ Directing the meetings;

> ➤ Ensuring the development of the organizational mission and goals;

> ➤ Monitoring progress toward meeting the goals; and

> ➤ Serving as the organization's representative to national associations, local organizations, the media, and other groups.

The vice chair or vice president presides over events during the president's absence. This officer may be the president-elect and be "in training" for the role. Smaller boards may incorporate this position within other officer's responsibilities. The secretary records the minutes for the meetings; files annual reports if required by state regulations or other requirements; and maintains the bylaws, articles of organization or constitution, copies of policies, and a record of the board's decisions and agreements. The treasurer reports on the financial health of the organization on a regular basis, ensures that correct and complete financial records are developed and recorded, monitors the financial investments, and chairs the finance committee (if applicable).

Some boards combine officer positions, depending on the total number of board members. General board members will support the roles of the board as listed previously, serve on committees, report on issues related to the organization, and participate in the development of the mission and goals.

Members should represent the varying interests and characteristics of the organization and its stakeholders. They should not represent a particular interest group; rather, they should be advocates for the benefit of the complete organization.

One issue of concern is whether or not the board is too small or too large and cumbersome. The total number of board members will vary depending on the size and complexity of the organization. Groups of fewer than five physicians might have all of their physicians on the board. Groups with more than five physicians should select a few of them to serve on the board. A ten-physician practice may have three to five board members. If the board grows to seven or more members, you should consider forming an executive committee. Typically consisting of three to four members, the executive committee meets more often than the board, works more closely with the chief executive officer, and provides the board with recommendations on various issues.

Board evaluations and self-assessments should be conducted every one or two years. Questions to ask include

➤ Were the board's decisions effective and in compliance with the organization's mission and values?

➤ Was the president effective in conducting the board meetings, supporting decision-making, and providing direction and vision?

➤ Did the board stick to its strategy and policy role and leave operational issues to the practice administrator/executive?

➤ Was the board adequately aware of financial issues, and did it respond appropriately?

➤ Does the board represent the practice in membership and outlook?

➤ Do members represent the organization's interests over personal interests?

➤ What did the board do to maintain excellence?

➤ Were board meetings effective, addressing limited but pertinent issues?

➤ Were members in compliance with the attendance and participation requirements?

➤ Did the board recognize different perceptions and opinions among the members?

➤ Were any opportunities missed during the evaluation period?

➤ What changes could be implemented to improve the board and its decision-making?

Sources:

Dennis D. Pointer and James E. Orlikoff, *Getting to Great: Principles of Healthcare Organization and Governance* (San Francisco, CA: Jossey-Bass, 2002).

Hobart Collins, CMPE, "Framework for the Future: Assessing Your Practice's Governance Structure and Processes," *MGMA Connexion*, November/December 2007, www.mgma. com/WorkArea/mgma_downloadasset.aspx?id=15658 (accessed January 10, 2011).

Joan M. Ledzian, CMM, CPC, FACMPE, "The Evolution of the Governance Structure: An Essential Progression of the Expanding Group Practice," ACMPE Fellowship Paper, October 2006.

Nick Fabrizio, PhD, FACMPE, FACHE, "Objective Advice: Reduce Conflict — Clarify Board Duties," *MGMA Connexion*, November/December 2010, www.mgma.com/ WorkArea/mgma_downloadasset.aspx?id=40206 (accessed January 10, 2011).

Stephen L. Wagner, PhD, FACMPE, "Organization and Operations of Medical Group Practice," in *Physician Practice Management: Essential Operational and Financial Knowledge*, edited by Lawrence F. Wolper, MBA, FACMPE, 39–43 (Sudbury, MA: Jones and Bartlett Publishers, 2005).

QUESTION 51 We need to formalize the responsibilities of our managing partner. Do you have sample job descriptions or other resources?

Quite frequently, as a practice grows, the managing partner takes on more responsibilities, but his or her role is never formalized and can lead to confusion and conflicts with administrators and others in the practice. This physician is often the owner or senior member of the practice. Many practices rotate the position among senior physicians or hold an election or other selection process. Developing a job description for the physician-leader role will clarify current responsibilities and ease the succession process as new physicians take over the role.

Unfortunately, each practice is different in how they envision the role, responsibilities, and title of its physician leader or leaders. Many different titles are used, including managing partner, physician leader, or medical director. For larger practices, there may be one or more medical directors as well as managing partners.

MGMA RESOURCES

Medical Directorship and On-Call Compensation Survey: 2010 Report Based on 2009 Data (Englewood, CO: Medical Group Management Association, 2010)

Information Exchange Item #6601, "Medical Director/Managing Partner Duties and Compensation," includes sample job descriptions

MGMA Member Community libraries or discussion groups (MGMA.com)

In some practices, the physician leader serves as a contact for the practice administrator to review strategy and financial and operations decisions. This reporting structure provides physician input without requiring the board's involvement, leaving the board to discuss major issues, strategic planning, and vision. You should also decide if the managing partner or the administrator or both will present to the board. In larger practices with executive committees, the managing partner may also serve as chair of the executive committee.

The job descriptions for the administrator and managing partner should clarify the daily financial and operational functions that the administrator manages, and the types of decisions and discussions with which the physician leader will be involved. The more the administrator handles, the more time the physician has for patient care and other revenue-generating responsibilities.

MGMA's *Medical Directorship and On-Call Compensation Survey Report* helps define the role and responsibilities of medical directors in group practices. Some of this can be applied to managing partners' descriptions. The report defines a medical director as

> ➤ A position that requires a licensed physician;

> ➤ A senior medical administrative position within the group practice;

> ➤ Having responsibilities that are divided between administrative duties and the delivery of healthcare services;

> ➤ Responsible for all activities related to the delivery of medical care and clinical services such as cost management, utilization review, quality assurance, and medical protocol development;

> ➤ Typically overseeing the group's physicians, including recruitment and credentialing; and

> ➤ Usually reporting to the governing body of the organization or the physician CEO/president.

The reported responsibilities for medical directors in descending order according to the MGMA report were

---

Case Study

Central Vermont Medical Center in Berlin, Vt., had a senior physician at each of its locations, but there were no job descriptions or performance expectations. This resulted in problems with communication, teamwork, decision-making, and training. With board approval, the physician leaders met and wrote job descriptions for a site medical director that specified the following responsibilities:

➤ Support the office supervisor;

➤ Mentor new physicians;

➤ Manage site productivity and operations;

➤ Participate in the evolution of a productivity-based physician compensation system;

➤ Develop and manage a budget, including presenting monthly financial reports to practice staff with the support of administration;

➤ Lead physician and staff recruitment for the site; and

➤ Spearhead site operational-improvement efforts, including policy development and quality projects.

According to Donna G. Izor, MS, vice president of physician services, the result was many improvements, including improved relationships with the board and senior management, better understanding and communication of group objectives, increased cooperation with site directors and office supervisors, and improved physician recruitment and relations with new providers.

➤ Attend standing meetings (board, committee, and so on);

➤ Monitor quality and appropriateness of medical care;

➤ Provide guidance and leadership for performance guidelines;

➤ Develop policies and procedures;

➤ Manage strategic development;

➤ Oversee clinical peer review;

➤ Oversee documentation and care planning;

➤ Manage physician relations and/or representation;

➤ Handle clinical patient complaints;

➤ Address emergency issues;

➤ Support physician education;

➤ Manage community relations;

➤ Handle physician behavior and impairment issues; and

➤ Oversee equipment selection, maintenance, and planning.

Once the position's responsibilities are clarified, the group will have to decide if and how the managing partner/medical director is compensated. This decision will be based on the rotation method for the position, the amount of time spent managing the responsibilities, and the compensation model among the physicians in the practice. Compensation based on clinical productivity alone may have to be adjusted to allow for time spent on administrative responsibilities. If the model already includes compensation for nonclinical activities, no changes may be required.

PHYSICIAN–ADMINISTRATOR TEAMS

Many practices have evolved their leadership responsibilities into physician–administrator teams. Indeed, having an effective physician-administrator team managing the organization is one of the keys in better-performing practices. While maintaining clearly defined roles, the closer the physician leader and chief administrator work together and support each other, the more effective the practice management becomes with the combination of clinical and financial knowledge.

Virginia Mason Medical Center in Seattle, Wash., has been run by the physician–administrator team of Gary Kaplan, MD, and Sarah Patterson for 25 years. They've identified several keys to successful team leadership, including

➤ Setting clear, measurable performance goals for the leadership team;

> ➤ Clearly dividing assignments for the team versus individuals, and physician-led versus administrator-led tasks;

> ➤ Awarding bonuses based on leadership team performance; and

> ➤ Using a physician-manager leadership structure throughout the organization.

They credit the physician–administrator team approach for the successful implementation of Virginia Mason's shift to an organization-wide management method focusing on quality, safety, and waste elimination.

Sources:

Donna G. Izor, MS, FACMPE, "Defining the Role of a Site Medical Director," *MGMA e-Source*, February 12, 2008, www.mgma.com/article.aspx?id=16586 (accessed January 12, 2011).

Gary Kaplan, MD, FACMPE, and Sarah Patterson, "The Physician-Administrator Team: Still an Optimal Model for Leading Medical Practices," *MGMA Connexion*, November/December 2009, www.mgma.com/WorkArea/mgma_downloadasset.aspx?id=31843 (accessed January 12, 2011).

Medical Group Management Association, *Medical Directorship and On-Call Compensation Survey: 2010 Report Based on 2009 Data* (Englewood, CO: Medical Group Management Association, 2010).

Medical Group Management Association, "Party Line: What's the Role of a Managing Partner?" *MGMA Connexion*, September 2009, www.mgma.com/WorkArea/mgma_downloadasset.aspx?id=30232 (accessed January 12, 2011).

Nick A. Fabrizio, PhD, FACMPE, FACHE, "Got Authority? An Administrator Needs to Know Scope of Power," *MGMA Connexion*, November/December 2009, www.mgma.com/WorkArea/mgma_downloadasset.aspx?id=31872 (accessed January 12, 2011).

Robert C. Bohlmann, FACMPE, "Objective Advice: How Do You Develop a Governance System for a Growing Practice?" *MGMA Connexion*, November/December 2008, www.mgma.com/WorkArea/mgma_downloadasset.aspx?id=24326 (accessed January 12, 2011).

QUESTION **What information do you have to help me develop a succession plan for practice leadership?**

52

Organizational leaders and boards often wait until a CEO or other leader announces his or her planned departure to begin thinking about succession planning. This is too late to begin the process. Succession planning is not replacement planning; its purpose is not to select someone to replace an executive but to identify the needs and goals of the organization and who is the best individual to lead the practice toward those goals. Succession planning is also providing opportunities for training and mentorship to prepare individuals for potential leadership. Preparing ahead of time lessens the shock and upheaval when a leader announces retirement or in cases of disaster or emergency that impact practice leadership.

Although this section deals with the executive or board chair role, many of the same principles should apply to recognizing the potential of and developing leaders for other roles. Nursing managers, billing office managers, and similar leadership positions are vital to the success of a medical practice. Use the ideas presented here to identify future managers and implement skill development for any managerial position. Recognize that exceptional managers at any level may become future executives or board members.

An important part of succession planning is developing future leaders within the organization. There are several keys to creating successful leadership development programs:

➤ Identifying the corporate culture and the leadership style to match;

➤ Appreciating diverse ideas, experiences, and backgrounds;

➤ Hiring people for their leadership possibilities, not just the required skill set;

➤ Encouraging current leaders to identify others with potential; and

➤ Providing a setting that encourages education and opportunity.

The development of future leaders begins soon after hiring. Recognizing potential leaders early will provide more time for education and mentorship and ensure retention of those individuals. Assess the competencies and knowledge desired in a leader and needed by the practice. Use the annual performance reviews as opportunities to discuss leadership interest, areas of concern, and opportunities for developing new skills. There are several competencies and qualities for successful leaders that should be recognized:

- ➤ Technical skills;
- ➤ Emotional intelligence, including self-awareness, accurate self-assessment, self-confidence, emotional control, empathy, and influence;
- ➤ Ability to inspire and lead others; and
- ➤ Vision.

Develop a leadership training program within the practice by rotating personnel in management or committee roles, encouraging participation in community-related activities, and offering mentoring by experienced individuals. Large practices and health systems have developed internal training programs, but there are other opportunities for training, including physician MBA programs, general leadership courses, and conferences or seminars sponsored by practice management and other associations.

Current practice leadership, from the CEO or administrator to the governing board, should recognize that leadership development is a large part of their responsibilities. The leadership development program is the first step in succession planning. Additional steps for leadership transition include

- ➤ Establish a succession committee, usually a subset of the governing board.
- ➤ Determine the experience and qualities needed in a new leader based on the goals and weaknesses of the organization in handling today's environment. For example, the increasing emphasis on quality management may lead to the selection of a leader with experience in overseeing or implementing quality programs.
- ➤ Review what worked in previous transitions, or learn from the experiences of other practices.
- ➤ Identify potential leaders within your organization, and determine whether the leadership development program has prepared an individual for the role or if you'll have to

A LOOK AT THE NUMBERS . . .

Methods Used to Develop Physician Leaders

Leadership development method	% of better-performing practices
Conducted formal training	7.53%
Involved new physicians in leadership roles	40.36%
Involved physicians in community outreach/charity programs	14.16%
Partnered new physicians with mentors	31.33%
Paid for leadership education programs	17.47%
Rotated board appointments to provide involvement in decision-making	31.93%

Source: Medical Group Management Association, *Performances and Practices of Successful Medical Groups: 2010 Report Based on 2009 Data* (Englewood, CO: Medical Group Management Association, 2010).

look at external candidates to obtain the experience and qualities the organization requires.

➤ Transition the physician stepping down into a new role within the practice. Since group practices often use rotating physician leaders, a transition plan will ease the physician away from the leadership role while maintaining his or her active participation within the practice.

After the transition from one leader to another has been accomplished, use the opportunity to discuss what went well and what could be learned to improve future transitions. Identify what was lacking in the leadership training program and how to fill the gap. Incorporate these ideas in the succession plan and ensure that it is available when needed the next time.

Sources:

Ana Dutra and Joe Griesedieck, "Succession Success: Start Planning for Your Next CEO," *Leadership Excellence*, V. 27, No. 5 (May 2010): 14–15.

Brent R. Phillips, MBA, FACMPE, "Developing the Next Generations of Leaders," *MGMA Connexion*, September 2007, www.mgma.com/WorkArea/DownloadAsset.aspx?id=14504 (accessed January 10, 2011).

Dennis Wipperling, "Moving On . . . or Moving Out? How You Can Develop a Physician Leadership Retention and Transition Plan," *MGMA Connexion*, V. 7, No. 10 (November/December 2007): 34–37.

William Rothwell, "The Future of Succession Planning," *T+D*, V. 64, No. 9 (September 2010): 50–54.

QUESTION 53 We need to modify our physician compensation plan to ensure physicians are compensated for their leadership time and other nonclinical activities. What are other practices doing?

Because of the time commitment to participate in practice leadership or other nonclinical activities, it is often best to provide some compensation as an incentive and recognition for the service. Smaller practices may not be able to afford additional compensation for managing partners, especially if the total practice revenue declines due to reductions in the physician leaders' productivity. Two other options are (1) changing the compensation system so the physician is not penalized or (2) rotating the responsibilities among all the physicians.

Some practices require that physicians participate in practice leadership or other nonclinical activities and assume that compensation will be equalized when all are involved in these activities. If the latter is the case, the practice should provide benchmarks within the compensation formula or employment agreement to ensure physicians achieve the expected commitment or number of hours of participation.

Practices that base compensation more on productivity or have fewer expectations for nonclinical commitments may choose to financially recognize the hours spent on leadership and other activities. There are three options that can be used to determine compensation:

➤ Market-based annual or monthly stipend;

➤ Hourly or time commitment calculation; or

➤ Incentive and leadership pool.

The market-based method looks at survey data to determine a market value for the services and can be used for medical director or physician leadership activities. MGMA has several resources, and other surveys are available that provide compensation data for medical directors and other leadership positions in medical practices. Your medical director's compensation should be adjusted to the market data depending on the size of the practice, the number of hours served, and the types of responsibilities.

A time commitment method determines a pool of money to be divided among physicians depending on the number of hours they've spent on nonclinical activities. A list of appropriate activities is developed and physicians' time is tracked. This is a good method for rewarding time served on community boards, charitable activities, resident training, and leadership in medical societies and organizations. The pool can be a set amount per hour or a total for the group practice that is divided based on the percentage of nonclinical hours for each physician.

A LOOK AT THE NUMBERS . . .

MGMA conducted an Information Exchange (an informal survey) asking groups if their managing partners and medical directors received additional compensation and, if so, how they determined the amount. In practices where physicians spent 5 percent or less of their time on administrative responsibilities, 55 percent received no additional compensation, while 32 percent received a predetermined amount each month. When the time commitment increased to between 5 percent and 10 percent, about 50 percent of the practices provided a specific amount. Physician leaders spending 50 percent to 100 percent of their time on administrative responsibilities were most frequently compensated by straight salary. Generally, only the largest practices (averaging 85 physicians) had a physician devoting the majority of his or her time to these responsibilities.

The incentive or leadership pool is similar to the time commitment method, but the pool of money is based on reaching goals rather than an hourly commitment. Performance goals or expectations are developed for each physician, such as serving on the strategic planning committee, researching or implementing a new development in the field, or leading an organization-wide effort like hospital integration. The incentive pool is divided by a method decided upon by the group at the beginning of the year. Options include a set amount per physician or a weighted amount per goal. This method uses subjective tactics to reward attaining subjective goals and so must be managed carefully. The bonus pool should be limited to a defined percentage of the salary or total compensation.

MGMA RESOURCES

Current-year *Medical Directorship and On-Call Compensation Survey Report*

Current-year *Management Compensation Survey Report*

"Managing Partner/Medical Director Duties and Compensation Methods," *Information Exchange*, Item #6601

Bruce A. Johnson, JD, MPA, and Deborah Walker Keegan, PhD, FACMPE, *Physician Compensation Plans: State-of-the-Art Strategies* (Englewood, CO: Medical Group Management Association, 2006)

Sources:

Bruce A. Johnson, JD, MPA, and Deborah Walker Keegan, PhD, FACMPE, *Physician Compensation Plans: State-of-the-Art Strategies* (Englewood, CO: Medical Group Management Association, 2006).

Medical Group Management Association, *Medical Directorship and On-Call Compensation Survey: 2010 Report Based on 2009 Data* (Englewood, CO: Medical Group Management Association, 2006).

QUESTION **Some physicians in the practice want to add a non-physician provider (NPP) to the group. How are other group practices using NPPs?**

Many physicians and medical practices are looking for options to deal with a tight physician market and the need to raise production and revenue to survive in an environment of tight reimbursement and rising operating costs. Also called physician extenders, nonphysician providers are training and adapting to work in a variety of environments and specialties.

Nurse practitioners (NPs) are advanced practice nurses trained to provide healthcare services similar to those of a physician. The scope of practice for NPs and supervisory requirements depend on state regulations, but they are typically more independent than physician assistants. According to the American Academy of Nurse Practitioners, NPs can provide the following services:

- ➤ Order, perform, and interpret diagnostic tests such as lab work and X-rays;

- ➤ Diagnose and treat acute and chronic conditions such as diabetes, high blood pressure, infections, and injuries;

- ➤ Prescribe medications and other treatments;

- ➤ Manage patients' overall care;

- ➤ Spend time counseling patients; and

- ➤ Help patients learn how their actions affect their health and well-being.

Physicians assistants (PAs) handle a variety of medical duties that are within the physician's scope of practice depending on the PA's training and experience. State regulations require a physician to supervise PAs but generally allow physicians broad delegating authority. For example, PAs can see their own patients, but physicians must sign off on the patient's chart and be available for consultation. PAs are authorized to prescribe in all 50 states.

Certified nurse midwives, nutritionists, physical therapists, and surgeon assistants are other nonphysician providers that have been incorporated into group practices.

There are several advantages for hiring nonphysician providers. NPPs' salaries are lower than physicians, but they can take on a variety of responsibilities and free up the physicians' time for more productive activities. Analysis of data from the MGMA Cost Survey reports shows that productivity for practices with NPPs is higher than productivity for practices without and proportionately higher than the increased operating costs. This trend

continues until the practice reaches 0.6 or more full-time-equivalent NPPs per full-time physician. After this, the operating costs
related to the increased number of NPPs (additional support
staff, increased facility size, and NPP compensation and benefits)
begin to weigh down the productivity increase.

Medicare reimburses NPP services at 85 percent of the physician's fee schedule depending on the services. Other payers differ
on how they handle NPPs: some credential them and pay 60 to
100 percent of the physician fee schedule. Others do not accept
billing for their services, and "incident-to" billing guidelines must
be followed. Check with each payer prior to starting an NPP
within your practice.

How NPs and PAs are utilized in practices depends on the specialty and physicians' choices about what to delegate and how
to team with NPPs. Both are used to conduct physicals, identify
and treat illnesses, manage preventive and follow-up care, order
and interpret tests, and educate patients. NPPs conduct rounds
in hospitals and nursing homes, if the facilities allow it, and
conduct post-operative visits that the surgeon wouldn't normally
receive compensation for, since they are included as part of the
surgical fee.

In one urology practice, one NP is the primary assistant for
robotic surgery and another is the clinical research coordinator.
Another urologist uses a PA in the operating room and to see
uncomplicated office visits, freeing up the physician's time.

In dermatology practices, NPPs may do biopsies; excisional surgeries; IVs; some noninvasive cosmetic procedures, such as Botox
and some facial fillers; or close incisions or removals conducted
by the physicians.

The majority of PAs and NPs practice in primary care settings.
Primary care practices often use NPs and PAs for uncomplicated
patient visits or to coordinate care for patients with chronic
conditions, collaborating with other NPPs, and conferring with
physicians. One internist has his NP assist at the hospital doing
rounds and coordinating discharge by writing scripts, home
instructions, and discharge summaries. NPPs' roles as team

A LOOK AT THE NUMBERS . . .

"Better-performing practices identified in the MGMA annual Cost Survey report know how to utilize NPPs. Almost 66 percent of better performers said NPPs helped them accommodate patient demand vs. about 56 percent of other groups. Some 57 percent of top-flight groups reported that NPPs boosted revenues, compared with 47 percent of their peers."

Source: Matthew Vuletich, "Top-Performers Outpace Their Peers in More than a Dozen Areas," *MGMA e-Source*, January 11, 2010, www.mgma.com/article. aspx?id=40604 (accessed January 16, 2011).

---

members in preventive care and chronic care management will become increasingly valuable with the growth of patient-centered medical homes.

Sources:

American Academy of Nurse Anesthetists, www.aana.com (accessed January 15, 2011).

American Academy of Nurse Practitioners, "FAQs about Nurse Practitioners," www. aanp.org/NR/rdonlyres/A1D9B4BD-AC5E-45BF-9EB0-DEFCA1123204/4271/ FAQsWhatisanNP83110.pdf (accessed January 15, 2011).

David N. Gans, MSHA, FAMPE, "The Data Mine: Nonphysician Providers — It's Possible to Have Too Much of a Good Thing," *MGMA Connexion,* February 2010, www.mgma. com/WorkArea/mgma_downloadasset.aspx?id=32533 (accessed January 15, 2010).

Karen Nash, "Dermatology Physician Assistants' Ranks, Responsibilities Grow," *Dermatology Times,* September 1, 2010, www.modernmedicine.com/modernmedi- cine/Modern+Medicine+Now/Dermatology-physician-assistants-ranks-responsibil/ ArticleStandard/Article/detail/684855 (accessed January 15, 2011).

Karen Nash, "Physician Assistants, Nurse Practitioners Gain Stature, Value in Urology Practices," *Urology Times,* August 1, 2009, www.modernmedicine.com/modernmedicine/ article/articleDetail.jsp?ts=1313442658575&location=http%3A%2F%2Fwww. modernmedicine.com%2Fmodernmedicine%2FModern%2BMedicine%2BNow%2FPhysic ian%252Dassistants%252Dnurse%252Dpractitioners%252Dgain%252Dstat%2FArticleStan dard%2FArticle%2Fdetail%2F614294&id=614294 (accessed January 15, 2011).

Mari Edlin, "NPs and PAs Extend the Reach of PCPs," *Managed Healthcare Executive,* V. 20, No. 4 (April 2010): 18–20.

Susanne Madden, "Do You Need a Nurse Practitioner?" *Physician's Practice Pearls,* September 30, 2010, www.physicianspractice.com/pearls/content/article/1462168 (ac- cessed January 15, 2011).

QUESTION 55 We've decided to hire a nonphysician provider. What resources do you have related to compensation, employment agreements, and billing for nurse practitioners and physician assistants?

Prior to interviewing for and hiring a nonphysician provider, evaluate the role that the NPP will have in the practice and what skills you will be looking for. Some candidates for the position will have different experience than others and may be employed in more advanced settings. Determine whether the NPP will rotate in call coverage and perform hospital rounds.

Use local associations for PAs and NPs as contact points for your job announcement. Look for candidates who emphasize customer service and have a passion for the field. Have a physician or nurse manager conduct reference checks to assist in determining their clinical competencies.

During the interview, provide a copy of the job description and employment agreement. These documents should specify the expectations for clinical responsibilities, relations with supervising physicians, proper conduct, and contributions to the practice.

A LOOK AT THE NUMBERS . . .

The MGMA *Physician Compensation and Production Survey Report* tracks compensation for nonphysician providers as well as physicians.

Specialty	Nurse practitioner	Physician assistant
Primary care	$86,944	$ 92,767
Surgical	$90,154	$106,108
Nonsurgical, nonprimary care specialty	$86,471	$ 94,961

Note: Compensation figures are medians and include bonus and incentive payments.

Source: Medical Group Management Association, *Physician Compensation and Production Survey: 2011 Report Based on 2010 Data* (Englewood, CO: Medical Group Management Association, 2011).

Methods for determining compensation and the benefits will also be described.

Deborah Hosilyk, PAHM, MGMA member and practice administrator at Advancements in Dermatology in Edina, Minn., has four NPPs who contribute significant revenue to the practice. She offers the following questions when interviewing NPPs:

➤ What experience do you have in our specialty?

➤ Describe your clinical strengths. Would others agree?

➤ How would your patients describe you? What would they say you do best?

➤ Have you had any malpractice suits?

➤ Have you ever been reported to the medical board?

➤ Can you provide us with documents confirming your certification, current state license, and DEA number (if appropriate)?

Compensation for NPPs can be a straight salary, but most practices find a productivity-based system or a base salary plus a bonus or incentive to be an effective model assuming adequate patient demand. Make sure the NPP compensation plan doesn't create an environment of competition for patients between the physicians and NPPs. According to an informal survey of MGMA members, 27 percent of responding practices compensate their NPPs with a straight salary while 50 percent use a base salary with a productivity or discretionary bonus. Practices that include an incentive system in the NPP compensation plan use a variety of incentives (see the following table).

NPP incentive plan option	% of responding practices
Productivity-based incentive	71%
Incentive based on practice productivity	30%
Incentive based on quality measures	13%
Incentive based on practice efficiencies	11%
Incentives incorporating nonclinical activities (administrative duties, meetings, outreach activities, and so on)	7%

Source: Medical Group Management Association, "Nonphysician Provider (NPP) Compensation and Incentive Plans," *Information Exchange* Englewood, CO: Medical Group Management Association, 2011.

As with any new provider, have the NPP attend an employee orientation session and promote his or her arrival to patients, hospitals, and referring physicians. Select a mentor who will introduce the new hire to practice operations and clinical responsibilities. Check frequently with the NPPs during the first few months to ensure they are settling in and that no issues arise that would lead to job dissatisfaction.

Feedback on the performance of the NPP should be provided frequently, especially during the first months after starting. Formal performance reviews should be conducted on a regular basis, with a preliminary review at six months and then annual reviews. Examples of valuation criteria include

➤ Completes charges and dictation in a timely and accurate manner;

➤ Receives acceptable ratings with patient satisfaction;

➤ Demonstrates knowledge and skills in specialty area;

➤ Follows best practices and quality-of-care guidelines;

➤ Has appropriate utilization numbers;

➤ Participates in continuing education; and

➤ Shows good interpersonal skills with physicians, staff, and others.

INCIDENT-TO BILLING

You will have to do your homework to ensure that your NPP's services are recognized and reimbursed by Medicare and other payers. Begin the credentialing process with your payers as soon as possible, and find out how they handle services provided by NPPs. Learn the details of Medicare's "incident-to" provisions. To qualify as a service provided incident to a physician's care, it must be

➤ Part of the physician's regular plan of care, initiated by and requiring the continuing involvement of the physician;

➤ Supervised by a physician available in the office; and

➤ Normally included within the charges for a physician's service.

Medicare recognizes NPPs as physicians in the previous definition, with their ability to supervise other clinical staff and provide services within their scope of practice. The service must be billed under the NPPs ID or that of a supervising physician. If the NPP provided the care under the previous definition, then Medicare will reimburse the practice at 100 percent of the physician fee schedule rather than the 85 percent for other NPP services. To ensure reimbursement for incident-to services, document the provider who developed the care plan, the SOAP (subjective, objective, assessment, and plan) note describing what was provided, and the name of the supervising provider.

Check for current Medicare regulations before assuming billing and supervisory requirements for NPPs. There have been discussions regarding changing these billing definitions. In 2008, Medicare released proposed changes due to findings that NPPs were billing for services for which they didn't have the required licenses, certifications, or training. The proposed changes were rescinded due to objections from MGMA and other organizations, but a modified proposal may reappear.

The growing shortage of primary care physicians and the adoption of patient-centered medical homes are increasing the demand for NPP services and on a more independent basis. For current information, go to MGMA.com or CMS.gov and search "incident-to."

Sources:

Deborah Hosilyk, PAHM, "How You Can Find — and Keep — Nonphysician Providers," *MGMA Connexion*, August 2009, www.mgma.com/WorkArea/mgma_downloadasset.aspx?id=30054 (accessed January 16, 2011).

Gail Garfinkel Weiss, "PAs and NPs: How They Boost Practice Earnings," *Contemporary OB/GYN*, July 1, 2007, www.modernmedicine.com/modernmedicine/Practice+Management/PAs-and-NPs-How-they-boost-practice-earnings-Medic/ArticleStandard/Article/detail/440133 (accessed January 15, 2011).

Laurie A. Desjardins, CPC, PCS, "Code of Conduct: Avoiding the Pitfalls of Medicare's 'Incident-To' Rules," *MGMA Connexion*, November/December 2008, www.mgma.com/WorkArea/mgma_downloadasset.aspx?id=24310 (accessed January 16, 2011).

"National Physician Assistant Census Report," American Academy of Physician Assistants, 2009, www.aapa.org/images/stories/Data_2009/National_Final_with_Graphics.pdf (accessed January 16, 2011).

QUESTION

56

How do I prepare my practice for the changes brought about by healthcare reform and reimbursement changes?

The health industry in the United States is going through fundamental changes. Some of the issues have been around for several years: shifting reimbursement from per procedure to quality performance, the introduction of EHRs, declining reimbursement relative to costs, and a shortage of physicians, especially in primary care. The Patient Protection and Affordable Care Act (PPACA) and other regulations in recent years have instituted some of the changes while pushing others to the forefront. Medical practices must rethink ways of operating to adapt to a different environment. Although not all practices have felt the full impact yet, the new reimbursement methods are expected to become more widely adopted in the near future. It is imperative for practices to prepare now.

Adapting to the changing healthcare environment involves a two-pronged approach:

1. Instituting structural changes, and

2. Getting providers and staff to adapt to and embrace the change.

The first aspect of change is the easiest, although it may still involve major changes within the organization. Structural changes, discussed elsewhere in this book, include

➤ Implementing an EHR;

➤ Optimizing data and reports from EHRs and practice management systems to become an information-driven organization;

➤ Adopting patient-centered care management;

➤ Considering alignment with hospitals or other practices;

➤ Employing a full-care team of NPPs and nurses;

➤ Maximizing organizational productivity and efficiency; and

> ➤ Shifting from emphasis on payment by procedure to payment by quality and outcomes.

The second aspect of implementing change is obtaining physician and staff buy-in and acceptance of change. This involves a shift in thought and actions that not everyone is willing to accept, but most can be brought along with patience and persistence.

For example, the concept of patient-centered care means that the patient comes first and everyone else is second. Although it has always been said in the medical field that a patient's care comes first, it was usually done at the convenience of the physicians and the facilities. Virginia Mason in Seattle, Wash., demonstrated its shift to patient-centered care by placing patients in window-filled rooms while interior rooms housed staff. The physicians, nurses, and lab techs come to the patients rather than forcing the patients to navigate the halls looking for the various services they were assigned. Virginia Mason also limits the number of people in its reception or waiting rooms by sending patients directly to service areas upon their arrival. Cleveland Clinic publishes its outcomes on its Web site to provide patients and the public with comparative figures and ensure that it accomplishes results that it can be proud to publish.

This type of shift in thinking and operations is never easy and must be done in steps. Physicians and staff must be convinced of the need to change and agree upon a shared vision for the future of the medical practice. They see the future as a challenge to their authority and autonomy.

There are five stages in the process of accepting change, and they are applicable to physicians:

1. **Precontemplation.** Hearing about a change without fully understanding its meaning or implications. Physicians are not ready to discuss its impact on them.

2. **Contemplation.** Thinking and talking about the change. Physicians may be curious about the new concept and are open to new information.

3. **Preparation.** More information is gathered and discussed. Attitudes and opinions begin to form affected by rumors

and misinformation. This is the time for open discussion on reasons and goals for change in order to enlist engagement and support. Use the 4-E model that was developed to improve physician-patient relations: Engage, Empathize, Educate, and Enlist.

4. **Action.** Once support is obtained, move into meetings and forums for ideas to implement change. Actively engage those supporting the change, and address concerns from those resisting change. Listen to the reasons for resistance, address the rumors or misinformation, and identify means of reducing fears.

5. **Maintenance.** During and after implementation of changes, ensure that supporters maintain their positive attitudes by addressing any issues that arise. Modify detractors' negative attitudes by continuing to seek their participation and incorporating some of their ideas. Ensure the negative attitudes don't spread to others.

Physicians will be in different stages and travel between stages at their own rates. Assess the various stages by listening to physicians: Have they heard about the changes, and are they discussing the implications to them? Ensure the topic is included in meetings at a level acceptable to their stage of accepting change. Physician leaders should be aware of casual gatherings where physicians may discuss their true feelings, both positive and negative. Use these opportunities to promote the change rather than allow negativism to fester.

During discussions, you'll hear several reasons why they are resisting change, but there are answers for addressing these concerns:

Reason 1. *I want to know what I'm doing and do it well. I don't want to look incompetent.*

Answer: Physicians who identify and embrace the need for change and demonstrate good leadership skills should be identified early in the process. These physician champions should develop the path for change, lead the discussion, and provide reassurances. They should hold physician-only meetings to discuss the changes, worries, what the future brings, and so on. Emphasize that all physicians are going through the change.

Reason 2. *This will interfere with my work and decrease my productivity.*

Answer: Ensure that physicians have the skills necessary to deal with changes, even if it's as minor as improving typing and computer skills for EHRs. Reduce other interferences, and promote improvements that will be achieved after the change.

Reason 3. *I don't see why we have to change; what we've been doing has worked well.*

Answer: Discuss the issues related to the current healthcare system and how changes are meant to improve the system. Help physicians recognize that it's not a personal attack on them but a systemic problem. As there are new ideas for clinical care options, so it is time for new ideas in care management and reimbursement.

Reason 4. *It's Congress's or the president's fault. I don't see why I have to suffer because of their decisions.*

Answer: Don't let physicians get caught up in a blame game that increases negativism and doesn't encourage change. Physicians should recognize that the patient's needs are first and changes will improve patient care.

At times, the amount of changes will seem overwhelming to you and the others around you; it is a large-scale change to the industry. Break down the changes into manageable pieces and move from one to the next. Prioritize the steps by the current situation in your practice, ideas presented by participants, and willingness to accept specific changes. For example, is there support for a new practice management system in your practice that could be expanded to include an EHR? Are physicians overworked and open to the idea of hiring NPPs or empowering nurses to take on more responsibilities? Are payers introducing pay-for-performance, requiring a shift in your data-tracking capabilities and physician compensation model? You should have already made your practice aware of these upcoming changes to help staff and physicians enter Stage 1, and now you're ready to move to Stage 2 or 3.

Sources:

Barbara Le Tourneau, "The Five Stages of Physician Reaction to Change," *Journal of Healthcare Management*, V. 50, No. 1 (2005): 5–7.

Barbara Le Tourneau, "Managing Physician Resistance to Change," *Journal of Healthcare Management*, V. 49, No. 5 (2004): 286–88.

Gary Bradt, MD, "Defining Your Profession: How to Lead Your Practice through Uncertain Times," *MGMA Connexion*, July 2010, www.mgma.com/WorkArea/mgma_downloadasset.aspx?id=34098 (accessed January 17, 2011).

Marc D. Halley, MBA, "4 Business Imperatives to Manage Dynamic Change in the New Healthcare Environment," *MGMA Connexion*, July 2010, www.mgma.com/WorkArea/mgma_downloadasset.aspx?id=34103 (accessed January 17, 2011).

Thomas H. Lee, "Turning Doctors into Leaders," *Harvard Business Review*, V. 88, No. 4 (2010): 50–58.

QUESTION 57 We know that the practice needs to change to compete in our community and deal with all the changes in healthcare, but we don't know if we want to join the hospital that has approached us or what our options are. Help!

Healthcare in the United States is going through major changes. Increasing government regulations and the complexity of information technology are driving up operating costs while there is pressure to reduce healthcare costs. Recent health-reform legislation and changes in reimbursement are threatening paradigm shifts in how practices will operate and compensate physicians. It is increasingly difficult for medical practices to operate as before, and many are looking for options to align or grow in order to be better positioned to deal with these changes.

There are many options for alignment, and identifying which is right for your medical practice will involve assessing the healthcare market in your community and the current position and goals of your practice, as well as understanding general healthcare trends.

What are the characteristics of your group practice? Are you a primary care practice or multispecialty practice? Do you lack the

A LOOK AT THE NUMBERS . . .

Hospital-owned MGMA member practices increased by 25 percent from 2003 to 2008 and reached 11 percent of MGMA member practices in 2010.

The average number of physicians per medical practice stands at 18.8 full-time-equivalent physicians (for nonhospital-owned practices). The average number of physicians in hospital-owned medical groups increased to 70 FTE physicians in 2010.

The number of solo practices declined from 41 percent to 23 percent from 1997 to 2008.

Sources: Medical Group Management Association, "State of Medical Practice — Hospital Ownership Increases among MGMA Member Practices," *MGMA Connexion*, January 2011, www.mgma.com/WorkArea/DownloadAsset. aspx?id=40639 (accessed January 15, 2011).

Medical Group Management Association, "State of Medical Practice — Integrated Delivery Systems," *MGMA Connexion*, January 2010, www.mgma.com/ WorkArea/DownloadAsset.aspx?id=32156 (accessed December 17, 2010).

time or clout to negotiate with payers and vendors? Are you having difficulty recruiting physicians to your practice?

What are the dynamics of your marketplace? How many hospitals are in your community, and what are their strategies for the future? Whom are they hiring? Are they limiting out-of-system referrals? Is there an IDS in place now or under development? Are your patients and the community asking for more integrated services?

Are there large medical practices that dominate your market, making it difficult for you to compete? What types of services do they provide?

Is your practice positioned for the future? Do you have an EHR in place, or are you purchasing one? Are you prepared to make the shift to clinical integration that health reform is demanding? Is the practice culture open for alignment or integration?

Since you've asked the question regarding alignment strategies, you've reached a necessary first step by recognizing the possible need for change. It is time to look at the options, including forming a larger practice, joining an independent practice association (IPA), or aligning with a hospital.

One option is to form a larger group practice, usually by merging your practice with other practices. Advantages include

- ➤ Continued autonomy of an independent group practice;

- ➤ Governance by the group's physicians;

- ➤ Opportunities to improve coordination of care;

- ➤ Increased patient volume to support the development of ancillary services;

- ➤ Increased efficiencies from centralizing functions, including business operations and regulatory management;

- ➤ Increased access to capital for purchasing information systems or offering additional services; and

- ➤ Having a competitive edge in negotiating with payers and recruiting physicians.

There are still risks associated with merging and forming a larger practice. To succeed, the participants must identify with the benefits of a larger practice, acknowledge the need to compromise to achieve organizational goals, and be fully committed to the success and future of the organization.

IPAs blossomed during the 1980s and 90s to meet the demands of managed care organizations while maintaining practice independence. With the decreasing influence of managed care and the changing healthcare environment, IPAs have struggled to define their role. Many are shifting their goals to emphasize the business administrative tasks of member practices. The organization may still support payer contract negotiation but also provide EHR purchase and management, human resources, group purchasing, credentialing, and other functions. Other IPAs are developing alignment options for leading the way in healthcare reform.

The increasing number of hospital-affiliated practices shows that there are potential benefits for hospital-physician integration, including

➤ Providing a continuum of care for improved quality and to position for the changing healthcare environment;

➤ Assistance in purchasing and managing EHR and practice management systems;

➤ Gaining market share and increased visibility;

➤ Improved ability to negotiate with payers; and

➤ Guaranteed physician income promised by the hospital.

Potential disadvantages include governance by another structure that may have different goals and the difficulty in merging practice and hospital cultures. If you are considering the hospital's offer, ensure that they are committed to physician engagement in the organization's governance and that there is adequate trust on both sides for the affiliation to succeed.

A LOOK AT THE NUMBERS . . .

1
2
3

Hospitals seek closer ties with physicians for several reasons, but one is the potential inpatient and outpatient revenue that physicians generate for the hospital. A Merritt Hawkins survey of hospital chief financial officers found a median estimated net revenue from primary care physicians of $1,385,775 and $1,577,764 from specialty physicians.

Source: Merritt Hawkins, *2010 Physician Inpatient/Outpatient Revenue Survey*, www.merritthawkins.com/pdf/2010revenuesurvey.pdf (accessed February 11, 2011).

Sources:

Caren Baginski, "Why Medical Practices Should Consider Integrating with Health Systems," *MGMA In Practice blog*, May 19, 2010, http://blog.mgma.com/blog/bid/33015 (accessed December 17, 2010).

David A. Gregory, FACHE, "Integrate or Disintegrate: Integrated Delivery Systems a Reemerging Trend," *MGMA Connexion*, November/December 2010, www.mgma.com/WorkArea/DownloadAsset.aspx?id=40221 (accessed December 17, 2010).

Lisa L. Jensen, MHBL, FACMPE, CPC, "Survival Strategies of IPAs," ACMPE Fellowship Paper, October 2008.

Michael Chisholm, MSHA, FACMPE, "Is Your Market Ripe For An IDS? 2 Tools Help You Evaluate the Likelihood an IDS Will Emerge in Your Area — and How Physicians Might Respond," *MGMA e-Source*, July 27, 2010.

Stuart Kertzner, CPA/ABV, CVA, and Lee Ferber, CPA, "United We Stand: The Formula for Creating a 'Megagroup,'" *MGMA Connexion*, March 2010, www.mgma.com/WorkArea/mgma_downloadasset.aspx?id=33005 (accessed December 17, 2010).

QUESTION **We are considering affiliation with a hospital in our community. What are the best options for structuring physician-hospital integration?**

58

There are several models available for physician-hospital partnerships, including direct employment and forms of subsidiary models. Determining which model is best depends on your practice's goals and culture and the structures in place in your marketplace.

With the direct employment model, physicians are employees of the hospital after signing an employment contract. They assign the professional services component to the hospital and are compensated based on fair market value of the services provided. The practice is incorporated in the legal identity of the hospital, often as a division within the hospital, and the physician's support staff members are hospital employees.

A variation of the direct employment option is the full-practice professional services agreement (PSA). In this model, hospitals own and operate a medical practice and contract with an independent physician or physicians to provide professional services to the practice. As with direct employment, the hospital bills for services and pays the physicians based on productivity or other factors.

Subsidiary models for physician-hospital alignment usually enable medical practices to maintain more independence than employment models. The captive subsidiary model maintains two legal entities: the hospital and the practice, which is a separate entity owned and controlled by the hospital. Physicians bill as a medical practice and can operate ancillary services. However, hospitals may limit the ancillary services that practices can provide, preferring to keep the services and revenue themselves.

Variations of the subsidiary model are the foundation model or health-system parent-subsidiary model. The parent organization is a foundation or health system under which both the hospital and the medical practices operate and report. The larger organization may provide financial support, and the practice may operate fairly independently.

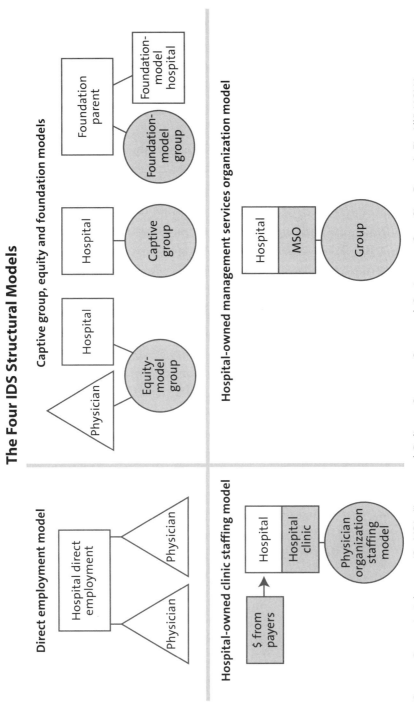

The Four IDS Structural Models

Captive group, equity and foundation models

Direct employment model

Hospital-owned management services organization model

Hospital-owned clinic staffing model

Source: Bruce A. Johnson, JD, MPA, "Integrated Delivery Systems Structural Options — One Size Doesn't Fit All," *MGMA Connexion*, January 2008, www.mgma.com/WorkArea/mgma_downloadasset.aspx?id=15826 (accessed December 17, 2010).

The subsidiary models benefit from an organizational governing board, which should represent all components of the integrated system, physician practices, and hospital. Group practices benefit from the relative independence to concentrate on practice operations while maintaining close ties and goals within the IDS.

Another option is a management services organization (MSO) in which the hospital provides management and operation functions for the practice via the MSO. The practice maintains financial and legal independence, but the weak tie between hospital and practice may not be sufficient to obtain the integration needed in the changing healthcare environment.

Whichever model is chosen, it must comply with federal regulations and any state-specific regulations affecting relationships among healthcare providers. According to Bruce Johnson, JD, MPA, of MGMA's Health Care Consulting Group, there are four principles underlying these regulations:

➤ Compensation in business transactions must be consistent with fair market value, involve commercially reasonable terms, and not vary based on physician referrals;

➤ Physicians can receive returns on their investments and compensation for services they personally perform;

➤ Tax-exempt organizations must promote their charitable missions and protect their charitable assets, which include using "reserve" and similar powers; and

➤ The physician compensation, incentive, and governance structures available to integrated systems will be restricted by an IDS's structure and how it receives external reimbursement.

Sources:

Bruce A. Johnson, JD, MPA, "Integrated Delivery Systems Structural Options — One Size Doesn't Fit All," *MGMA Connexion*, January 2008, www.mgma.com/WorkArea/mgma_downloadasset.aspx?id=15826 (accessed December 17, 2010).

Cordell Mack and Craig D. Pederson, MHA, MBA, "Together Yet Separate: The Full-Practice Professional Services Agreement (PSA)," *MGMA Connexion*, August 2009, www.mgma.com/WorkArea/mgma_downloadasset.aspx?id=30050 (accessed December 17, 2010).

Nick A. Fabrizio, PhD, FACMPE, FACHE, with Robert C. Bohlmann, FACMPE, *Integrated Delivery Systems: Ensuring Successful Physician-Hospital Partnerships*, 10–14 (Englewood, CO: Medical Group Management Association, 2010).

QUESTION 59

How do I ensure that our proposed alignment with the hospital will succeed? How do we maintain physician involvement once we join the IDS?

IDS have been around long enough to provide examples of what leads to success and what causes failure. In the past, hospitals chose to combine with practices by purchasing practices or forming physician-hospital organizations for financial reasons: Hospital leaders dreamed of the additional revenue from physician services and their related ancillary services and strength in negotiation. Hospital leaders tried to manage physician practices in the same manner as the hospital. Physicians were looking for options with normal working hours and less stress.

Now, IDS are forming with the shared goal of providing a continuum of quality care to adjust to the changing healthcare environment. IDS leadership recognizes that medical practices operate differently, and physicians operate best under systems that provide the right incentives. Even with these general changes in attitude, structure, and operations, there is no guarantee that the IDS or hospital alignment that you are entering into will succeed. Now is the time to address several concerns on both sides to ensure that there is trust, alignment of goals, and shared governance prior to finalizing the IDS.

A key step to successful physician-hospital partnerships is to ensure there is adequate physician involvement in the planning discussions between your practice and the IDS and that involvement will continue in the ongoing organizational governance. The MGMA "Integrated System Performance Self-Assessment Tool" offers several questions you should be asking now:

➤ Are physicians well represented in system management and on your boards and committees?

➤ Do they have genuine authority and accountability in the system?

➤ Do they have the opportunity to share in system success?

➤ Are both primary care physicians and specialists represented in governance and strategic planning?

➤ Are appropriate primary care networks and specialist af-
    filiations in place, and are they organized to accept risk and
    manage patient care?

➤ Are physicians actively involved in developing and imple-
    menting these strategies?

IDS often use committees as a means of incorporating physician
involvement and overseeing the business functions and communications with the IDS physician practices. The operations
committee, or whatever it is called, should include key physicians
or directors from the practices, a representative from the hospital
or health system, and several office managers. According to Nick
Fabrizio, MGMA healthcare consultant, the committee's responsibilities should include

➤ Monitoring the operations of the member medical groups
    and the system of groups as a whole;

➤ Recommending policies and procedures for the medical
    practices to the executive committee;

➤ Monitoring productivity and recommending course-
    correcting strategies;

➤ Managing cost and overhead;

➤ Working with underperforming physicians to improve
    their outcomes;

➤ Developing clinic budgets across all the practices; and

➤ Recommending strategic initiatives to the board.

While expecting the IDS to include physician participation in
organization and governance, medical groups should be committed to providing active participation. Since past IDS failures were
often due to physicians wanting to hand over operations and
governance, your practice must be dedicated to providing constructive participation in the governance and financial success
of the organization. To accomplish this, you need to ensure that
the governance structure and physician participation within the
practice are strong enough to carry it through the challenges of
the alignment and into the future. Physicians selected to serve in
IDS leadership positions must be more committed to the success

of the organization and to providing quality of care than to their personal interests.

If the IDS is forming to ensure continuum of care and to participate in accountable care organizations or similar incentive programs, it will need governance and infrastructure to ensure the success of these efforts. Will there be an integrated EHR for sharing outcomes and quality data? What will be the process for applying quality and outcomes data to improve patient wellness and quality of care across the organization? How will pay-for-performance or quality incentive payments be distributed? Will the executive committee or governing board have representatives from the community to keep the focus on patients and providing for the community's health? Do the practice and IDS leaders have a shared understanding of the changing healthcare market and how to position for the future?

Answering these questions now will lead to the trust, practice involvement, and organizational commitment that are required for IDS success.

Case Study

Dartmouth-Hitchcock Health in New Hampshire is an integrated system that includes a hospital, academic medical center, and a multispecialty group practice. The system is "designed to efficiently coordinate resources and enhance the value and quality of care in communities throughout New Hampshire and eastern Vermont."

The board of trustees consists of public trustees, clinic physicians, and presidents of the clinic, hospital, medical center, and parent health system. All of the trustees are members of the Dartmouth-Hitchcock Assembly of Overseers, a 400-member body of stakeholders. The system co-presidents are clinicians, an RN, and a physician with years of clinical and administrative experience. The Dartmouth-Hitchcock Clinic (DHC) is a not-for-profit organization with a commitment to physician leadership and representative governance.

DHC established a single unifying vision and strategic plan as part of a new direction. Christine Schon, MPA, FACMPE, vice president of Community Group Practices, participated in a leadership retreat of five senior physicians and six administrators in order to plan the implementation of organizational goals. Combining physician and administrative leaders led to a unified message and commitment to the identified priorities.

Source: Dartmouth-Hitchcock Web site, www.dartmouth-hitchcock.org/

Sources:

James Hamilton, FACMPE, "Will Your Physician Hospital Alignment Strategies Succeed? Tips on Predicting a Workable Union," *MGMA Connexion*, May/June 2010, www.mgma.com/WorkArea/DownloadAsset.aspx?id=33806 (accessed December 21, 2010).

Nick Fabrizio, PhD, FACMPE, FACHE, "10 Questions about Governance to Ask before Hospital Integration," *MGMA In Practice blog*, December 15, 2010, http://blog.mgma.com/blog/?Tag=integrated%20delivery%20systems (accessed December 21, 2010).

Nick A. Fabrizio, PhD, FACMPE, FACHE, "Creating Key Committees to Drive Successful Integrated Delivery Systems," *MGMA Directions Newsletter*, Summer 2009, www.mgma.com/WorkArea/DownloadAsset.aspx?id=29922 (accessed January 10, 2011).

Nick A. Fabrizio, PhD, FACMPE, FACHE, "Love and Logic: Why Some Integrated Delivery Systems Succeed and Others Fail," *MGMA Connexion*, October 2007, www.mgma.com/WorkArea/mgma_downloadasset.aspx?id=14778 (accessed December 21, 2010).

QUESTION 60 What are accountable care organizations and how, or should, my practice participate?

CMS defines an accountable care organization (ACO) as:

> *a recognized legal entity under State law and comprised of a group of ACO participants (providers of services and suppliers) that have established a mechanism for shared governance and work together to coordinate care for Medicare fee-for-service beneficiaries. ACOs enter into a 3-year agreement with CMS to be accountable for the quality, cost, and overall care of traditional fee-for-service Medicare beneficiaries who may be assigned to it.*

The PPACA specified that a Medicare Shared Savings Program be developed using ACOs and gave the CMS until January 2012 to establish the program. The program is based on the CMS

Physician Group Practice Demonstration project and is intended to encourage coordination of care and improved quality. If the ACO demonstrates savings in providing care, it will receive an incentive payment in proportion to the savings. Savings can be reached through reducing unnecessary services, switching to lower-cost providers, and other methods.

The PPACA specified which types of organizations can participate in the program:

➤ Physicians and other professionals in group practices;

➤ Physicians and other professionals in networks of practices;

➤ Partnerships or joint-venture arrangements between hospitals and physicians/professionals;

➤ Hospitals employing physicians/professionals; and

➤ Other forms that the secretary of HHS may determine appropriate.

The CMS proposed rule providing more details on ACOs was released on April 7, 2011. Due to the complexity of the rule and possible changes in the final rule, refer to mgma.com/policy or cms.gov/sharedsavingsprogram for more detailed and current information. In order to participate, organizations must be committed to the program for at least three years and must have in place

➤ A formal legal structure to receive and distribute shared savings, repay shared losses, and otherwise implement the ACO requirements;

➤ A governing board with members from ACO provider participants and Medicare beneficiary representatives;

➤ A sufficient number of primary care professionals for the number of assigned beneficiaries (with a minimum of 5,000 beneficiaries). Beneficiaries will be assigned to an ACO based on their primary care physician's participation;

➤ Defined infrastructure and processes to (a) promote evidenced-based medicine, (b) report the necessary data

> to evaluate quality and cost measures, and (c) coordinate care; and

➤ The ability to demonstrate that the organization meets patient-centeredness criteria, as determined by the HHS secretary.

Quality and cost measure reporting could incorporate requirements of other programs, such as the PQRS, Electronic Prescribing (eRx), and EHR. Quality standards might include measures in such categories as clinical processes and outcomes of care, patient experience, and utilization (amounts and rates) of services.

According to the proposed rule, eligibility for shared savings is determined by comparing the average per capita Medicare costs for "assigned" beneficiaries for the first year of the ACO agreement with the costs for the three years prior to the ACO agreement. If savings beyond a minimum savings rate are achieved, the ACO will share in a percentage of the additional savings. The proposed rule created two models. ACOs participating in the one-sided model aren't liable for shared losses during the first two years. Two-sided model participants are eligible for a greater percentage of savings but are also liable for losses.

You may not be prepared to join an ACO at this time, but there are steps that you and your practice can take to prepare for a future with an ACO or a similar organization as the country transitions from silos of healthcare providers and a volume-based payment structure to continuum of care and quality-driven reimbursement. A first step is information orientation: developing the information technology and data-gathering capabilities to support future trends. EHRs, prescription management systems, and other programs to track patient visits and health will help position you for ACO participation and the new environment. Implement and begin exploring these programs' capabilities for organizing, accessing, and reporting information related to quality of care and outcomes. You may need to add a data warehousing, data mining, or BI program for additional analytical capabilities.

The second step is developing the processes to shift from a system based on increasing the number of procedures and patients to a system based on ensuring the quality of care provided. After you begin gathering data, share the data in discussions on patient care and practice operations. Identify what steps can be implemented to incorporate clinical standards and evidence-based medicine.

A CLOSER LOOK . . .

Medicare's Demonstration Shared Savings Program

Medicare's Medical Group Practice Demonstration Program began in 2005 with 10 multispecialty practices representing 5,000 physicians. It tracks 32 healthcare quality measures including preventive services, such as breast screenings and immunizations, and follows heart disease, diabetes and hypertension, and other chronic conditions. The demonstration project encouraged coordination of Medicare Part A and Part B services, increased efficiency through information technology and other investments, and rewarded physicians for demonstrated quality.

In the first year, two of the groups earned $7.3 million as their share of $9.5 million in Medicare savings due to improvements in quality and cost efficiency. In the fourth year, all participating groups achieved benchmark performance levels in 29 out of 32 measures. The groups shared in a total of $31.7 million as their portion of the Medicare savings.

Participating groups include the Everett Clinic in Washington; Geisinger HealthCare System in Danville, Pennsylvania; Marshville Clinic in Wisconsin; Park Nicollet Health Services in St. Louis Park, Minnesota; and the University of Michigan Faculty Group Practice in Ann Arbor.

Source: DHHS Centers for Medicare & Medicaid Services, "Medicare Physician Group Practice Demonstration," December 2010, www.cms.gov/DemoProjectsEvalRpts/downloads/PGP_Fact_Sheet.pdf (accessed February 9, 2011).

Sources:

Bruce A. Johnson, "Accountable Care Organizations and Beyond," *MGMA Connexion*, April 2010, www.mgma.com/WorkArea/mgma_downloadasset.aspx?id=33266 (accessed December 19, 2010).

Centers for Medicare and Medicaid Services, "Shared Savings Program Overview," www. cms.gov/sharedsavingsprogram (accessed May 9, 2011).

Centers for Medicare and Medicaid Services, Office of Legislation, "Medicare 'Accountable Care Organizations' Shared Savings Program — New Section 1899 of Title XVIII: Preliminary Questions & Answers," www.cms.gov/OfficeofLegislation/Downloads/ AccountableCareOrganization.pdf (accessed December 19, 2010).

Mark C. Shields, Pankaj H. Patel, Martin Manning, and Lee Sacks, "A Model For Integrating Independent Physicians into Accountable Care Organizations," *Health Affairs*, December 2010, http://content.healthaffairs.org/content/early/2010/12/15/ hlthaff.2010.0824.full.html (accessed December 19, 2010).

Melanie Evans, "Being Held Accountable," *Modern Healthcare*, V. 40, No. 20, May 17, 2010.

Powers, Pyles, Sutter, and Verville, PC, "Memorandum: Accountable Care Organizations: Analysis and Implications," to Medical Group Management Association, April 13, 2011, www.mgma.com/WorkArea/linkit.aspx?LinkIdentifier=id&ItemID=1248594&lib ID=1248594 (accessed May 9, 2011).

CHAPTER 6

Patient Care Systems

QUESTION 61 We are looking for ideas to increase the productivity of our physicians. We already have a productivity-based compensation formula, but the physicians say they can't fit in any more visits. How else can we improve operations to increase the number of office visits?

There are two ways of analyzing operations related to number of visits: The first is patient flow from an operational viewpoint, and the second is by analyzing the physicians' time. The first is addressed in another question (Question 63). In this question, we'll assess means of increasing the efficiency of the physicians' time.

Sherry Anderson Delio offers seven keys to maximizing physician time in her book *The Efficient Physician: 7 Guiding Principles for a Tech-Savvy Practice, 2nd Edition.* While analyzing physician time and productivity, keep in mind the organizational mission related to providing quality patient care and the increasing emphasis on quality and outcomes.

1. **Real-time work.** This is defined as doing today what can be done today rather than putting it off. Any task that is delayed adds time by increasing the number of times it is thought about and touched but not completed. Physicians' tasks that should be completed daily include dictation, chart completion, billing, and handling messages.

    Technology can assist in task completion, especially EHRs. Physicians should use EHRs during and immediately after a patient visit or procedure to complete the notes and send the chart for coding reconciliation and documentation checking so the bill can be submitted. EHR use should automate prescription and referral management. Ensure the physicians are optimally using the EHR to minimize delays and time demands. Provide additional training opportunities to ease their use of the technology, or look for additional ideas to incorporate, including improving templates.

2. **Making a time commitment.** There are two parts to this principle: the physician's time and the patient's time in the office. Conduct an analysis of the physician's schedule by calculating the number of days in a year the physician is practicing medicine (number of work days in a year, subtracting vacation and holidays) and the number of hours in the office, in the hospital or other facility, and any traveling in between. Use an employee- or physician-scheduling program or application available for computers or electronic personal devices (smart phones, and so on) to assist. Analyze time spent in each location and ways to increase time in productive activities. How much time is spent traveling between facilities? Is there downtime between activities that can be decreased?

   Patient time assesses the time from a patient's arrival in the practice, the amount of time with the physician, and check-out. EHRs, stopwatches, or synchronized timepieces can be used to record the minutes between each step. Analyze the amount of time per patient, time with the physician, and so on to identify irregularities and areas for improvement. Also, compare this data with data from previous years to assess whether productivity has improved or declined.

3. **Balancing workloads.** Use an annual or monthly schedule to ensure that the practice will experience predictable workloads by having the same number of physicians in the practice from day to day. This involves scheduling days off, hospital rounds, and other reasons for being out of the office so there are a predictable and maximum number of physicians in the office on a daily basis to increase the number of patients seen.

4. **Decreasing unnecessary variation.** Minimize the variations in a practice due to physician or staff personal preferences. Although some accommodations need to be made for individual differences, the practice will operate more efficiently with standardized forms, schedules, procedures,

layouts, and so on. Standardization should also ensure that all patient information and tools needed to complete a visit or procedure are in place so the physician isn't wasting time looking for them.

5. **Distributing tasks appropriately.** The concepts of rightsizing, delegation, and the appropriate use of NPPs combine to ensure the physician is doing only physician-appropriate activities while other tasks are assigned to NPPs, RNs, LPNs, medical assistants (MAs), and others. Each position should have responsibilities specified in clear job descriptions, and the physicians should delegate as many tasks as possible.

6. **Creating an interdependent team.** Practices may use a set team of clinical staff to support each physician, increasing communication and teamwork; however, most practices work as one team with physicians utilizing all clinical staff. To increase team style, build a staff that is trusted and competent, standardize operations, and utilize communication tools. Frequent, short meetings to confer on patient issues and practice styles can increase teamwork.

7. **Allocating resources by volume of work.** Provide the support staff and exam space equal to the productivity of the providers. Ensure that physicians who see more patients are allocated staff and exam space to support their level of visits and that NPPs receive the resources demanded for their capabilities.

    Combinations of technology applications, task and resource delegation, standardization, and empowering others in the team can improve physician productivity while ensuring quality patient care.

Source:

Sherry Anderson Delio, MPA, FACMPE, HSA, *The Efficient Physician: 7 Guiding Principles for a Tech-Savvy Practice, 2nd edition* (Englewood, CO: Medical Group Management Association, 2005).

QUESTION 62 What is the typical patient panel size by specialty? How do I know how our panel size compares with other practices?

Determining the panel size for physicians is important for several reasons:

➤ Patients are more satisfied if appointment wait times and access to physicians is within expectations;

➤ Helps in determining patient demand;

➤ Ensures that physicians within a group have an equitable share of patients and workload;

➤ Exposes differences in physician performance if there are wait-time or scheduling issues for physicians with similar panel sizes; and

➤ Physicians can identify more with patients within their panel size to improve continuity of care.

You can calculate the panel numbers for your practice by assigning patients to the same physicians they saw for most or all of their visits during an 18-month period. This time period will include patients who don't visit a practice every year. Determine the average number of visits per patient per year. You can then back into a calculation of the expected panel size for your practice by determining the number of patient visits per day per physician multiplied by the number of days worked per year and divided by the average number of visits per patient per year.

$$\frac{(\text{\# of visits/day} \times \text{\# of days/year})}{(\text{\# of visits per patient/year})}$$

For example, if a physician averages 10 visits per day, 240 days per year, and his or her patient population averages two visits per patient per year, then the panel size would be 1,200 patients.

When comparing physicians and their panel sizes, it's important to look at their patient demographics, since visit frequency varies with age, gender, ethnicity, and so on. The following chart shows changes in the number of physician office visits per 100 persons per year.

Patient characteristics	Number of visits per 100 persons per year
Age 15–24 years	174.8
Age 25–44 years	225.8
Age 45–64 years	345.0
Age 65 years and over	645.3
Female, all ages	355.1
Male, all ages	256.0
White	323.9
Black or African American	235.4
Hispanic or Latino	295.5

Source: National Center for Health Statistics, Centers for Disease Control and Prevention, "National Ambulatory Medical Care Survey: 2006 Summary," www.cdc.gov/nchs/data/nhsr/nhsr003.pdf (accessed January 17, 2011).

The MGMA *Cost Survey Report* and *Performance and Practices of Successful Medical Groups Report* track the number of patients per full-time-equivalent physician. For the purposes of the survey, a patient is defined as "a person who received at least one service from the practice during the 12-month reporting period, regardless of the number of encounters or procedures received by that person." Therefore, a practice may see a person who will be counted as a patient for one visit only and not become a "panel member." Also, there are many variables that can affect the patient-per-physician number, including patient population demographics (age and gender), physician working style, patient loyalty, scheduling systems, and organization type. Use the following numbers as a general reference rather than a benchmark.

Patients per FTE physician

Specialty	Better-performing groups	Other practices
Cardiology	2,747	1,573
Orthopedic surgery	1,762	1,518
Primary care	2,609	2,878
Family practice		2,196
Internal medicine		2,435
Obstetrics and gynecology		2,015
Pediatrics		2,886

Note: Numbers reflect medians for responding practices.

Source: Medical Group Management Association, *Performance and Practices of Successful Medical Groups: 2010 Report Based on 2009 Data* and *Cost Survey for Single-Specialty Practices: 2010 Report Based on 2009 Data* (Englewood, CO: Medical Group Management Association, 2010).

Use appointment access time to determine whether or not your practice is operating at peak panel size. If wait times for appointments are longer than average and patients are complaining about the wait times, then your physicians may have more patients in their panel than they can handle. If this is the case, you can decide to close the practice to new patients or look for ways to increase efficiencies to handle more patients. Options include hiring a nonphysician provider or increasing other clinical staff to maximize the physicians' productivity. Sometimes the strain is relieved when patients from one physician's panel are shifted to another physician's.

Sources:

Diwakar Gupta, Sandra Potthof, Donald Blowers, and John Corlett, "Performance Metrics for Advanced Access," *Journal of Healthcare Management*, V. 51, Issue 4 (July/August 2006): 246–58.

Mark Murray, Mike Davies, and Barbara Baoshan, "Panel Size: How Many Patients Can One Doctor Manage?" *Family Practice Management*, V. 14, Issue 4 (April 2007): 44–51, www.aafp.org/fpm/2007/0400/p44.html (accessed January 17, 2011).

QUESTION How do I improve patient flow in my group practice?

Patient flow covers all aspects of interaction with the patient and involves many different processes. As identified by patient flow expert Elizabeth W. Woodcock, MBA, FACMPE, CPC, patient flow encompasses the physician's time, telephone operations, scheduling, patient access, reception services, waiting, patient time with the physician, prescriptions, tests, check-out, and follow-up. All processes are tied together with technology. Maximizing patient flow and practice productivity means assessing these various operations and their interactions.

Conducting a time flow study will help in understanding current patient flow and identify possible bottlenecks. You can conduct time flow analyses by asking a set number of patients to record times in the process of their visit or having staff members note times in paper or electronic charts. Record the times arrived in office, greeted by receptionist, taken to exam room, seen by physician, end of physician's visit, and departure from practice.

In *Mastering Patient Flow: Using Lean Thinking to Improve Your Practice Operations, 3rd Edition*, Elizabeth W. Woodcock suggests starting with four steps to ensure the right strategy in improving patient flow:

➤ Embrace the concept that your physicians' time is the practice's most valuable asset;

➤ Create an environment in which the patient encounter provides value for the patient;

➤ Root out waste and inefficiency while looking for new ways to accomplish things; and

➤ Redesign the core processes of your practice so they work more seamlessly to bring value to the patients.

Many of the components of patient flow are discussed in other answers. We'll discuss some of the other concepts here, including patient access, reception services, waiting, patient time with the physician, prescriptions, tests, check-out, and follow-up.

Patient access is ensuring that a patient requesting to see a provider is seen within a reasonable time. Key indicators for patient access are time to the next available appointment, new versus established patient ratios and wait times, and fill rates. Maximizing a schedule to capacity while incorporating no-shows and cancellations and minimizing physician cancellations will enhance patient access. Patient access is closely tied with physician productivity.

Reception services incorporate pre-registration, insurance verification, the reception area, and the check-in process. Since this involves the initial contact with patients, customer service is very important. Pre-registration collects necessary information at the time of the appointment, decreasing the time needed at check-in. Include registration information and forms on your Web site, and train your employees to remind patients that this option exists. Check with your practice management vendor regarding a Web portal; the interactive technology increases efficiency and effectiveness. The practice can mail the forms if preferred by patients.

Many payers have online insurance verification that can be checked prior to the patient's arrival, enabling the practice to have information about copayments and deductibles to improve time-of-service collections. Another resource to help with pre-visit eligibility and benefits checking is your clearinghouse; check with them regarding this functionality.

Prescription management can be improved with the use of technology. Electronically submitted prescriptions minimize the chance of errors in reading a physician's writing and conflicts with a payer's formulary or a patient's other prescriptions. EHRs can track prescriptions and ensure they are recorded in the chart accurately and at the time they are given. There is also a Medicare financial penalty for not using electronic prescribing by June 2011. Processing renewal requests can be handled with a dedicated telephone line or voice mail going to the nursing staff or by patients entering the request through the practice Web site or patient portal. Protocols should be developed for pre-approval of renewal requests depending on the patient, the prescription, and the time between office visits. For example: Allergy medication for Mrs. Jones can be renewed twice between annual office visits.

Automation should also be used for ordering and tracking tests and results. Computerized order entry eliminates delays and confusion and often can be submitted directly to the lab or imaging center. Scheduling the patient for the test should be part of the process rather than another step. Charts should be tagged to watch for test results, but EHRs should do this automatically. If a follow-up visit will be needed, schedule this at the same time as scheduling the test results to eliminate another step. Patient-centered practices frequently schedule the tests prior to the visit to have the results available during the visit.

The patient check-out process is the time to wrap up the visit, ensure payments have been made, and that patients understand the next steps. Clinical staff should confirm that patients understand the next steps related to tests, referrals, and follow-up visits. Ask if there are additional questions, and confirm that the patient's prior questions were answered completely. This is the opportunity to confirm that the appropriate educational materials are provided and understood. Patient outcomes are dependent in part on patients complying with the instructions.

Appropriate fees and other payments should be collected in a courteous manner. The patient should have been informed of the financial policy and expected fees prior to the appointment and confirmed upon the patient's arrival. Financial expectations should be posted on the practice Web site. Copayments and deposits are frequently collected during check-in. Outstanding balances should be noted, and the front desk staff should be trained to collect past-due balances prior to every appointment. They should also be trained to explain the reasons for the balances. The patient can be referred to a billing department employee at check-in or check-out. Check-out is also the time to share a patient satisfaction survey.

Technology is key in every step of improving patient flow and practice efficiency. However, the main point is to ensure that patients and their time and needs are respected. Evaluate every step in a patient's contact with the practice to smooth the process and eliminate later questions or unnecessary follow-up contacts. Capture data for charge entry, tests, labs, and next steps at the time of visit. Focusing on these ideas satisfies patients' needs while improving practice operations.

Sources:

Donna Izor, MS, FACMPE, "Action Plan: 10 Tips to Improve Your Patient Schedule," *MGMA Connexion*, January 2011, www.mgma.com/WorkArea/mgma_downloadasset.aspx?id=40531 (accessed January 18, 2011).

Elizabeth W. Woodcock, MBA, FACMPE, CPC, *Mastering Patient Flow: Using Lean Thinking to Improve Your Practice Operations, 3rd Edition* (Englewood, CO: Medical Group Management Association, 2009).

Rosemarie Nelson, MS, "Top 10 Tips to Improve Overall Practice Work Flow, *MGMA In Practice blog*, August 11, 2009, http://blog.mgma.com/blog/bid/24623/Top-10-tips-to-improve-overall-practice-work-flow (accessed December 19, 2010).

QUESTION 64 What are some new ideas for improving the appointment and scheduling process?

Some of the new ideas for increasing scheduling efficiencies are based on old ideas but with the advantage of new technologies for assistance. Use your automated scheduling system or other in-house technologies to track patient and referral demand for schedules and not just how the current scheduling system confines appointments. Patient demand will show time frames (day of week and time of day) that are requested most frequently. Consider adjusting schedules to fit patient demands rather than fitting demands to your schedule. Develop policies and provide training to clarify priority of appointments, matching schedules to length of time per procedure, and ensuring patients arrive on time. Maximize efficiency by tracking the following key indicators for scheduling:

➤ Capacity utilization;

➤ On-time starts;

➤ Slot utilization rates;

➤ Wait time to next appointment by slot; and

➤ No show/cancellation reason and recovery rates.[1]

Computerized scheduling programs frequently include algorithms to maximize scheduling efficiency. Utilize the programs to track overbooking and excess time scheduled for certain appointment types, and to remind schedulers to include additional needed services (lab work or second imaging test) or confirm medical necessity and insurance eligibility at time of scheduling.

OPEN ACCESS

Open access, also called advanced access or same-day appointments, is still a popular option among some practices. MGMA's *Performance and Practices of Successful Medical Groups: 2010 Report Based on 2009 Data* found that better-performing medical groups implemented open access scheduling at a higher rate than other practices. Open access eliminates the concerns related to no-shows and late cancellations.

Once patients are trained about its existence and that a same-day appointment is guaranteed, requests for appointments may actually drop. Kaiser Permanente facilities reportedly noticed a 40 percent reduction in appointments after implementing open access. Some practices adjust staffing levels and appointment slots to known busy times, such as Monday morning and Friday afternoons. Most practices blend open and advanced scheduling, for example, reserving one-fourth to one-third of the daily appointments for advanced scheduling and the remainder for same-day appointments.

ONLINE SCHEDULING

Online appointment and scheduling systems enable patients to schedule their own appointments at their convenience rather than during the hours the scheduling department is open. The forms utilized for requesting appointments can also include registration information, eliminating another step. A 2008 Deloitte Center for Health Solutions survey found that 60 percent of respondents want physicians to provide online appointment scheduling. One option is to use centralized online scheduling systems. The American Academy of Family Physicians developed a patient portal for its member physicians to use. The system, developed in partnership with Med Fusion, includes online appointment scheduling along with other services. The vendor reported that participating physicians have reduced no-show rates from 10 percent to an average of 4 percent.

Online appointment requests rank in the top three most frequently used services in the Kaiser Permanente member Web site. At Medical Associates of Northwest Arkansas, patients can use the practice Web site to select the time and date of their preference and whether or not to receive an e-mail or telephone confirmation. A staff member checks online appointments before the practice opens each morning. The practice has noticed increased patient satisfaction with the convenience of the service compared to dealing with hold times and busy signals when patients were required to call for appointments.

CENTRALIZED VERSUS DECENTRALIZED SCHEDULING

Many large practices have implemented central call centers or access centers that handle referral and patient requests for appointments. The centralized center provides one location for requests as diverse as scheduling, prescription renewal, and test results. The difficulty is in dealing with customized schedule requests for separate departments. One multispecialty practice overcame this issue by switching to the centralized access center one department at a time, building in the custom needs as the conversions occurred. Even with the careful work with specific departments, the call center still handles only about 50 percent of the patient appointments. A hybrid centralized/decentralized scheduling system works well for this practice.

Success of centralized scheduling depends on the operation of the central call center. Adjust the staffing levels to the demand. For example, calls may be heaviest first thing in the morning, and increased staffing will reduce hold times and busy signals. Ensure that quality of service is emphasized and not just quantity of calls handled.

Centralized scheduling should emphasize the needs and concerns of patients over preferences of the departments and staff. It enables the coordination of reception and registration areas with the service areas so patients for several departments aren't arriving at the front desk at the same time. Call center staff should be trained on exchanging more information during the initial call so the need for later telephone calls is decreased and the practice will notice increases in efficiency of actual appointment time. For this reason, many practices obtain pre-registration information at the time of request.

Reference:

1. Daniel P. O'Neill and Peter B. Kenniff, "Centralized Scheduling: An Unanticipated Revenue Cycle Opportunity," *hfm (Healthcare Financial Management)*, V. 61, Issue 9 (2007): 82–87.

Sources:

Anna-Lisa Silvestre, Valerie M. Sue, and Jill Y. Allen, "If You Build It, Will They Come? The Kaiser Permanente Model of Online Healthcare," *Health Affairs*, V. 28, No. 2 (2009): 334–44.

California Health Foundation, *Delivering Care Anytime, Anywhere: Telehealth Alters the Medical Ecosystem*, November 2008, www.chcf.org/~/media/Files/PDF/T/PDF%20 TelehealthAltersMedicalEcosystem.pdf (accessed February, 1, 2011).

George A. DeLange Jr., CMPE, "A Whole-Person-Care Campus Gets Serious about Service," *APA Matrix*, V. 17, No. 4, September 2003, www.mgma.com/article. aspx?id=1784 (accessed February, 1, 2011).

Grand Central Scheduling, *Health Management Technology*, V. 25, Issue 10 (October 2004): 50–52.

Ken Terry, "Online Appointment Reminders Reduce No Shows," *InfoTech Bulletin*, V. 1, No. 4, October 13, 2006, http://medicaleconomics.modernmedicine.com/memag/article/ articleDetail.jsp?id=377804 (accessed February, 1, 2011).

Medical Group Management Association, "Utilizing Technology to Create a Positive Patient Experience," in *Performance and Practices of Successful Medical Groups: 2009 Report Based on 2008 Data*, 53–54 (Englewood, CO: Medical Group Management Association, 2009).

"Open Access Works," Patient Care Conference Update, October 3, 2007, http://patient-care.modernmedicine.com/patcare/aafp07/Open-access-works/ArticleStandard/Article/ detail/462422?ref=25 (accessed February, 1, 2011).

"Survey Indicates Consumers Want to See Major Changes in Healthcare Design and Delivery, "*Managed Care Outlook*, V. 21, No. 7 (2008): 1–9.

QUESTION 65 What are other practices doing to reduce the number of patient no-shows and late cancellations? Can we charge patients a no-show fee?

Practices that track no-shows and cancellation rates averaged less than 5 percent for no-shows and 5 percent for their daily cancellation rate, according to an MGMA Information Exchange conducted in April 2009 (an informal survey with voluntary participation). To reduce the number of no-shows, responding practices used the following patient-appointment-reminder techniques:

➤ 66 percent have staff make telephone calls;

➤ 18 percent send postcards/mailers;

➤ 29 percent have an automated attendant system make calls; and

➤ 9 percent have a vendor handle reminders and confirmations.

When patients miss an appointment,

➤ 65 percent of practices do not charge the patient;

➤ 12 percent charge but with staff discretion;

➤ 10 percent charge after one missed appointment; and

➤ 2 percent charge every patient, every time.

For those that charge for missed appointments, 27 percent charged a flat fee of $21 to $50.

Tracking the number of no-shows is important, but it is also essential that the practice follow up with the patients to monitor why they did not present for the appointment. Knowing why the patient failed to show for an appointment will allow the practice to take steps and change faulty processes that may have contributed to the no-show.

Elizabeth W. Woodcock, MBA, FACMPE, CPC, offers the following suggestions to reduce the number of no-shows in the book *Mastering Patient Flow*:

➤ Schedule appointments within a reasonable time of the patient's call. The longer the lapse, the greater the chance of a no-show.

➤ Switch to open or advanced access scheduling to provide patients same-day appointments (see Question 64).

➤ Remind patients of their appointment, and ask them to confirm their commitment to the appointment.

➤ Monitor your no-shows. Are they more apt to be covered by one insurance carrier, seen on a particular day of the week or by one physician, or is there some other factor that prevents them from honoring their appointment?

➤ Develop a policy for dealing with repeat offenders. Specify how future appointments will be handled.

➤ Develop strong relationships with patients to increase their commitment to your practice. Suggestions include sending birthday or holiday cards and assigning nurses to specific patients.

➤ Lead by example. The more cancellations your physicians have, the more the patients will think it is acceptable.

Additional suggestions include

➤ Have patients complete and submit registration and health history forms prior to the appointment. Pre-registration of patients decreases the number of no-shows. Use your practice Web site or e-mail system to ease completion, submission, and tracking.

➤ Assign one person to track and follow up on no-shows. This keeps the duty from falling through the cracks. This employee should contact the patient after the missed appointment to reschedule and confirm the patient's commitment to the practice.

➤ Create a no-show tracking code in your computer system to make it easier to identify characteristics of no-show patients.

New technologies offer new opportunities for reminding patients of their upcoming appointments. Automated systems can tie into the practice management or electronic medical record system and still provide patients with an option to talk to a staff member. These systems can use e-mail or other social media and also contact patients when lab or test results are available. Your information systems should also help you identify individuals with a history of no-shows or late cancellations.

Another no-show strategy is "strategic overbooking." Elizabeth W. Woodcock describes this as overbooking a schedule during periods of high no-show rates, on Friday afternoons, for example, or during times when patients with histories of cancelled or missed appointments are scheduled. The other option is to overbook a frequent offender.

Charging patients who miss appointments may not be the best policy, especially for first-time offenders. It may cost the practice more to bill the patients than the amount to be collected (a typical charge is $21 to $50), and patients may choose to leave the practice. Other options include contacting the patient for reasons for missed appointments and reiterating the value of the physician's scheduled time; scheduling repeat offenders at times that will impact the practice less, including double-scheduling their time; and discharging the patient after multiple no-shows with attempts by the practice to contact the patient. Whatever policy your practice develops, make sure that it is widely publicized to all patients.

A CLOSER LOOK . . .

2007 Medicare Ruling on Charging for No-Shows

A no-show charge policy needs to apply to both Medicare and non-Medicare patients. Charge the same amount to all patients, and do not bill Medicare for the missed appointment. Instead, bill the patient directly.

Sources:

Elizabeth W. Woodcock, *Mastering Patient Flow: Use Lean Thinking to Improve Your Practice Operations, 3rd Edition* (Englewood, CO: Medical Group Management Association, 2009).

Elizabeth W. Woodcock, MBA, FACMPE, CPC, "Prevent Draining Revenue by Addressing Missed Appointments," *Dermatology Times*, August 1, 2010, www.modern-medicine.com/modernmedicine/Modern+Medicine+Now/Prevent-draining-revenue-by-addressing-missed-appo/ArticleStandard/Article/detail/680502 (accessed December 30, 2010).

Karen Zupko, "Make No-Show Prevention a Priority," *Plastic Surgery Practice*, V. 20, No. 1 (2010): 28–29.

Kathleen Quinn, MBA, RN, "14 Tips to Prevent No-Shows," *MGMA e-Source*, November 25, 2008, www.mgma.com/article.aspx?id=24026 (accessed December 30, 2010).

Medical Group Management Association, "Patient No-Shows and Cancellations," *Information Exchange* #4574 (Englewood, CO: Medical Group Management Association, April 2009).

QUESTION 66

Our patient satisfaction survey showed concerns with waiting times and delays in scheduling appointments. Do you have comparable data for benchmarking and ideas on improving wait times for my practice?

Ask your scheduler to calculate the next available appointment time for new patients, for physical exams and follow-up appointments. To assess waiting time during an appointment, have the receptionists record the time when a patient checks in at the desk, when the nurse or medical assistant escorts the patient to the exam room, and when the patient checks out. This information can be recorded on the charge ticket or other form used during the appointment.

After you've gathered enough data, compare your numbers with benchmarks, including the following:

Average time to next appointment for new patient

Specialty	Days to appointment
Cardiology	15.5
Dermatology	22.1
OB-GYN	27.5
Orthopedic surgery	16.8
Family practice	20.3

Source: Merritt Hawkins & Associates, "2009 Survey of Physician Appointment Wait Times" (Irving, TX: Merritt Hawkins & Associates, 2009), www.merritthawkins.com (accessed January 4, 2010).

According to a survey by Press Ganey, the average waiting time upon arrival at a medical practice to see a physician is 23 minutes, but the range by specialty was from 17 minutes for optometry to 30 minutes for neurosurgery. This time was the total amount of time spent in the waiting area and exam rooms until the physician arrived.

The Press Ganey survey identified an inverse correlation with wait times and patient satisfaction: As the wait time increased, patient satisfaction decreased. The lower the patients rated the comfort and pleasantness of the waiting area, the more they were dissatisfied with their visit. The survey also identified factors that improved patients' satisfaction with their visit:

➤ A short wait in the exam room;

➤ An accurate assessment of the wait time upon arrival;

➤ Comfortable seating in the waiting or reception area; and

➤ Entertainment options in the waiting area, including Internet access.

Since you have heard patients' comments regarding unsatisfactory wait times, you should take steps to decrease the wait times in your practice. Consider taking one or more of the following actions:

➤ Add another physician or NPP, especially if your physicians are seeing more patients than the benchmarks;

➤ Extend office hours to accommodate more patients per day;

➤ Hire additional staff to support the physicians;

➤ At check-in, provide patients with a form to write down what they want to discuss with the physician in order to make their time with the physician more efficient;

➤ Identify opportunities to maximize patient flow and increase the number of patients seen per day;

➤ Encourage your staff and physicians to express their ideas for eliminating delays; and

➤ Modify your appointment system to schedule patients more efficiently and more accurately, or implement advanced access to offer same-day appointments (see Question 64).

Sources:

Elizabeth W. Woodcock, MBA, FACMPE, CPC, *Mastering Patient Flow: Using Lean Thinking to Improve Your Practice Operations, 3rd Edition*, 300–307 (Englewood, CO: Medical Group Management Association, 2009).

Press Ganey Associates, Inc., *2010 Medical Practice Pulse Report: Patient Perspectives on American* 2010, http://pressganey.com/Documents_secure/Pulse%20Reports/ MPPulseReport_11-2010.pdf?viewFile (accessed January 4, 2011).

Roger T. Anderson, Fabian T. Camacho, and Rajesh Balkrishnan, "Willing to Wait? The Influence of Patient Wait Time on Satisfaction with Primary Care," *BMC Health Services Research* 2007, 7:31, www.biomedcentral.com/1472-6963/7/31 (accessed January 4, 2011).

QUESTION 67 One of my physicians wants to offer online visits. Are other practices doing virtual visits, and how does it work?

Some practices offer virtual visits or e-consultations. State regulations often require the establishment of a patient-physician relationship prior to online communication, thereby limiting the service to established patients. E-visits are frequently accessed through a secure patient portal to ensure compliance with HIPAA patient privacy regulations. The AMA created a

CPT code (0074T) for online patient consultations in 2004, and a few payers started reimbursing for e-visits soon after. In 2010, payers were using reimbursement rates of $25 to $35 per online visit. Confirm with your payers regarding their reimbursement practices and rates for online visits. While fees for online consultations are less than office-visit rates, the time savings and patient satisfaction can make it worthwhile.

Precautions should be taken to ensure liability risks aren't increased when the patient isn't seen in person. Some online consultation vendors cover the malpractice insurance for physicians subscribing to their services.

Not all patients are willing to use e-mail to conduct a visit with their physicians and some object to paying. However, there may be enough patients within the practice that it will lessen the number of telephone calls and decrease the demand on physicians' time. Another option is to offer streaming video and Web cams so physicians and patients can see each other during an online visit. This service may be slower to be accepted as fewer patients have Web cameras.

Maureen Whelthan, MD, of Comprehensive Women's Medical Center, Florida, charges $35 for a Web visit. Patients fill out an online questionnaire and receive responses within eight hours and occasionally after hours. The practice uses an online vendor to manage the visits and collect the fees. The vendor stores the e-mail interaction, but the practice also copies the communications into the EHR. All interactions are handled through the secured area of the Web site. Only one patient's insurance reimburses for the visit, but other participating patients felt the virtual visit fee was worth the convenience.

Glenwood Medical Associates, Colorado, implemented the virtual visits after one physician suggested it would offer more quality time with patients, reduce telephone calls, and add a competitive advantage. The service, called Virtual Doc Visit, is promoted on the Web site as an opportunity for "patients to visit with their physicians, presenting their medical concerns or requests for medications or appropriate web-based treatment." RNs field the e-mail requests for appropriateness as a virtual visit and to clarify the request. The service was offered at an introductory cost of $20 per visit, and response was promised within a few hours during business operating hours.

Sources:

Maureen Whelthan, MD, "Making Web Visits Work for Your Practice," *MGMA Connexion*, May/June 2009, www.mgma.com/WorkArea/mgma_downloadasset. aspx?id=28896 (accessed February, 1, 2011).

Mike Colias, "Virtual Access," *Modern Healthcare*, V. 34, Issue 4 (January 26, 2004): 48–49.

Patricia Brown and J. Larry Shackelford, CPA, FACMPE, "Virtual Virtues," *MGMA Connexion*, V. 8, No. 6 (July 2008): 40–43.

Yvette M. Cole, "Controlling Crowds with E-Visits," in *MGMA Buyer's Guide 2010*, 46–47 www.mgma.com/WorkArea/mgma_downloadasset.aspx?id=34325 (accessed February, 1, 2011).

QUESTION 68 I think our practice is experiencing a high rate of patient turnover. Are there industry benchmarks for turnover rates that I can use to compare my practice?

Unfortunately, there are no current data on average patient retention or turnover rates in medical practices. However, another way of looking at the question is by comparing established- and new-patient visits in medical practices.

Percentage of new vs. established patients

Specialty	New	Established
Primary care	10%	90%
Surgical specialties	24%	76%
Medical specialties	18%	82%

Source: Centers for Disease Control and Prevention, National Centers for Health Statistics, *National Ambulatory Medical Care Survey: 2007*, November 2010, Number 27, Table 8, www.cdc.gov/nchs/data/nhsr/nhsr027.pdf (accessed February 2, 2011).

There are some factors that could lead to a high patient turnover rate that are beyond your control, especially if your practice serves a population that moves or changes jobs frequently. Medicaid enrollees with limited enrollment periods cannot afford regular office visits and change doctors with each enrollment period.

However, if your practice has unusually high turnover without the previously mentioned factors, you should look for issues within your practice. A patient satisfaction survey (see Question 79) will help identify potential reasons, as will talking with patients who have announced that they will be changing doctors.

Reviewing factors that affect patient loyalty toward their physicians provides insights on what patients are looking for from their physicians. Frequently cited reasons given by patients who planned to change physicians include

> ➤ Dissatisfaction with the length of the visit;

> ➤ Physician did not listen to what the patient said;

> ➤ Inadequate explanation of purpose of prescription;

> ➤ Physician's explanations were not understandable; and

> ➤ Physician did not provide enough medical information.

Patients were more likely to stay with physicians when they reported a high level of trust. Patients felt this trust for the following reasons:

> ➤ The physician listened;

> ➤ The physician shared a higher level of information;

> ➤ The physician told them what to do if the symptoms continued, worsened, or returned;

> ➤ Patients felt involved in the decision-making; and

> ➤ The physician spent adequate time with them.

Patients also expressed more trust with physicians and intent to stay with a physician when they perceived similarities with the physicians in terms of ethnicity and personal beliefs and values. Because of the ethnic factor in patient trust, Street and O'Malley found that minority patients often reported less trust in their physicians.

After a doctor/patient relationship has developed, patients are able to overcome some of these factors and continue the relationship. Therefore, it is important for practices to be aware of the factors affecting patient satisfaction and trust with their physicians during the new-patient visits.

After reviewing these studies, there are several steps that practices can implement with the goal of increasing patient retention:

➤ Increasing physician time with patients;

➤ Coaching physicians on listening to patients and their
concerns;

➤ Ensuring physicians are explaining diagnoses, treatments,
and prescriptions in a comprehensive and understandable
manner;

➤ Involving patients in decision-making; and

➤ Providing a diversity of providers to match the diversity of
your community.

Sources:

A.D. Federman, et al., "Intention to Discontinue Care among Primary Care Patients:
Influence of Physician Behavior and Process of Care," *Journal of General Internal
Medicine*, V. 16, No. 10 (2001): 668–74.

Hector P. Rodriguez, PhD, William H. Rogers, PhD, Richard E. Marshall, MD, and Dana
Gelb Safran, ScD, "The Effects of Primary Care Physician Visit Continuity on Patients'
Experiences with Care," *Journal of General Internal Medicine*, V. 22, No. 6 (2007): 787–93.

Nancy L. Keating, Diane C. Green, Audiey C. Kao, Julie A. Gazmararian, Vivian Y. Wu,
and Paul D. Cleary, "How Are Patients' Specific Ambulatory Care Experiences Related to
Trust, Satisfaction, and Considering Changing Physicians?" *Journal of General Internal
Medicine*, V. 17 (2002): 29–39.

N.L. Keating, T.K. Gandhi, E.J. Orav, D.W. Bates, and J.Z. Ayanian, "Patient Characteristics
and Experiences Associated with Trust in Specialist Physicians," *Archives of Internal
Medicine*, V. 164, No. 9 (2004): 1015–20.

R.L. Street Jr., K.J. O'Malley, L.A. Cooper, and P. Haidet, "Understanding Concordance
in Patient-Physician Relationships: Personal and Ethnic Dimensions of Shared Identity,"
Annuals of Family Medicine, V. 6, No. 3 (2008): 198–205.

QUESTION **Our recent patient satisfaction survey showed some
69 dissatisfaction related to our telephone system. How
can I improve our telephone operations? Are there
benchmarks for hold time, time until call is answered,
and so on?**

An individual's first impression of your practice is gained
from their initial contact, which is usually over the telephone.
Therefore, it is important that you pay attention to the customer
service provided via telephone. Did the satisfaction survey

provide clues as to the reasons for the dissatisfaction? Several telephone-related issues could be the problem:

➤ Delays in returning telephone messages;

➤ Telephone calls not being answered;

➤ Long wait times;

➤ Rude or unhelpful personnel; or

➤ Automated systems that are more confusing than helpful.

To get at the root of the issue, you may want to conduct a more detailed patient survey, interview individual patients, hold a patient focus group, or use a "mystery patient." The latter should be an outsider or contractor who will call the practice several times over different periods of the day.

In the meantime, start gathering data on call volume, hold time, and number of dropped calls using your telephone service provider or automated telephone system. Ask your telephone vendor to suggest software that can be added (or already exists) to your telephone system that can help you monitor time on hold, abandonment rate, and do-not-disturb time by operator. The telephone service provider should assist you in analyzing the data. Do you have adequate lines for the volume? Are there peak times for calls that may require additional staffing? Is the length of time before answering or hold time too long?

A LOOK AT THE NUMBERS . . .

It's difficult to track telephone benchmark data for medical practices. Physician referral and telephone triage call centers have been surveyed on their metrics. These benchmarks may be similar to what patients are experiencing with other businesses and what they'll expect from your practice. The average time for an incoming call to be answered was less than 15 seconds for 31 percent of responding call centers and between 15 and 30 seconds for 44 percent of respondents. Fifty percent of responding call centers had an abandoned call rate of 4 percent or less.

Source: "Structure and Metrics Results from 2009 Healthcare Call Center Survey," in *Physician Referral & Telephone Triage Times*, V. 9, No. 8 (2009): 1, 3, 5, 7.

Have staff record data on the topics of incoming calls, the number of calls that need transferring, and patients' comments about the number of transfers or unreturned calls. Review this information to identify potential solutions. An automated system could be implemented to direct patients to the most frequently requested topics. If a current automated system is confusing rather than helpful, work with the vendor and your staff on ideas to improve it.

Messages that are never returned will also create dissatisfaction. Ensure the practice has procedures in place to record incoming messages, and verify that they are transferred to the appropriate person who then follows up within an appropriate time. The patient survey or mystery patient should help identify bottlenecks in this flow. Whoever takes messages should be trained on all the information to record to assist with the call back.

Steps can be implemented to eliminate the need for patients to leave messages. Nurse triage services or call centers let patients speak with someone on almost every call rather than leaving messages for physicians. Providing nurses with training and access to requested information, such as quick access to the medical record and a doctor's notes, decreases the need for a physician to return the call.

Assess customer-relations issues in how personnel answer the telephones and direct calls. Well-trained staff should know appropriate departments for specific questions or be able to address more questions themselves to decrease the number of transfers. Some practices develop scripts for employees to use for standardized means of answering billing questions or prescription renewals. Ideas on how to handle patient complaints should be shared with staff. Technology can be used to improve telephone operations. Voice mail systems can eliminate the need for paper messages or lengthy hold times but might be more appropriate in billing departments than the clinical area. Sophisticated telephone systems can sense increasing call volume and change the routing protocol or provide alarms to increase the number of personnel answering the telephones.

NEW TECHNOLOGY AND PATIENT COMMUNICATION

Advanced automated communication systems convert the telephone conversation to digital computer format. It can then be tracked as an assigned task transferred to the appropriate personnel or integrated into an EHR. This eliminates concerns about losing paper messages or the time involved in recording telephone calls in patients' charts. The system can also be used to automate outbound calls. These systems can be used by contracted call centers as well as within the practice.

Practice Web sites can be utilized to reduce the number of times patients must call for information. Some practices have automated scheduling and make it available online so patients can book their own appointments. Patient portals offer secure access to test results and e-mail communication.

Telephones are still a vital link between your practice and its patients. If they aren't functioning correctly, it threatens to sever the link.

Case Study

Provena Health System, a large multispecialty clinic in Tacoma, Wash., identified problems related to response time to telephone messages. Team members interviewed staff and conducted time-motion studies, recording the number of times the message was passed and the average response time. Implemented changes included

➤ Redesigned message templates for recording information and simplifying transferring it to charts;

➤ Improved message flow that shifted responsibilities related to scope of practice. For example, MAs were tasked with handling prescription refill and lab result calls; and

➤ Development of a message pool that enabled all nurses and providers to access messages.

The result was a reduction in message-response time from more than 34 hours to an average of 11 hours and an increase in the number of same-day responses.

Source: Ilene V. Gilbert, FACMPE, "Improve Your Telephone-Message Response Time," *MGMA e-Source*, January 22, 2008, www.mgma.com/article.aspx?id=16192 (accessed January 19, 2011).

Sources:

Arthur W. Lane III, "Tech Talk: Put that Phone to Work," *MGMA Connexion*, July 2007, www.mgma.com/WorkArea/mgma_downloadasset.aspx?id=13730 (accessed January 19, 2011).

Elizabeth W. Woodcock, MBA, FACMPE, CPC, *Mastering Patient Flow: Using Lean Thinking to Improve Your Practice Operations, 3rd Edition* (Englewood, CO: Medical Group Management Association, 2009).

QUESTION 70

What is a patient-centered medical home, and how does my practice become one?

A patient-centered medical home (PCMH) is a "physician practice and patient partnership that provides accessible, interactive, family focused, coordinated and comprehensive care," according to Cynthia Dunn, RN, MGMA healthcare consultant. It provides a single source for a patient's medical information and revolves around the whole physician/patient relationship rather than being driven by episodic care. It is an effective means for the management of chronic care patients.

Any practice can become a PCMH, but it requires a shift in management, operations, and philosophy. Dunn describes some of the key concepts that your practice must adopt:

➤ Team-based coordinated care of the whole patient directed by a physician;

➤ Patient involvement in decision-making and self-management of chronic conditions;

➤ Planned, proactive visits (as opposed to episodic care or reactive visits);

➤ Enhanced access for patients (e-mail communication, open access scheduling, expanded hours); and

➤ Use of technology (EHR).

The team-based coordinated care usually involves a physician–nurse partnership, with the nurse preparing and reviewing the chart prior to the visit and participating in the consultation and care management with the physician. The nurse or other staff takes on additional responsibilities including dictation, chart completion, and prescription management to free the physician's time for developing the patient relationship.

Whole patient care and increased patient involvement require having all information available during the appointment. During chart preparation, the nurse ensures that lab work, test results, and specialist consultation information are available and reviewed prior to the visit. This involves scheduling lab work and diagnostic tests prior to the appointment.

Enhanced access is necessary to build the physician/patient relationship and ensure that potential issues are taken care of immediately instead of after the fact. E-mail communication builds the bond and provides an easy way for patients to keep in touch and express their concerns. Many practices converting to a PCMH have implemented open access or a rapid access system to provide same-day appointments with their physician or another in the practice if necessary.

The most difficult issue related to PCMH is the need to shift from reimbursement per procedure to reimbursement for patient outcomes and satisfaction. You will need to talk with payers to identify opportunities for pay-for-performance or other quality management programs. Medicare, various Blue Cross and Blue Shield plans, United Healthcare, and Aetna have implemented demonstrations of the medical home concept. One study identified four methods that payers are using to reimburse for medical home services:

➤ A supplemental fee, frequently a per-member, per-month fee. This is often in addition to a pay-for-performance payment or the medical practice's share of program savings.

➤ New service codes developed by payers for medical home services.

➤ Increased fee-for-service payments above current reimbursement rates. This is easy to implement but conflicts with the purpose of medical homes.

➤ Global or capitation payments.[1]

Case Study

Geisinger Health Plan (GHP) started a medical home pilot program in 2007 with selected medical practices and quickly expanded the program. The practices expanded hours until 7 or 8 each evening plus Saturdays. Nurse case managers, part of the care teams, identified the highest risk patients and partners with the provider to develop personalized plans of care. The case manager follows the patients through care transitions, especially post-discharge periods, and conducts medication reconciliations. Case managers and physicians also emphasize self-care and self-management, and GHP has developed a series of patient education tools to support these efforts.

GHP rewards providers for their participation in the program and supported practice infrastructure improvements and additional staff with a $5,000-per-month allowance per 1,000 Medicare patients. GHP's operating costs increased with the medical home implementation, but "the clinical and efficiency outcomes are going to more than cover operating costs," according to Janet Tomcavage, RN, MSN, vice president of health services.

Geisinger Health System modified its physician compensation model to link 20 percent of the compensation to quality, outcomes, and patient satisfaction. The remaining 80 percent is tied to the physicians' efficiency benchmarked with peer data. Each physician that participates in a medical home program receives an extra $1,800 per month for the additional work.

Source: Healthcare Intelligence Network, *Model Medical Homes: Benchmarks and Case Studies in Patient-Centered Care*, 22–28 (Sea Girt, NJ: The Healthcare Intelligence Network, 2009).

Besides reimbursement issues, there are other potential roadblocks to widespread implementation of the PCMH concept:

➤ Day-to-day demands on physicians and practices don't allow the time to make the switch to the time-intensive patient-relationship building;

➤ Smaller practices have less capital to invest in the information technology needed for the intensive care management; and

➤ Management changes are required to support the high levels of access and strong care team and relationship building.

Even if your practice and your major payers aren't ready for full PCMH implementation, there may be aspects of the concept that your practice can adopt to improve physician efficiency, patient quality, and everyone's satisfaction.

Several studies have shown the effectiveness of the medical home model. A ProvenHealth Navigator demonstration program using 11 primary care practices found that inpatient admissions were reduced by 18 percent and readmissions were reduced 36 percent for Medicare patients.[2]

ADDITIONAL RESOURCES

American College of Physicians (www.acponline.org) Medical Home Builder[SM] — The ACP Medical Home Builder "provides affordable, accessible online guidance and resources for practices involved in incremental quality improvement changes — or significant transformation of their practices."

Bridges to Excellence Medical Home Recognition Project, www.bridgestoexcellence.org

HealthTeamWorks, healthteamworks.com

National Center for Quality Assurance (www.ncqa.org) Physician Practice Connections® — Patient-Centered Medical Home™, includes medical home certification.

Healthcare Intelligence Network, *Model Medical Homes: Benchmarks and Case Studies in Patient-Centered Care* (Sea Girt, NJ: The Healthcare Intelligence Network). MGMA Item #8336

TransforMED, www.transformed.com — A subsidiary of the American Academy of Family Physicians, "TransforMED acts as a leader and catalyst to generate positive transformations in primary care."

Transformed Transformation Series publications including:

➤ *Is the PCMH Model Right for My Practice Workbook*, TransforMED and MGMA, 2010, MGMA Item #8195

➤ *Patient-Centered Medical Home Access Workbook*, TransforMED and MGMA, 2010, MGMA Item #8222

➤ *Patient-Centered Medical Home Care Management Workbook*, TransforMED and MGMA, 2010, MGMA Item #8223

➤ *Patient-Centered Medical Home Care Coordination Workbook*, TransforMED and MGMA, 2010, MGMA Item #8268

References:

1. Paula Haas, "Medical Home Model Calls for New Payment Methods," *AAFP News Now Special Report*, February 17, 2009, www.aafp.org/online/en/home/publications/news/news-now/pcmh/20090217pcmhpayment.html (accessed February 4, 2011).

2. Richard J. Gilfillan et al., "Value and the Medical Home: Effects of Transformed Primary Care," *American Journal of Managed Care*, V. 16, No. 8 (August 2010): 607–15.

Sources:

Cynthia L. Dunn, RN, FACMPE, "Objective Advice: There's No Place Like . . . A Patient-Centered Medical Home," *MGMA Connexion*, January 2010, www.mgma.com/WorkArea/mgma_downloadasset.aspx?id=32147 (accessed January 4, 2011).

Lisa H. Schneck, MSJ, "Home Is Where Your Doctor Is: Patient-Centered Medical Home Transforms the Office Visit," *MGMA Connexion*, April 2009, www.mgma.com/WorkArea/mgma_downloadasset.aspx?id=28012 (accessed January 4, 2011).

Robert A. Berenson et al., "A House Is Not a Home: Keeping Patients at The Center of Practice Redesign," *Health Affairs* V. 27, No. 5 (2008): 1219–30.

QUESTION 71 If my payers shift to pay-for-performance or quality-based reimbursement, we may be in trouble because of lack of patient compliance with the physicians' recommendations. How can I improve our patient compliance and education?

For years, practices have been providing patients with printed materials related to their conditions and medication and discussing care plans, including exercise and diet changes. But it has been accepted knowledge that a large percentage of patients simply don't comply. One study on hypertension found that only

50 percent of patients were following the recommended drug therapies. Other than the frustration and concern related to patients' attitudes, there haven't been consequences for practices under typical fee-for-service reimbursement. Patient compliance is becoming a major concern when practices are shifted from reimbursement per procedure to reimbursement related to patient outcomes and quality of care. If patients don't comply with treatment plans and their health doesn't improve, there are now consequences for the practice.

The first step is to understand the patient and reasons for lack of compliance. One reason may be the health literacy status of the patient. Many patients don't understand their care plans, medication instructions, or self-management guidelines. Factors that affect health literacy include education level, age, language barriers, or hearing disabilities. Patients are often too embarrassed to admit they don't understand or forgot a set of instructions.

Options for overcoming health literacy barriers and improving patient education and compliance include

➤ Provide written information as well as verbal instructions;

➤ Provide written materials in another language or provide an interpreter;

➤ Provide patients with a complete list of their prescribed medications;

➤ Ask patients to repeat instructions;

➤ Encourage patients to ask questions; and

➤ Train staff to recognize the signs of health illiteracy.

Patients have a variety of other reasons for noncompliance, and understanding these reasons provides a means of addressing their concerns and behavior. A study of patients suffering from hypertension and their levels of compliance with health regimens segmented the patients into six categories. The categories, which apply to others suffering from chronic conditions, and suggestions for working with these patients were

➤ **Proactive.** Participated in the drug regimen and only needed encouragement to continue.

➤ **Confident.** Felt they could control their condition in other ways and might discontinue the medications. Incentive programs to reward continuing the medication worked well with this group. Examples of rewards include gaining points per prescription or discounts on gym memberships.

➤ **Concerned.** Worried about the effects of the medications themselves. Needed reassurance on long-term safety and benefits of medication compared to consequences of not taking medication.

➤ **Confused.** Feel they lack control or don't have enough information to gain control of the condition and also have some distrust of physicians. Need to be provided with more education and opportunities to gain trust with physicians.

➤ **Resigned.** Believe changing their lifestyle is too much trouble, so it's easier to deal with the condition as it is. Providers need to explain the real dangers and risks of ignoring the condition and provide patients easier reminder tools for taking medication so it's "not too much trouble."

➤ **Skeptical.** Patients who think condition isn't serious and distrust the physicians and the medication. Need all of the above: more education on the seriousness of the disease, benefits of the medication, and easy tools to help them take the medication. True skeptics may continue to disbelieve, and other voices need to be brought in, including fellow sufferers, family members, or more medical literature.

Increasing patients' involvement in self-management is a key to improving patient compliance and outcomes. The four components for successful self-management are

➤ **Information.** Providing information regarding the patient's disease and available health and social services for managing it empowers the patient and provides him or her with more confidence for gaining control of their lives. With increased knowledge comes increased participation in patients' care planning. Providers should utilize the patients' knowledge about their condition and what makes them feel better or worse to modify plans accordingly.

➤ **Skills.** Provide patients with skills to help control their conditions through individual or group sessions.

➤ **Tools and devices.** Use medical devices and electronic tools to help patients self-manage.

➤ **Support networks.** Either organize groups within your practice or direct patients toward support groups within the community.

A variety of electronic tools are available to support self-management and to empower patients with information. EHRs can be used to schedule follow-up and regular care visits for chronic care patients who may forget to schedule appointments. Use technology to present data from previous visits to demonstrate trends and then bring up educational materials. These aids can engage the patient in discussions regarding their care management.

Physicians or nurse care managers can use e-mails to communicate with patients on a more regular basis or to send reminders to patients to take medication or follow other behaviors. Use e-mails to share information from new studies that support benefits of medication, care plans, or patient participation.

Some patients may prefer smart phone apps that deliver regular reminders for insulin tests or taking medication or that encourage exercise. Learning about these apps and encouraging their use may reach a new audience of patients.

Self-management support networks can be patient-led or facilitated by nurses or other "health coaches." Topics can include exercise, symptom management techniques, nutrition, fatigue management, community resources, dealing with emotions, and communication with health providers. Programs that have recorded success incorporate weekly action plans followed by feedback and group problem solving. The group approach often improves participants' conditions because of increased motivation to take control of their condition with the support of or pressure from peers.

A Des Moines, Iowa, family practice was successful in managing conditions of chronic care patients and increasing the revenue of the practice by instituting a population health coach (PHC) program. The practice, with 10 physicians and 5 PAs, had witnessed an increase in chronic care patients until 5 out of 30 of daily patient visits were those with chronic conditions. A nurse with strong patient rapport became a PHC to provide medical education. The program, directed by the physician with the largest chronic care patient population, included a schedule of regular testing to monitor status and progress followed by one-on-one visits between the PHC and patients. The program expanded to include shared medical visits and an additional PHC. The practice billed for the appropriate E&M visit, and grant money was received for contributing data to a patient registry. The PHCs generated additional revenue by promoting the service in the community and developed patient education classes for local businesses. Physicians were pleased with the improved patient quality of life and being able to devote more of their time to acute care and well-patient visits.

The difficulty is that patient education and chronic care management are not adequately reimbursed at this time. Some practices have incorporated the self-management programs in group visits called shared medical appointments. Billing is handled the same way as similar one-on-one visits because most payers don't distinguish group from individual visits. It is vital to accurately document who was present and what occurred to warrant the CPT code, including codes for prolonged visits requiring face-to-face contact with the patient.

The greater benefit will be from reducing costs with improved patient care. Under Medicare and other payer's quality or pay-for-performance programs, the savings or incentive payments will eventually cover the costs of these patient education and compliance programs.

Sources:

Eric Lundin, FACMPE, "Utilizing Population Health Coaches to Improve the Lives of Patients with Chronic Health Conditions," ACMPE Fellowship Paper, October 2009.

Jessica Hopfield, Robert M. Linden, and Bradley Tevelow, "Getting Patients to Take Their Medicine," *McKinsey Quarterly*, Issue 4 (2006): 14–17.

John Mendez, MBA, "Removing Barriers So Patients Understand Their Care," *MGMA Connexion*, September 2008, www.mgma.com/WorkArea/mgma_downloadasset. aspx?id=21834 (accessed January 18, 2011).

Matthew Vuletich, "More Doctor Communication Equals Better Patient Care," *MGMA e-Source*, July 13, 2010, www.mgma.com/article.aspx?id=34121 (accessed January 18, 2011).

Maureen McKinney, "Coaching with Care," *Modern Healthcare*, V. 40, No. 33 (2010): 30–32.

Nicola J. Davies, "Improving Self-Management for Patients with Long-Term Conditions," *Journal of Nursing Standard*, V. 24, No. 25 (2010): 49–56.

Paul Shank, MBA, "Patients Treated Together Can Improve Together," *MGMA Connexion*, March 2010, www.mgma.com/WorkArea/DownloadAsset.aspx?id=33004 (accessed January 18, 2011).

QUESTION 72

One of my physicians is complaining about a non-compliant patient. Should we dismiss the patient, and what's the proper way to do it?

Having patients who don't follow the recommendations of the physicians is a fairly common occurrence. They are the patients who don't return to the practice for recommended tests or procedures or don't show signs of improvement after receiving a treatment plan. Their noncompliance requires extra staff time and raises the liability risks and should be addressed.

The first step in dealing with difficult patients is to find out the reasons for their noncompliance. There are three major reasons for patients not following physicians' instructions:

➤ **Limitations in understanding the instructions.** These patients may have language problems, hearing disabilities, or memory problems. These issues can be addressed by writing down instructions, engaging a family member, hiring interpreters with the patient's permission, and asking the patient to repeat the instructions. Some patients may have mental health issues that need to be addressed.

➤ **Economic and environmental reasons.** The patient may not be able to afford the medications or prescribed treatment. He or she may be unable to take time off work or get transportation to the facility. Individuals are often reluctant to explain these barriers. The practice should be aware of public assistance programs, the use of medication samples, or other alternatives that may work for the patient.

➤ **Personal reasons.** Many patients will not follow physicians' orders because they are "too hard," they don't like taking medications, or they "don't want to." These patients are more difficult to approach and change their compliance. The physician can continue to explain concerns of consequences related to noncompliance and try various methods to encourage participation.

Additional methods for dealing with these noncompliant patients include soliciting help from other providers or staff in the practice. The patient may have a different relationship with other staff members who will have insights into handling the patient. Ask the patient if there are alternatives that they would participate in. Use pictures or other visuals to demonstrate consequences of noncompliance.

If the patient still refuses to follow the physician's recommendation, it may be time to dismiss the patient from the physician's care. Confer with your legal counsel and state medical board to ensure you're aware of and complying with legal provisions and medical board expectations. To make sure that race, gender, sexual preference, or religious affiliation are not factors in the decision to dismiss a patient, develop a policy defining under which circumstances patients may be dismissed. Review the documentation that tracks the patient's noncompliance and efforts to educate the patient and gain his or her compliance. Additional documentation to reduce liability exposure includes signed copies of written instructions and informed consent forms. Complete and accurate documentation will help protect the practice in case of liability suits.

The patient should be notified with a termination letter, reviewed by legal counsel, advising the patient to find another physician within 30 days. It should be sent via certified mail and a return receipt requested with the receipt filed in the patient's chart. The letter should explain the reasons for the dismissal and state that the practice will continue to provide care for another 30 days. List the conditions for which the patient should seek care, and include a list of hospitals or other sources for finding another physician. Provide an authorization form to send his or her medical records to a new physician.

Sources:

Diane Weber, "How to Dismiss a Noncompliant Patient," *Medical Economics*, August 1, 2008, www.modernmedicine.com/modernmedicine/article/articleDetail. jsp?ts=1295822577438 (accessed January 23, 2011).

Shelly K. Schwartz, "In Practice: Do As I Say . . . Pretty Please?" *Physicians Practice*, March 1, 2008, www.physicianspractice.com/compliance/content/article/1462168/1586310 (accessed January 23, 2011).

Theodore Passineau, JD, "How to Manage Noncompliant Patients," *MGMA e-Source*, February 26, 2008, www.mgma.com/article.aspx?id=17152 (accessed January 23, 2011).

QUESTION **73** How can we increase the number of referrals we receive from primary care physicians?

Prior to referring to your practice, primary care physicians need to know about your physicians, their specialties, and what makes your practice unique. They are more apt to refer patients to physicians with whom they have developed a relationship. Flashy promotional brochures and gifts are not as effective as name recognition.

You can use options already in place to increase your physicians' visibility in the community. Physicians should be encouraged to attend hospital-sponsored events and rounds. They should participate in hospital committees and lecture programs or write articles for hospital newsletters. Local medical societies' meetings and newsletters are a great way to meet more physicians and increase awareness.

Your practice may want to sponsor an open house or an educational series to demonstrate how your practice is unique or to inform primary care physicians about new procedures or new techniques. Consider handing out small items, like a referral note pad or informational items, to keep your name in front of the physicians.

After you've created awareness, you need to secure the referring relationship. The physicians, an administrator, or a referral manager should be available to welcome new referrers and build the relationship. Share information on your practice's hours, your physicians' expertise, the insurance plans you accept, and so on. Inform referrers of procedures or areas your physicians don't handle to limit confusion. Learn as much as possible about the referring physicians and their practice. Send thank-you notes stating appreciation of their referrals.

Meet with referring physicians to discuss opportunities to smooth the referral process. Together, develop a form to gather information prior to the visit about

➤ The patient's medical condition and test results;

➤ Any special needs or concerns, including hearing impairments or language difficulties;

➤ Insurance verification and referral authorization, including appropriate numbers; and

➤ Information on how to contact the referring physician's office.

Referring physicians will have several expectations of your practice, which your practice should meet or exceed; these include

➤ An easy process for setting up appointments, which includes having a direct telephone number or a dedicated extension for referrals, and a process for returning telephone calls as soon as possible;

➤ A reasonable time frame for available appointments;

➤ Frequent communication about the patients' status, with initial calls and follow-ups made on a regular basis;

➤ A professional and friendly staff; and

➤ Respect for the referring physician and an appreciation of their referrals.

Investigate means of automating these processes to ease referrers' access to your appointment system and physicians. Many practices utilize secure Web sites or practice portals for physicians to submit referral requests and communicate in a secure manner with their physicians. Include the referral information form discussed above. EHRs can be utilized to track the referral process and share information with referring physicians or at least alert the provider of the need to contact the referrer regarding their patient's status.

To ensure a continuing relationship, conduct annual referring-physician satisfaction surveys. Include questions about communication, ease in setting up appointments, quality of care, and the relationship with staff. The survey will help in identifying problems that need to be corrected.

Sources:

Cynthia Dunn, RN, FACMPE, "How You Can Improve the Referral Management Process," *MGMA Connexion*, April 2009, www.mgma.com/WorkArea/mgma_downloadasset. aspx?id=28004 (accessed February 11, 2011).

Elizabeth W. Woodcock, MBA, FACMPE, CPC, *Mastering Patient Flow: Using Lean Thinking to Improve Your Practice Operations, 3rd Edition* (Englewood, CO: Medical Group Management Association, 2009).

Linda Rickey, FACMPE, "How an 'Invisible' Practice Reversed Declining Patient Volumes and Boosted Revenue," *MGMA e-Source*, August 10, 2010, www.mgma.com/article. aspx?id=34365 (accessed February 11, 2011).

QUESTION 74

I'm getting dragged into a battle regarding call schedules and call coverage. How are other administrators dealing with the issue?

Call schedules and ensuring adequate call coverage at hospitals are contentious issues in medical group practices. New scheduling tools are available to develop and distribute call schedules, but they don't deal with the personal issues and areas of conflict. Call schedules are areas of disagreement because they affect physicians' personal lives, can be seen as unfair by participating physicians, and bring up multigenerational differences. Senior physicians want to decrease call, and younger physicians don't want to take as much call.

Developing a call schedule policy sets the standards and expectations of the practice and how the processes related to call coverage will be handled. MGMA member Karen Retchless, COO of Clearwater (Florida) Cardiovascular & Interventional

Consultants, develops the schedule for her 20 physicians by following five core principles:

➤ Never lose sight of our mission to provide quality care;

➤ Understand that our practice operates 24 hours a day, 365 days a year;

➤ Understand that taking call is the most demanding responsibility my physicians have;

➤ Never deviate from the call guidelines or rules established by the physicians; and

➤ Remain unbiased.[1]

Items to include in a policy are

➤ Hospital rotations;

➤ Office rotations;

➤ Specialty and subspecialty coverage;

➤ Weekend and weeknight call;

➤ Holiday schedules;

➤ Nonphysician providers included in the call schedule; and

➤ Notification requirements for time off and no call.

Practices may want to include options for no-call requests to block out time for evening or weekend family events or commitments. If changes in time off or no call are requested after a schedule is written, it should be the individual physician's responsibility to find someone to cover. The schedule developer should ensure that holiday coverage is evenly distributed within and between years.

Multispecialty practices or single specialties with subspecialties have the additional difficulties of scheduling to ensure adequate coverage of all specialties. Specialties that are frequently called during off hours may rotate call on a daily basis. Those called less frequently, such as allergy or rheumatology, often use a weekly rotation. One of the goals in forming group practices is to ensure an adequate number of physicians by specialty to provide reasonable call schedules. Developing IDS may also incorporate call coverage factors in determining the right mix of specialties and subspecialties.

Group practices in rural areas are under additional strain, since there is frequently only one physician of a particular specialty at a time. Patricia Richesin, MHA, administrator of Internal Medicine Group PC in Cheyenne, Wyoming, uses locum tenens occasionally to assist with call coverage. She says, "It's an expensive alternative, but that's what needs to happen to give our doctors a break."

NPPs may be incorporated in the schedule depending on practice or physician preference and state regulations regarding their responsibilities. Some practices have the after-hours calls go to the NPP first. The physician is contacted if the issue isn't resolved over the telephone. The NPP may also do floor rounding during the weekend for patients in the hospital or assist the physician on emergency room visits.

On-call compensation varies depending on the type of coverage and the practice's preferences. Call coverage within the practice is usually incorporated in the physician's general compensation plan. Practices may include separate call compensation when physicians are allowed to decrease compensation for family or health reasons (see Question 23 on part-time physician policies).

A LOOK AT THE NUMBERS . . .

An informal survey of MGMA member practices in 2008 found that 26.8 percent of responding practices include call coverage as a factor in physician compensation. Of those that did, 34 percent include call coverage compensation within the physician compensation plan, while 21.8 percent had a set compensation amount per call shift.

A September 2007 HHS Office of Inspector General (OIG) advisory opinion allowing hospitals to provide compensation for on-call coverage increased the number of hospitals providing this compensation. The MGMA's *Medical Directorship and*

On-Call Compensation Survey: 2010 Report Based on 2009 Data found that compensation for call coverage varied depending on specialty:

Specialty	% of respondents receiving compensation
Primary care	43.4%
Nonsurgical specialty	51.5%
Surgical specialty	72.46%

For those receiving compensation, the following methods were the most common:

Compensation method	% of respondents receiving compensation
Daily stipend	33%
Annual stipend	14%
Hourly rate	8%
Monthly stipend	4%

Rates for call coverage varied widely by specialty and location. For example, the daily rate went from $100 for family practice without OB to $1,670 for neurological surgery, and the hourly rate ranged from $62 for primary care to $225 for nonsurgical specialties.

Kenneth T. Hertz, FACMPE, MGMA principal healthcare consultant, warns that hospital compensation for call coverage may not occur in hospital-affiliated practices. He says "as the trend toward physician employment within integrated systems increases, the separate on-call payment disappears from the formula and instead, is integrated in the overall compensation package."

Reference:

1. Lisa H. Schneck, MSJ, "Call of the Riled: Physician Call Schedules," *MGMA Connexion*, April 2008, www.mgma.com/WorkArea/DownloadAsset.aspx?id=17580 (accessed January 14, 2011).

Sources:

Matthew Vuletich, "Physician Compensation Differs for Medical Directorship Duties, On-Call Coverage," *MGMA e-Source*, April 13, 2010, www.mgma.com/article.aspx?id=33318 (accessed January 14, 2011).

Medical Group Management Association, *Medical Directorship and On-Call Compensation Survey: 2010 Report Based on 2009 Data* (Englewood, CO: Medical Group Management Association, 2010).

Medical Group Management Association, "MGMA: 43.4% of Primary Care Provider Survey Respondents Receive Additional Compensation for On-Call Coverage," MGMA Web site, April 28, 2010, www.mgma.com/press/default.aspx?id=33505 (accessed January 14, 2011).

QUESTION 75 I need to write a policy for managing medication samples in my practice? Do you have some example policies I can use?

Providing physicians with samples of medications is a frequent marketing tool used by pharmaceutical representatives. Most physicians and practices accept the samples and distribute them among patients. Perceived benefits of the samples include providing medication to those who can least afford it, determining the efficacy of the prescription prior to prescribing it for a patient, and having the opportunity to start the medication immediately. However, several studies on the use of samples question the benefits to patients and society. Physicians who accepted and distributed more samples were found to have more prescriptions in general and to more frequently prescribe the newer, more expensive drugs. The patients receiving samples and the same drug via prescription did not always show better outcomes.

For these and related reasons, practices are evaluating the use and management of medications samples and meetings with pharmaceutical representatives. A policy related to meetings with pharmaceutical representatives should include

➤ Contact person within the practice, frequently a nurse manager;

➤ Specific dates and times when physicians or contact person are available to meet with representatives;

➤ Reference to sample medication policy for representatives and practice to follow; and

➤ Statement on what the practice can accept from representatives.

The federal government is looking at sample medication use, as well. Beginning in 2012, the PPACA requires pharmaceutical manufacturers and distributors to report the identity and quantity of drug samples requested and the name and address of the practitioner making the request.

To ensure there is no abuse of medication samples in your practice, you should maintain internal controls for managing them as controlled substances. The controls should ensure that samples do not expire and that employees' access is monitored and limited to a few personnel.

The *MGMA Operating Policies & Procedures Manual* includes a Sample Medication Controls policy that helps identify what should be included in your policy:

> ➤ Medications are distributed only under order of a practice provider;

> ➤ A locked cabinet is used to store samples and prescription pads;

> ➤ Only designated employees have access to sample medications;

> ➤ Logs are used to record the arrival of samples and who orders their distribution;

> ➤ There is a double-check system to ensure one employee is not abusing the samples by having a physician or second employee sign and review the medication logs; and

> ➤ Recording which patient received the sample medication and the treatment reason along with the physician's signature.

The check-in log should include pharmaceutical name, representative, name of prescription, quantity, employee checking in the sample, date, and total amount in inventory. Distribution of a sample should be recorded in the patient's chart, including the name of the drug, strength, date, and directions for use.

In addition to these controls, you might want to implement a program to monitor prescription management among the physicians and providers in your practice. The medical director or quality officer should review the sample medication distribution log, frequency of distributions, type of prescriptions by provider, and patient outcomes. This data might provide training opportunities for the physicians on managing quality outcomes and costs, which are becoming increasingly important in the changing healthcare environment.

For indigent patients in need of medications, you can also use the pharmaceutical manufacturers' patient assistant programs. For more information, go to www.rxassist.org.

Sources:

Barbalee Symm, PhD, RN, et al., "Effects of Using Free Sample Medications on the Prescribing Practices of Family Physicians," *Journal of the American Board of Family Medicine*, V. 19, No. 5 (2006): 443–49, www.medscape.com/viewarticle/545405 (accessed January 4, 2011).

Elaine J. Beeble, FACMPE, "Trust Is Not an Internal Control: Understanding, Assessing, and Implementing Internal Controls in a Medical Practice," ACMPE Fellowship Paper, October 2007.

Elizabeth W. Woodcock, MBA, FACMPE, CPC, and Bette A. Warn, CMPE, *MGMA Operating Policies & Procedures Manual for Medical Practices, 4th Edition*, 278–80 (Englewood, CO: Medical Group Management Association, 2011).

Mary C. Shaw, MHA, FACMPE, *The Ethical and Economic Implications of the Pharmaceutical Industry on Medical Profession Practices*, ACMPE Fellowship Paper, October 2007, www.mgma.com/WorkArea/mgma_downloadasset.aspx?id=16404 (accessed January 4, 2011).

CHAPTER 7

Quality Management

QUESTION 76 One of our payers has announced it will implement a pay-for-performance incentive program. Can you provide me with some information on the topic prior to my meeting with the representative?

Pay-for-performance (P4P) was initiated by CMS as a means to compensate physicians for quality not quantity. As healthcare costs in the United States continued to expand more than other costs, many demanded a shift away from compensating providers based on quantity of services rather than quality or outcomes. Although the success of the program in reducing costs and increasing quality is still being studied,[1,2] many private payers are adopting the concept.

P4P programs in private payers have taken a variety of forms based on the local environment, medical specialties, and the payers' prior experience or lack thereof. Typically, the plans are based on three criteria in the physician's practice:

➤ Presence of infrastructure or care delivery systems to support quality care. Example: An EHR is used to record and analyze patient care data.

A LOOK AT THE NUMBERS . . .

Thirty-seven percent of better-performing group practices participated in a P4P plan in 2009 compared to 24 percent of other practices responding to an MGMA survey. Responding better-performing groups said that the plans measured the following:

Infrastructure that supported quality care	27.9%
Clinical processes	68.2%
Medical care outcomes	42.6%

Source: Medical Group Management Association, *Performance and Practices of Successful Medical Groups: 2010 Report Based on 2009 Data* (Englewood, CO: Medical Group Management Association, 2010).

➤ Providers follow treatment plans and processes that are consistent with accepted quality indicators or clinical best practices. Example: The practice consistently reminds diabetic patients to have annual foot and eye exams.

➤ Outcome measurements are tracked and are within recommended ranges.

To thrive in P4P and shared savings reimbursement plans, practices must switch the emphasis from financial benchmarking to clinical outcomes measurement and creation of treatment standards by diagnosis. A practice must become as data-driven in its clinical arenas as it is in its financial endeavours. Timely, accurate, and accessible data brings with it an immense power for clinical process improvements and enhanced efficiencies. You may need to utilize a data warehousing, data mining, or BI program for additional analytical capabilities.

Deborah Walker Keegan offers the following advice to practice executives preparing for P4P:

➤ Develop a strategy to compete for the insurers' P4P funds;

➤ Ensure that your information systems permit you to track the course of care for patients typically measured by these programs — e.g., diabetic, asthmatic, cardiac — and that your clinical staff is actively engaged in this work;

➤ Ensure that your diagnosis and procedural coding is accurate, as that data are used to screen for quality and efficiency, resulting in differential reimbursement; and

➤ Increase efforts to involve patients in maintaining their own health and wellness.[3]

In addition, P4P demonstration projects identified the following implementation requirements from a medical practice administrative level:

➤ Senior practice leadership must be committed and engaged in the program.

➤ Providers and staff must be educated on the importance of P4P.

➤ Organizational priorities must be aligned with performance goals. Data gathering and reporting tools must be redesigned to incorporate P4P priorities.

➤ Set aside funds or investigate financing options for EHR investment.

➤ Initiate implementation of clinical measurement tracking and process improvement.

➤ Work with hospitals and other healthcare partners to improve coordination of care and information sharing.

QUESTIONS TO ASK REGARDING THE P4P PROGRAM

If you are ready to meet with the payer's representative, there are several items you'll want to understand prior to signing on to a P4P plan. The agreement must be clear on which quality measures will be used. Are the measures widely accepted and developed by physicians' professional organizations, or did the payer develop the measures? Is the emphasis on patient quality and safety or cost reduction? Will the physician performance data be adjusted for sample size and case-mix composition, including factors of age/sex distribution, severity of illness, and number of co-morbid conditions and other features of physician practice and patient population that may influence the results?

Will the practice be required to gather and report its data or will the insurer? If the insurer is gathering the data, will you have an opportunity to review and correct it? Have other practices participated in the program, and what experiences can they share?

What are the details on how reimbursement will be handled? Does it reward physician participation, including physician use of EHR and decision-support tools? Are there penalties as well as bonuses? How is the reimbursement bonus pool determined? Is it adequate to provide enough incentive compared to the increased administrative costs for the practice?

Will the data gathered for the program be utilized for other reasons, such as diverting patients to lower-cost physicians or otherwise penalizing physicians?

The Harvard School of Public Health found that P4P programs are shifting from ensuring that physicians follow recommended processes to assessing the actual outcomes. For example, rewards that were based on physicians providing prescriptions for cholesterol or hypertension are now given based on actual cholesterol levels and blood pressure rates among the physicians' patients. Unfortunately, there is too much variety in the indicators that payers use in their P4P programs. A PricewaterhouseCoopers study found that not one indicator was used by all of the plans surveyed.[4]

A CLOSER LOOK . . .

Bridges to Excellence, a Pioneering P4P Program

Bridges to Excellence (BTE) is a partnership program developed with the Leapfrog Group, the collaborative effort of major corporations, health plans, and medical professionals. BTE consists of recognition programs based on chronic conditions and recommended primary care standards. Once practices report data on complying with the recommended care standards, they are recognized for the specific programs. Its Physician Office Link module requires doctors to use e-prescribing, automatically track laboratory results, and receive electronic patient care reminders regarding medical guidelines for managing chronic conditions. Practices can also qualify for "medical home" recognition.

After completing several recognition programs and the Physician Office Link module, the provider's name is reported to participating payers who provide cash and distinction rewards. The status of BTE-recognized providers and medical practices can be shared with patients as a factor in selecting physicians from a payer's network. Health plans participating in the P4P program include Aetna, Anthem-Wellpoint, Blue Cross Blue Shield (in several states), Cigna, and United Healthcare. From 2003 to 2009, $12.4 million in rewards were paid to over 13,000 participating providers.

BTE also developed the PROMETHEUS Payment® model for rewarding providers that deliver value and improved incomes. The payment is a bundled payment, called Evidence-Informed Case Rate™ (ECR), for all providers involved in an episode of care. Pilot projects were in place at the time of this writing to evaluate the effectiveness of the ECR payment.

Sources: Bridges to Excellence Web site: www.bridgestoexcellence.org.

Julie Miller, "Provide a Good Product or Go Out of Business," *Managed Healthcare Executive*, V. 20, No. 1 (2010): 12–18.

References:

1. Tim Doran, "Lessons from Early Experience with Pay for Performance," *Disease Management & Health Outcomes*, V. 16, No. 2 (2008): 69–78.

2. Kathleen J. Mullen, Richard G. Frank, and Meredith B. Rosenthal, "Can You Get What You Pay For? Pay-for-Performance and the Quality of Healthcare Providers," *RAND Journal of Economics*, V. 41, No. 1 (2010): 64–91.

3. Deborah Walker Keegan, PhD, FACMPE, "Are You Ready for the Perfect Storm? Align Your Practice with the Changing Healthcare Environment," *MGMA Connexion*, January 2008, www.mgma.com/WorkArea/mgma_downloadasset.aspx?id=15816 (accessed December 19, 2010).

4. Richard K. Miller and Kelli Washington, "Chapter 40: Pay-for-Performance," in *Healthcare Business Market Research Handbook*, 87–88, 2010.

Sources:

Medical Group Management Association, Government Affairs, "Pay for Performance Toolkit," www.mgma.com/WorkArea/DownloadAsset.aspx?id=8720 (accessed December 19, 2010).

Michael Goler, MD, MBA, "Pay-for-Performance as a Medical Quality Initiative," ACMPE Fellowship Paper, October 2006, www.mgma.com/WorkArea/mgma_downloadasset. aspx?id=12438 (accessed February 8, 2011).

QUESTION 77 How do we locate quality measurement tools and practice guidelines if we want to participate in pay-for-performance or other quality recognition programs?

There are several medical societies, nonprofit organizations, government agencies, payers, and large healthcare purchasers that are involved in developing and implementing quality measurement programs. To participate in P4P programs, it is recommended that you contact your payers to understand their quality measurement tools and indicators, since many payers are developing their own. The following organizations are leaders in quality research, measurement, and implementation programs.

MEDICAL SOCIETIES

Many specialty societies and medical associations are involved in developing specialty-specific or physician-based quality measures.

American Medical Association-Physician Consortium for Performance Improvement (AMA-PCPI) — The AMA-PCPI was developed to enhance the "quality of care and patient safety by taking the lead in the development, testing, and maintenance of evidence-based clinical performance measures and measurement resources for physicians." It is comprised of medical specialty societies, state medical societies, American Board of Medical Specialties, professional organizations, and federal agencies. It was instrumental in developing many quality measurements used by the CMS PQRS. For more information, go to www.ama-assn.org and search "PCPI."

OTHER ASSOCIATIONS AND ORGANIZATIONS

Accreditation Association for Ambulatory Healthcare (www. aaahc.org) develops "standards to advance and promote patient safety, quality and value for ambulatory healthcare through peer-based accreditation processes, education and research." The AAAHC Institute for Quality Improvement is involved in clinical performance measurement tools designed specifically for the ambulatory care environment. AAAHC also offers medical home certification.

The Joint Commission on Accreditation of Healthcare Organization (JCAHO.org or www.jointcommission.org) accredits more than 15,000 healthcare organizations and programs. The Joint Commission maintains many standards related to quality and safety of care. It developed a Disease-Specific Care (DSC) Certification program offered to health plans, disease management companies, hospitals, and other providers that offer disease management and chronic care services. The program includes asthma, diabetes, congestive heart failure, coronary artery disease, chronic obstructive pulmonary disease, skin and wound management, and primary stroke care. The Outcome Recording to Yield eXcellence (ORYX) program integrates outcomes and other performance data in the accreditation process for hospitals.

Leapfrog Group, founded in 2000 by the Business Roundtable, includes over 174 U.S. corporations and public health benefit purchasers. It developed seven demonstration P4P programs and concluded that the concept can increase quality of care. The P4P partnership program Bridges to Excellence (BTE) is discussed in Question 76. BTE has extensive care guidelines and quality measures for its recognition programs, available on the Web site www.bridgestoexcellence.org.

Integrated Healthcare Association (IHA) (www.iha.org) includes six managed care plans in California. Participating physicians in the state are eligible for a total of $50 million annually in incentive payments. IHA publishes its measure set each year on its Web site.

National Center for Quality Assurance (NCQA) focuses on certifying managed care organizations. It developed Health Plan Employer Data and Information Set (HEDIS), standardized measures to simplify comparing the healthcare performance of managed care plans. NCQA developed many of the clinical quality measures used in the CMS PQRS program. The Web site, www.ncqa.org, includes information on the HEDIS measures and compares them with measures used by Medicare and insurance companies. It also certifies medical groups under the Physician Organization Certification Program and the Physician Practice Connections® — Patient-Centered Medical Home™.

Institute for Healthcare Improvement (IHI.org) works with JCAHO and other quality organizations to standardize P4P measures and evidence-based practices.

National Association for Healthcare Quality (NAHQ.org) is a professional association with more than 10,000 members dedicated to the advancement of the profession of healthcare quality, patient safety, and the individual professionals working in the field.

National Quality Forum (NQF) is also working to standardize healthcare quality measures and ensure consistent evidence-based practices and comparable data. The list of endorsed healthcare performance measures is available at www.qualityforum.org.

URAC (www.urac.org) accredits health plans, preferred provider organizations, and other healthcare organizations. It is involved with the "development of quantitative measures for accreditation programs and the analysis and reporting of measure results." URAC also offers a Patient Centered Healthcare (Medical) Home (PCHCH) Program.

GOVERNMENT AGENCIES

Agency for Healthcare Research and Quality (AHRQ) (www.ahrq.gov) offers two valuable clearinghouses: (1) National Quality Measures Clearinghouse (information available at www.qualitymeasures.ahrq.gov) and (2) the National Guidelines Clearinghouse (information at www.guideline.gov). A recent AHRQ initiative is the Comparative Effectiveness Research (CER) looking at the difference in costs and outcomes of various treatment options for the same conditions.

Medicare's PQRS Web site lists its annual quality measures (170 in 2011) at www.cms.gov/PQRI. CMS also offers a Quality Improvement Organizations page at www.cms.gov/QualityImprovementOrgs.

QUESTION

78

My physicians are discussing participating in the Medicare PQRS. Can you provide me with more information about it and practices' experiences with it?

The Physician Quality Report System (PQRS) is a voluntary quality-reporting program for providers participating in Medicare. It began as the Physician Voluntary Reporting Program (PVRP) in 2005 before becoming the Physician Quality Reporting Initiative (PQRI) in 2007. The name was changed to PQRS in 2011. CMS describes the system as a step to transform Medicare "from a passive payer into an active purchaser of high-quality care by linking payment to the value of care provided." The goal is to have physicians track and submit their patient care data to a system that will help them evaluate and improve the quality of care they provide.

An additional benefit in participating in PQRS at this time is to prepare the practice for a future of required quality measurement participation. In 2014, CMS will begin penalizing practices that don't participate in the program. Many commercial payers are also implementing P4P or quality reimbursement programs based on quality measure tracking and reporting.

PQRS includes quality measures for

- ➤ Diabetes mellitus;
- ➤ Coronary artery disease;
- ➤ Heart failure;
- ➤ Stroke and stroke rehabilitation;
- ➤ Perioperative care;
- ➤ Osteoporosis screening and therapy;
- ➤ Asthma;
- ➤ End-stage renal disease (ESRD);
- ➤ Adoption and use of EHRs;
- ➤ E-prescribing; and
- ➤ Coordination of care for various cancers.

Initially, the Medicare claims processing system was modified to include the submission of specific quality data codes (QDCs) for the PQRI. To address physicians' concerns, options for data submission were expanded. Physicians and NPPs can choose to report their quality measure data to

- ➤ CMS on their Medicare Part B claims;
- ➤ A qualified Physician Quality Reporting registry; or
- ➤ CMS via a qualified EHR product.

Registries are databases with data on patients with chronic conditions including asthma and diabetes or data on specific medical tests, such as Pap smears and mammograms. Since many physicians and practices already participate in medical or patient registries, it simplifies the process for reporting data to CMS. Physicians enter their data as part of regular clinical activities.

State public health departments, professional associations, and insurance companies maintain the registries. With registries, CMS created measure groups that allow smaller samples of patients with a particular diagnosis, making PQRS reporting easier. CMS maintains a list of qualified registries for PQRS, along with the certified EHR products.

Large medical group practices have been able to participate in the Group Practice Reporting Option (GPRO) if they have at least 200 eligible professionals (EPs). By the end of 2011, CMS will develop Group Practice Reporting Option II (GPRO II) for medical practices with 2 to 199 eligible professionals. Information about the self-nomination process is available at www.cms.gov/pqri.

In order to encourage participation, CMS developed an incentive program. Participants that submit data into the system and qualify are eligible for

- ➤ **2011:** 1 percent of the Medicare Part B allowed charges for professional services for the reporting period

- ➤ **2011–2014:** An additional 0.5 percent is available if the individual professional participates via a "continuous assessment program"

- ➤ **2012–2014:** 0.5 percent incentive

- ➤ **2015:** –1.5 percent penalty if practices are not successfully participating

- ➤ **2016 and beyond:** –2 percent penalty

In 2011, CMS also began additional participation methods and incentives through continuous assessment programs or Maintenance of Certification (MOC) programs, such as the American Board of Medical Specialties Maintenance of Certification (ABMS MOC) program. By January 2012, CMS must improve its timely feedback to PQRS participants.

Also in 2011, CMS launched a searchable online physician directory for Medicare patients called Physician Compare. The site includes information on physicians' addresses; gender; medical specialty; where professionals completed their degrees, residency, or other training; and whether the professional speaks languages besides English. Additionally, Physician Compare shows whether physician practices have submitted data to CMS via PQRS. Medical practices and physicians should review their data in Physician Compare, as several inaccuracies have been reported. Beginning in 2013, this Web site will also start reporting on

> ➤ Measures collected under PQRS;

> ➤ Assessment of patient health outcomes and the functional status of patients;

> ➤ Assessment of the continuity and coordination of care and care transitions, including episodes of care and risk-adjusted resource use;

> ➤ Assessment of efficiency;

> ➤ Assessment of patient experience and patient, caregiver, and family engagement;

> ➤ Assessment of the safety, effectiveness, and timeliness of care; and

> ➤ Other information as determined appropriate by the secretary.

To improve the reporting process, CMS publishes an annual PQRS (PQRI) Common Errors Report. Reviewing this report will help medical practices identify problems with previous submissions that they should avoid when submitting their data.

MGMA member practices participating in PQRS reported high levels of frustration in dealing with the system in 2008. Participants reported difficulty accessing their feedback reports, were dissatisfied with the information presented, and felt there was a lack of guidance to improve patient care. MGMA continues to work with CMS on improvements for the PQRS process.

ADDITIONAL RESOURCES

CMS Physician Quality Reporting System Web pages: www.cms.gov/PQRS

MGMA's PQRS Resource Page: www.mgma.com/pqri

Sources:

DHHS Centers for Medicare & Medicaid Services, "Physician Quality Reporting Initiative: 2007 Reporting Experience," December 3, 2008, www.cms.gov/PQRI/Downloads/PQRI2007ReportFinal12032008CSG.pdf (accessed September 15, 2011).

Medical Group Management Association, "Medical Practices Express Continued Frustration with PQRI Program," press release, February 17, 2010, www.mgma.com/press/default.aspx?id=32798&kc=WAC (accessed August 31, 2011).

MGMA Government Affairs, "Final 2011 Medicare Physician Fee Schedule Analysis," www.mgma.com/WorkArea/mgma_downloadasset.aspx?id=40300 (accessed September 15, 2011).

Richard Gliklich, MD, and Francis Campion MD, FACP, "Patient Registries: They May Ease the Challenges of PQRI Reporting," *MGMA Connexion*, January 2010, www.mgma.com/WorkArea/mgma_downloadasset.aspx?id=32150 (accessed September 15, 2011).

QUESTION 79 We'd like to conduct a patient satisfaction survey but need some advice before continuing. Also, do you have sample questionnaires?

Assessing patient satisfaction with your practice operations and physicians is important to retaining current patients who often become your best promotional tool. Many studies have also found that patient dissatisfaction related to the physician-patient relationship increases the risk of malpractice suits. Strong physician-patient relations are also a factor in patient compliance and outcomes. It is important to conduct patient surveys on a regular basis and in a manner that paints an accurate picture of patients' perceptions of your practice and relationship with physicians.

Steps in developing and implementing a patient satisfaction survey include

➤ Ensure physician and administrative members are included in planning and implementing the survey and following up on survey results.

➤ Determine if the survey will ask about one specific visit or the overall experience with the practice.

➤ Determine the budget for the survey and if it will be managed in-house or conducted by a contractor. The latter may have nationwide data for benchmarking your practice.

➤ Decide if the questionnaire will be mailed; handed out at the end of a visit; or conducted via telephone, e-mail, or

Web site. Also determine the percentage of patients who will receive the questionnaire. Using more than one format or survey device may increase the response from different patient populations.

➤ Select the frequency of survey distribution: annually, quarterly, or monthly.

➤ Develop the questions to be asked based on practice priorities. Contractors' questionnaires may be standardized.

➤ Decide how results will be shared and utilized. Who will be responsible for addressing issues raised by the results, or will individual departments be responsible? Share the results with patients and employees, and include information on how the practice plans to address concerns. This information can be posted on the practice Web site or distributed in the reception area.

The most difficult aspect is determining which questions should be included. The questionnaire should be short enough that patients don't feel burdened to complete it but long enough to gather pertinent information for practice improvement. Identify the goal of the survey and which questions best address the goal. Questions that ask for a ranking (1 to 5 or poor to excellent) will provide more information than yes/no questions. Include space for comments, especially for low rankings. End the survey with one or two open-ended questions, such as, "What can we do to improve your experience with our practice?"

Most surveys will be anonymous, but you should include an opportunity to provide name and contact information for further follow-up. This opportunity may lead to more insight on reasons for satisfaction or dissatisfaction. Assign someone to respond to these patients in a reasonable time frame.

New technology means new methods of distributing questionnaires. Ask patients if they will share their e-mail addresses to receive satisfaction surveys or communications from their physicians. Set up a computer kiosk in the check-out area for patients to complete a short survey rather than handing out a paper questionnaire.

Medical practice satisfaction surveys typically ask questions in the following areas:

➤ **Appointments and registration.** Ask about timeliness of appointments, waiting time upon arrival and in the exam room, hours of operation, and the check-in process.

➤ **Relations with staff.** Address several types of employees (receptionists, billing personnel, and so on), their professionalism, friendliness, and communication style.

➤ **Communication.** Include telephone service, returning messages, promptness of delivering test results, and after-hours issues. Determine if the Web site is easy to navigate and has the sought-after information.

➤ **Relation with physician.** Ask whether the doctor listens, is courteous and respectful, spends an adequate amount of time with them, demonstrates knowledge and skill, and sufficiently explains the diagnosis and treatment.

➤ **Facility issues.** Ask about adequate parking, difficulties in finding the practice or the specific department within the building, and the comfort of the waiting room and exam room.

After the responses are tabulated, administration and physician leaders should review the results to identify areas that need to be addressed. Decide if further surveying or analysis is necessary to identify the specific reasons for less-than-satisfactory ratings in some areas. Inform patients about the changes that are made in response to the surveys to let them know you listened and care about their comments. Begin planning the next survey to track changes in the responses and success in implementing changes.

SOURCES FOR SAMPLE SATISFACTION/PATIENT LOYALTY QUESTIONNAIRES

Star-Studded Service: 6 Steps to Winning Patient Satisfaction, by Kevin Sullivan and Meryl Luallin, Medical Group Management Association, Item #6635

MGMA.com, search for "Example Patient Satisfaction Survey" or samples shared by MGMA members in the Member Community

SullivanLuallin Healthcare Consulting, MGMA AdminiServe Partner, www.sullivan-luallin.com or 619.283.8988. Standardized survey forms and benchmarking with the MGMA-SullivanLuallin database

Sources:

Janice Chase, PHR, FACMPE, "Implementing a Patient Satisfaction Survey System," ACMPE Fellowship Paper, October 2007, www.mgma.com/WorkArea/mgma_download-asset.aspx?id=16182 (accessed February 2, 2011).

Medical Group Management Association, "Tips for Conducting a Patient Satisfaction Survey," www.mgma.com/WorkArea/mgma_downloadasset.aspx?id=30086 (accessed February 2, 2011).

 QUESTION Our patient satisfaction survey showed some issues with our employees' and physicians' relations to patients. What are other group practices doing to improve customer service?

Customer service is a major factor in satisfaction with medical practices, and employees and physicians are both involved. Contact with employees is often the first impression with the practice, from the first telephone call to the practice to the greeting at the reception desk. Patients' satisfaction with their physician relationship is a key to retention in the practice and reducing the risk of malpractice. Emphasis on service excellence should be pervasive throughout an organization; it should be part of the organization's mission, vision, and/or values statement and demonstrated by the top leadership.

To implement a plan for improving customer relations, decide which steps are needed to bring about changes. Identify the organization's goals and means of measuring progress toward the goals. Key performance indicators (KPIs) can be used to identify areas of patient dissatisfaction and be aligned with the satisfaction survey. Examples can include, "Do staff clearly describe the next step in care?" or "Are staff adequately trained to provide consistent and accurate communication?" Implement plans to address the KPIs, share the goals with physicians and employees, and monitor progress toward achieving success.

Many practices incorporate patient satisfaction in employee and physician performance appraisals or reward and incentive programs. It's important that clear and measurable factors be included in formal appraisal and reward programs. Performance reviews can be tied to an organization-wide goal of improving patient satisfaction scores. Informal reward programs can be used for immediate or frequent recognition of specific instances of outstanding customer service. For example, you might provide a small reward or public recognition for an employee's careful handling of an unhappy patient encounter that ended with a satisfactory outcome.

Impress upon physicians the importance of their relationships with patients and that excellent clinical skills are not enough. Physicians' communication styles affect patient compliance and outcomes and are a major predictor of malpractice risk. Surveys of patients involved in malpractice cases have found dissatisfaction related to the physicians' clarity and accuracy of explanation and their lack of sympathetic manner. Common in malpractice deposition transcripts were complaints regarding physicians' failure to listen to patients' concerns or to provide information during an adverse event. Other communication-related issues included disrespect or distrust, disagreement regarding expectations or treatment plans, and lack of clear, adequate information. Researchers have found that many complaints could have been

---

A LOOK AT THE NUMBERS . . .

Better-performing practices' utilization of patient satisfaction survey results

Educate staff about behavior	63%
Educate physicians about behavior	63%
Benchmark to other practices	32%
Staff performance reviews	25%
Reward outstanding customer service	18%

Source: Medical Group Management Association, *Performance and Practices of Successful Medical Groups: 2010 Report Based on 2009 Data* (Englewood, CO: Medical Group Management Association, 2010).

resolved with an apology, additional information, or by acknowledging the patient's viewpoint after an incident or adverse event.

Keys to positive physician–patient relations include

➤ Creating a positive first impression: making eye contact, acknowledging patient by name, shaking hands, and asking questions to build a connection;

➤ Demonstrating concern and listening skills during the visit and not interrupting; and

➤ Providing information to the patient in a manner that he or she can understand that is not too technical. Physicians should provide accurate descriptions of what to expect, how long something will take, and what to do if no improvement is noticed or symptoms get worse.

Organization-wide changes that can be implemented include

➤ Repeatedly communicating an emphasis on excellent service;

➤ Using respected physicians as role models;

➤ Developing metrics for measuring physician performance; and

➤ Presenting physicians with individual patient satisfaction data compared to group and nationwide data.

Case Study

Physicians in the Sharp Rees-Stealy Medical Group in San Diego, Calif., were shocked to see their patient satisfaction scores in the 25th percentile of the nationwide database of survey scores. They initially questioned the data and then began working on new behaviors and ways to increase scores. The physician compensation method was updated to include patient satisfaction and quality measurements. Survey scores increased to the 72nd percentile, and the practice received a Number 1 ranking in the Blue Cross Quality Report Card in California.

RESOURCES FOR CUSTOMER SERVICE TRAINING

Customer service training is important for everyone in the practice.

MGMA DVDs and on-demand Webinars, MGMA.com

Customer Service that Rocks! DVD, Item #9021

Think Like a Patient Creating a Culture of Exceptional Customer Service Webinar, CD format, Item #8150 or On-demand Webinar, Item #E8150

The Office Manners Matter and Courtesy Counts Webinar, CD format, Item #8148 or On-demand Webinar, Item #E8148

Other Industry Resources

The Baird Group — Training Modules	www.baird-group.com
Chart Your Course International — Gregory P. Smith	www.chartcourse.com/healthcare-customer-service.html
Coastal Training Technologies Corp	www.coastal.com/healthcare-training
CRM Learning	www.crmlearning.com/In-Healthcare-C8837.aspx
The Customer Service Group, Healthcare Division	www.customerservicegroup.com/healthcare.php
The Studer Group	www.studergroup.com
SullivanLuallin	www.sullivan-luallin.com
Press Ganey	www.pressganey.com/researchResources
Enterprise Media	www.enterprisemedia.com
Healthcare Training Programs — Carlton's Training Solutions	www.healthcaretrainingvideos.com
Medcomm-Trainex	www.medcomrn.com
Media Partners	www.media-partners.com/customer_service

Sources:

Debra Roter, MD, PH, "The Patient–Physician Relationship and Its Implications for Malpractice Litigation," *Journal of Healthcare Law & Policy*, V. 9, No. 2 (2009): 304–14.

Jeff Eckert, MBA, CFM, CMA, "A Clear & Present Measure: Take Ownership of Patient Satisfaction," *MGMA Connexion*, September 2009, www.mgma.com/WorkArea/DownloadAsset.aspx?id=30229 (accessed January 15, 2011).

Quint Studer, "Keep Your Patients Coming Back," *MGMA Connexion*, August 2008, www.mgma.com/WorkArea/DownloadAsset.aspx?id=21260 (accessed January 15, 2011).

QUESTION 81 What is lean management, and how does it apply to medical practice management?

Lean management, also known as lean thinking or lean theory, evolved out of W. Edwards Deming's analysis of Toyota manufacturing processes and total quality management. It can be summarized as doing more with less. With costs increasing faster than reimbursement, many medical practices are turning to lean thinking to eliminate wastes, streamline processes, and cut costs.

It is difficult to imagine a manufacturing theory being applied to a service like healthcare, but both provide value to customers via a series of steps or processes.

The key is identifying waste in time, effort, and materials that is adding costs and slowing patient flow and other processes while still maintaining or increasing value for the customer. The ultimate customer is the patient, but other customers include staff members, vendors, and other healthcare providers.

You may think your practice is operating at peak efficiency, but there are always means of improving and streamlining processes. Cindy L. Dunn, of MGMA's Health Care Consulting Group, provides the following examples of waste in medical group practices:

➤ **Overproduction.** Healthcare services that do not add value to patients, including "just-in-case" work and printing paperwork or purchasing items before needed, resulting in inventory storage.

➤ **Material movement.** Excessive e-mail attachments; multiple handoffs and approvals; moving patients, specimens, or equipment; and too many trips to and from the computer, copier, or fax machine.

➤ **Waiting time for test results and medical records.** Physicians waiting for patients in the exam room or for results and records; nurses waiting on patients, physicians, or other departments; and precertification and system downtime.

➤ **Extra processing.** Repeat registration and form completion, retesting, re-entering data, making extra copies, creating unnecessary or excessive reports, and logging requests.

➤ **Inventory.** Patients or physicians waiting for anything, test scheduling and results, calls from other offices, filled "in" boxes (electronic and paper), office supplies, sales literature, batch processing transactions, and reports.

➤ **Defects — rework.** Order entry errors, design errors, employee turnover, wrong patient or procedure, missing or incomplete information, misdirected results, and billing errors.

➤ **Motion.** Excess reaching, walking, lifting, or bending; searching for charts, forms, or staff; and long hallways.

➤ **Untapped employee creativity/potential.** "Do what you're told," suppressed ideas and learning, excessive manuals/procedures, training not valued or offered, minimal communication, disengaged staff, and waiting for decisions.

The major tool in lean management is Value Stream Mapping (VSM), the analysis of the flow of materials and information to bring a product or service to a customer (patient). The goal is to identify the current process (current map) and envision the desired outcome (future map) while evaluating the value-added activities within the process.

The steps in VSM are

➤ Develop a team comprised of physicians and employees from several different departments.

➤ Select a process for analysis and improvement. Processes could be patient flow within the practice, referral management, test or lab ordering, and reporting results. Identify the start and end of the process.

➤ Determine who the customers are in the process. There can be more than one customer, and they can be internal or external.

➤ Map the process using input from team members and staff involved in the process. Make a note card for each step, and display them in chronological order.

➤ Analyze the current process.

   ➤ Look for places where work piles up, people are waiting, or other slowdowns. Mark the note cards with a "Q" for queues or similar notation.

   ➤ Note steps that require a check or review with a checkmark. Identify other options for completing the task.

   ➤ Walk through the process as if you are a document or patient in the process. Time the steps during the walk-through and note possible delays or variations. Concentrate on what occurs 80 percent of the time while minimizing what occurs during the remaining 20 percent.

   ➤ Count the number of steps, queues, handoffs, checks, and options to complete the process.

   ➤ Compare the identified process with written procedures. Are there any deviations, shortcuts, or inconsistencies due to personnel differences?

   ➤ Identify who is completing the tasks. Is it appropriate for their level of license, or should other staff be accomplishing it?

Draw the future map by identifying the ideal process based on the previous steps. Can steps be eliminated with new equipment, changing the order, or changing inputs or supplies? Can steps be combined? Future maps can be hand drawn or created by a computer program. The important thing is to illustrate the new process and steps within it.

If the future map identifies processes that can be eliminated or combined, then you've reduced waste and streamlined a process. After the identified changes are implemented, check on the process to ensure it operates smoothly but maintains the same results or improves them. As long as the goal is maintaining value for the customer, the VSM will succeed.

Elizabeth W. Woodcock, medical practice speaker and writer, reminds us that we need to focus on the people as well as the process for lean thinking to succeed. Involving staff from a variety of departments and positions in the VSM ensures several different viewpoints will be identified. Surprising ideas may come from employees who have the most contact with customers or those from outside the process looking at it with a fresh set of ideas. Employees may be concerned that lean thinking will mean lean staffing and a threat to their job security. These concerns need to be addressed.

Sources:

Cindy L. Dunn, RN, FACMPE, "Lean Healthcare: It Can Work in Your Practice," *Directions Newsletter*, Spring 2010, www.mgma.com/WorkArea/mgma_downloadasset. aspx?id=34036 (accessed February 2, 2011).

Elizabeth W. Woodcock, MBA, FACMPE, CPC, *Mastering Patient Flow: Using Lean Thinking to Improve Your Practice Operations, 3rd Edition*, 11–40 (Englewood, CO: Medical Group Management Association, 2009).

Owen J. Dahl, FACHE, CHBC, "Lean Theory Hits The News," *Directions Newsletter*, Spring 2010, www.mgma.com/WorkArea/mgma_downloadasset.aspx?id=34036 (accessed February 2, 2011).

Rosemarie Nelson, MS, "Lean Techniques Can Improve Practices' Operations, Bottom Lines," *MGMA e-Source*, February 9, 2010, www.mgma.com/article.aspx?id=32744 (accessed February 2, 2011).

QUESTION 82

We will be hiring a new physician soon. What steps can I take to ensure the credentialing process goes smoothly?

Credentialing is the process of having a physician accepted into a health plan network or onto a hospital's medical staff. The approval occurs after the payers or hospitals review and verify the doctor's credentials. Health plans conduct credentialing to protect themselves from providers' or patients' lawsuits, comply with accreditation requirements, and promote the quality of their provider network to consumers and employers. Medical practice administrators frequently complain about the delays and overhead commitments related to physician credentialing. One-fifth of MGMA members responding to a survey stated that dealing with Medicare and commercial payer credential processes was a considerable challenge.

Similar processes are involved for credentialing NPPs. Check with the hospitals and payers for NPP credentialing requirements and processes.

Prior to submitting the physician's credentials, ensure you've done the homework first. With the physician, verify

➤ Accuracy of the physician's information prior to hiring. Complete your own primary source check to ensure the certifications, specialty, and training are as stated, and there are no malpractice claims of concern;

➤ The curriculum vitae (CV) includes month, year, and location for all training and work history along with the start date at your practice; and

➤ That you have secured a copy of the NPI letter and Social Security card along with

➤ Licenses;

➤ DEA certificate and list of controlled substances, depending on state regulations;

➤ Proof and history of malpractice coverage;

➤ Specialty board certificate(s); and

➤ Proof of training.

Obtaining hospital privileges for the new physician is the first step, since it's often a prerequisite for payer's credentialing. Physicians must have access to the labs, radiology facilities, and hospital within a health plan's network, or they won't be added to the physician network. Hospitals obtain primary source information to verify credentials and have it reviewed by the credentials committee, medical executive committee, and board of directors. The process may take two to six months.

Health plans typically follow NCQA credentialing standards. The health plan's credentialing committee will review the primary source verification of the physician's credentials. If approved, the physician's NPI, tax identification numbers, location, and specialties are entered into the payer's database. If there are any errors, it will delay or stop reimbursement of any submitted claims. For example, only CPT codes associated with the physician's specialty will be paid.

The payer's process also takes two to six months and may include a site visit before the location is added to the database. A site visit will rate the office on factors such as quality of records, use of EHRs or other information technology, training, and overall condition of the office.

Hospitals, commercial payers, and medical practices may use a credential verification organization (CVO) to obtain and verify the credentials. They will ensure the integrity of the information and their report.

Medicare's credentialing process is even more involved. Providers may choose the Internet-based enrollment process or the paper forms. The Internet-based version of PECOS has many advantages including quicker processing and an audit function to check for all required information, plus it uses e-mails for missing information or other errors, and it can provide status updates.

Currently, there are three forms related to credentialing and one for electronic funds transfer (EFT):

➤ **855B** — to establish or change a practice group number or information including participating physician NPIs. This form is also used for ambulatory surgery centers, clinical laboratories, and diagnostic testing centers;

➤ **855I** — to establish or reactivate a physician or nonphysician provider's individual number to obtain Medicare billing privileges with the Medicare state or regional contractor;

➤ **855R** — to link the physician's individual number to the group or facility's number. This must be signed by the physician and the group's authorized official; and

➤ **588** — to receive payments via EFT, which is required for new practices and providers who do not reassign their benefits.

Because of the length of time involved and the importance of credentialing for billing and reimbursement, the process should begin as soon as the physician accepts the offer from your practice. Obtaining primary source verification and double-checking every form for accuracy and completeness will reduce the number of delays at a later time.

If some insurance companies haven't credentialed the new physician by the start date, you have three choices on how to proceed:

➤ Limit the physician to patients under the insurance companies that have credentialed him or her;

➤ Schedule any patient and hold claims until credentialing occurs; or

➤ Schedule some patients and assume the loss.

A few payers will reimburse the difference when credentialing is completed, but confirm this first. One practice scheduled some patients with their new physician and processed the claims as out of network but only charged the patients the in-network charge.

ADDITIONAL RESOURCES

Centers for Medicare and Medicaid Services, Medicare Provider-Supplier Enrollment Web page, www.cms.gov/MedicareProviderSupEnroll

National Center for Quality Assurance, www.ncqa.org

Healthcare Credentialing Handbook, Wolters Kluwer Publishers, MGMA Item #7001

"Physician Credentialing Policies and Procedures," *Information Exchange*, MGMA Item #8308 (informal survey with key findings)

Sources:

Medical Group Management Association and American Medical Association, "The Medicare Provider Enrollment Toolkit," August 2010, www.mgma.com/WorkArea/DownloadAsset.aspx?id=28064 (accessed February 2, 2011).

Medical Group Management Association, "Party Line: Credentialing Conundrum," *MGMA Connexion*, November/December 2008, www.mgma.com/WorkArea/mgma_downloadasset.aspx?id=24324 (accessed February 2, 2011).

Michelle McFarlane, MSN, MBA, "Street Cred: Smoothing Bumps in the Road to Physician Credentialing," *MGMA Connexion*, April 2009, www.mgma.com/WorkArea/mgma_downloadasset.aspx?id=28018 (accessed February 2, 2011).

QUESTION 83 Do you have information on patient safety programs in medical practices?

Developing a patient safety program in your practice benefits the practice by improving patient care and satisfaction while reducing the risk of malpractice. One adverse incident could ruin the reputation of your practice. MGMA, in cooperation with the Health Research and Educational Trust and the Institute for Safe Medication Practices, has developed the Pathways for Patient Safety™ program and a patient safety assessment tool.

Your practice may already be showing signs of patient safety issues if you have had malpractice claims, patient complaints, stories about close calls or adverse events, or if staff members have expressed concerns.

The first step in developing a patient safety program is fostering a culture of teamwork and good communication. Research in a variety of industries has shown that teamwork and communication reduce the risk of adverse events, and healthcare studies show that ineffective communication is the cause of most errors rather than individual actions. High-performance teams have effective leaders, monitor each other's performance, support the needs of others, and are aware of their surroundings and how conditions will affect safety.

The practice should have a designated safety officer and a safety team, but each employee should be a participant in the patient safety program. Every employee should feel comfortable in saying CUS — "I am *concerned* or *uncomfortable*" or "This is a *safety* issue" — whenever they spot or sense a potential safety breach. The safety officer and/or team should be ready to respond whenever they hear a CUS.

Patients should also be involved and listened to when they express their own concerns; they know when something does not seem right. Providers must ensure that they listen to patients' reservations, answer questions in understandable language, and ask patients to repeat care instructions to limit the chance of misunderstandings.

The second step in developing a safety program is to assess your current patient safety processes and operations. The Physician Practice Patient Safety Assessment™ (PPPSA) is available for free on the MGMA Web site. The tool also provides ideas for improving patient safety and compares your results with those of other participants.

The key areas to review while conducting an assessment are

➤ **Medications.** Items to review include

➤ Are lists of prescriptions in the patients' records complete and accurate?

➤ Are the lists given to and reviewed with patients on a regular basis?

➤ Are there barriers in patients obtaining or taking prescriptions?

➤ Are medications checked for interactions?

➤ **Handoffs and transitions.** The process of referring patients to or receiving patients from other providers and healthcare facilities. Incidents often occur with incomplete or miscommunicated information.

➤ **Surgery or other procedures.** Especially those involving anesthesia or sedation.

➤ **Personnel qualifications.** Practices should ensure providers have and maintain the education and skills to perform specific procedures and practice safe care, including appropriate continuing education.

➤ **Practice management or culture.** Ensuring patient safety and a culture of patient-centered care is instilled throughout the organization.

➤ **Patient education and communication.** Do patients have the health literacy to follow providers' instructions, and do they have a commitment to comply with the instructions and participate in their care plans?

The self-assessment will identify gaps and opportunities related to patient safety. The next step is to implement changes to fill in the gaps and educate employees about the changes. The final step is to develop an ongoing program that ensures safety is a continuous commitment, that safety reviews are conducted regularly, and that patient safety remains integral to practice culture.

Your patient safety program should include the steps to take when an adverse event occurs. Prior to any incident the patient safety officer and physicians should discuss how the practice will respond to the patient involved in the incident. Several states have regulations regarding the reporting and response to adverse events and patient safety issues. The Patient Safety and Quality Improvement Act (PSQIA) of 2005 led to the development of Patient Safety Organizations (PSOs) responsible for the collection and analysis of confidential medical-error information that healthcare providers voluntarily report. More information about the PSQIA is available at www.hhs.gov/ocr/privacy.

Case Study

Dartmouth-Hitchcock Medical Center and its Community Group Practices of Bedford, N.H., is an example of an organization that has instilled a culture of safety. They have committees on clinical quality and patient safety and track quality metrics as part of their balance scorecard. They've also implemented several steps that any group practice can implement to improve patient safety:

➤ Insisting on hand hygiene with regular hand washing or use of antibacterial hand solutions.

➤ "Ensuring that you're right — all the time." This means double-checking patient identification, medication dosage, the correct site, and treatment.

➤ Reporting test and lab results promptly.

➤ Reducing or eliminating latex products that may trigger allergic reactions.

➤ Measuring efforts against internal and external benchmarks.

Conducting a self-assessment and implementing simple steps can go a long way to improve patient safety within your practice. Soliciting participation from all employees, physicians, and patients and developing a culture of teamwork and safety will enhance patient safety even more.

Sources:

Christine Schon, MPA, FACMPE, "Safe, Sure and Savvy: Patient Safety is Part of Quality Management," *MGMA Connexion*, April 2009, www.mgma.com/WorkArea/mgma_downloadasset.aspx?id=27934 (accessed February 3, 2011).

Medical Group Management Association, Health Research and Educational Trust, and Institute for Safe Medication Practices, *Pathways for Patient Safety, Module One: Working as a Team* and *Module Two: Assessing Where You Stand*, 2008 www.mgma.com/pppsapathways (accessed August 31, 2011).

A CLOSER LOOK . . .

12 Questions Every Administrator Should Answer about Patient Safety

➤ Who is our patient safety advocate?

➤ How can I understand what safe care is?

➤ Are my goals and performance metrics providing an accurate picture?

➤ What should our patient safety goal be?

➤ What is the relationship between patient safety and the other practice-performance metrics?

➤ Can we measure our patients' exposure to adverse events, injury, and death?

➤ How can we create a culture that will allow the reporting of patient safety information?

➤ How do our clinicians view patient safety?

➤ What resources can we redirect to achieve our patient safety goals?

➤ Are we really committed to patient safety?

➤ Do our partners, stakeholders, patients, and families know that we are moving toward a culture of safety?

➤ Have we exempted anyone from the process?

Source: Bergitta Smith, "Patient Safety: 12 Important Questions," from "The High Road to Risk Reduction and Cost Savings" presentation at the MGMA 2007 Annual Conference, Philadelphia, PA, October 29, 2007, www.mgma.com/WorkArea/mgma_downloadasset.aspx?id=18780 (accessed February 3, 2011).

CHAPTER 8

Risk Management

QUESTION

84

I've been assigned to develop a risk management plan for the practice? What should I include in the plan?

Risk management in medical practices has typically concentrated on medical malpractice issues. However, there are other potential threats to the practice's assets including its financial assets, personnel, property, and reputation. Developing a risk management plan is only one step in the process of protecting the practice's financial assets, employee well-being, patient safety, and the ongoing trust and reputation of the practice.

There are four key components in the risk management process:

➤ **Risk assessment** — identification of potential threats and your exposure;

➤ **Loss control** — selection of options for addressing risks and reducing exposure;

➤ **Risk financing** — purchasing insurance or self-insuring; and

➤ **Monitoring** — ongoing behaviors to minimize risks and control potential losses.

To conduct a risk assessment and analysis, consult with insurance company representatives and risk management specialists. Discuss with staff and physicians areas of potential concern that they've noticed and complaints from patients. Conduct self-assessments from one of the published resources or insurance application forms. The latter alerts you to areas the insurance companies identify as high risks. An excellent resource in patient safety risk assessment is the PPPSA developed by MGMA and others. The safety assessment and other patient safety issues are discussed in Question 83.

Although patient safety issues attract the most attention in medical practices, they aren't the only risk. Other threats include natural disasters (see Question 85), employee injuries, and information technology failures. Assessments should include possibilities of human errors, system failures, and external issues, including influenza pandemics.

Loss control is addressed in developing and implementing plans and processes to minimize the chance of a risk occurring and the steps to mitigate the damage after an event occurs. Effective plans and processes should also minimize the consequences of Occupational Safety and Health Administration (OSHA) or other agency audits. Risk management plans should include

➤ Identification of potential risks addressed in the plan, not meant to be comprehensive but to create awareness;

➤ Methods and steps to eliminate or reduce each type of risk and the potential severity;

➤ Communication protocols for responding to an incident; and

➤ Monitoring to ensure ongoing risk reduction practices and compliance with practice policies and procedures.

Potential patient and employee safety risks to include in the plan are bloodborne pathogens; hazardous materials; hazardous wastes; ergonomics; personal protective equipment; respiratory safety; fire and other emergency responses; emergency exit planning, including patient evacuation; infection control; response to pandemic declarations; medication and prescription issues; lab safety and other issues; medical emergency response; workplace safety; workplace violence and security; and human relations issues. The latter includes drug testing, harassment, grievances, and privacy.

Additional patient safety steps should be in place, including ensuring that personnel are qualified for the procedures they perform, that all risks related to surgical and invasive procedures are minimized, and that checks are in place to confirm medications and effective patient communication. Risk management should be part of the organization's culture to ensure that every step and employee is in compliance with normal procedures and safety measures.

Loss control should also address business operations and the threat and response to the loss of business information in cases of natural disasters and information system failures. Inappropriate access to funds or private information should also be minimized. Management plans should include security and backup procedures.

Risk financing is usually done through contracts with commercial insurers for malpractice, natural disaster, business loss, or workers' compensation insurance. The company representatives will offer advice on recommended types of coverage, size of policy, and risk-reduction steps. What won't be covered must be clearly understood. Some organizations choose to self-insure for some incidents, particularly incidents with a predicted frequency and consistent value in the loss. Self-insurers must maintain sufficient funds to cover these losses.

The designated risk management officer and/or committee must conduct monitoring on a regular basis. The officer or committee is the contact point in the communication plan and should review the incident reporting form, responses to previous incidents, and documentation compliance. Besides monitoring implementation and compliance with the risk management plan, the officer or committee should address new issues that appear within the practice, potential new external threats, and new federal and state regulations. Hold periodic meetings with insurance representatives to review policies and new risk-reduction and mitigation ideas.

ADDITIONAL RESOURCES

Barbara J. Youngberg, editor, *Principles of Risk Management and Patient Safety* (Sudbury, MA: Jones and Bartlett Learning, 2011)

Carolyn Pickles, MBA, FACMPE, and Alys Novak, MBA, *Assessment Workbook for Medical Practices, 5th Edition* (Englewood, CO: Medical Group Management Association, 2011)

Lewis Lorton, *Risk Assessment and Management Guide for the Medical Practice* (Chicago, IL: American Medical Association)

Medical Group Management Association, *Body of Knowledge Review: Risk Management* (Englewood, CO: Medical Group Management Association, 2009)

Sources:

Carolyn Pickles, MBA, FACMPE, and Alys Novak, MBA, *Assessment Workbook for Medical Practices, 5th Edition* (Englewood, CO: Medical Group Management Association, 2011).

Health Research & Educational Trust, Institute for Safe Medication Practices, and Medical Group Management Association, *Pathways for Patient Safety™ Assessing Where You Stand, Module Two*, 2008, www.pathwaysforpatientsafety.org.

Medical Group Management Association, *Body of Knowledge Review: Risk Management, Volume 8* (Englewood, CO: Medical Group Management Association, 2009).

QUESTION 85   What should be included in a disaster plan, and do you have any samples?

Disaster plans, properly called disaster preparedness or recovery plans, should include sections on risk assessment, response, and business continuity. Risk assessment identifies the variety of disasters that threaten the practice with loss of property, medical and business records, human safety, and continuity of operations. The destructive hurricanes to hit U.S. coasts in recent years, including Hurricane Katrina, are a reminder of the potential devastation of natural forces and the difficulty in recovering, but they are only one type of disaster that may strike. Review other potential natural disasters that could occur in your location, including flooding, earthquakes, blizzards, and tornadoes. Even severe thunderstorms could cause power outages that impact operations and safety. Additional incidents that should be included are epidemics, chemical or biological attacks, and infrastructure failures (water leaks or computer system crashes).

It may help to separate the risks into categories of high-impact/high-likelihood, high-impact/low-likelihood, low-impact/high-likelihood, and low-impact/low-likelihood events. The categories will help in prioritizing the threats and preparing responses.

Disaster recovery plans should be developed incorporating ideas and concerns from several departments. They should include issues related to patient and employee safety, practice finances, and business continuity. The following is a checklist for plan development and implementation.

PATIENT SAFETY

➤ Does the medical group have detailed evacuation plans? Has it carried out practice evacuation drills with staff, using people simulating patients with various stages of mobility and without using the elevators?

➤ How is responsibility designated for ensuring the practice's evacuation and securing the premises?

➤ If the power goes off, what backup power system is in place?

➤ Do you have a contingency plan developed with other providers, clinics, and hospitals — including emergency departments — to accept the practice's patients?

➤ Have you discussed with supply vendors their capabilities during local, regional, or national emergencies?

EMPLOYEE SECURITY

➤ Have you designated an off-site location for employees to meet following an emergency?

➤ Is a list of employees, contact information, and emergency contacts maintained in a secure or off-site location accessible immediately after a disaster?

➤ Physicians and staff members worrying about loved ones will not function effectively during a crisis. Do you have a plan for the safety of employees' families?

➤ Do employees understand their roles in an emergency?

➤ Have you developed a chain of command that anticipates the loss of key personnel? Do employees know who will step up to assist management?

➤ Do managers and supervisors know their roles in tracking employees and patients during an emergency? Is their contact information accessible and secure?

➤ Do you have an employee assistance program to help employees deal with the aftermath of a crisis?

PRACTICE FINANCES

➤ How will you handle payroll, payments, and collections if the banking system shuts down? Have you contacted your banking representative to discuss backup plans?

➤ Does the practice have a safe to hold cash deposits while financial institutions are closed?

➤ Are duplicate financial and business records stored off-site?

➤ Have you designated backup personnel who can obtain off-site records if key personnel are not available?

PRACTICE CAPABILITY

➤ What backup system do you have for medical records? How will you access backup records immediately after the disaster?

➤ What plans do you have for accessing clinical information during power outages or other failures of the EHR?

➤ Does the disaster plan include a list of local health department and emergency manager points of contact? Will the list be accessible during a crisis?

➤ What is the role of the practice in the community disaster plan? Does a practice representative meet with community leaders on community response?

➤ Is the practice prepared to respond to public health outbreaks, like influenza pandemics, that might put employees and patients at risk for life-threatening illnesses?

➤ Have you developed plans for practice downtime? How rapidly could you establish a temporary clinic?

➤ How and who will inform patients of the disaster and how to contact the practice?

➤ Is there an off-site number employees can call for current information?

➤ Do you have arrangements to duplicate the practice computer system while a destroyed system is being replaced or rebuilt?

> ➤ Does the practice store key employee computer passwords and access codes off-site?

> ➤ Do you have a list of vendors who provide disaster recovery services?

With each item in the disaster plan, identify who has chief responsibility for monitoring compliance with the plan and taking the steps during or after the disaster. The plan should be tested, initially in small parts and then in a full-scale drill. Expect failures to occur and learn from them.

Smooth emergency evacuations occur with practice and clear assignments. Evacuation drills should be held periodically in cooperation with local fire departments. Assign employees with responsibilities to ensure safe patient evacuation and that all parts of the building are cleared and what items, if any, should be removed during an evacuation of the practice. The latter may include contact lists and resources vital to business continuity, including checkbooks, passwords, and backup tapes. If time allows, additional steps may mitigate the disaster including protecting computer systems, covering important files and equipment, turning off servers, and forwarding phones to the answering service.

It's impossible to fully prepare for major disasters, but having a disaster preparedness and recovery plan in place will help ensure patient and employee safety and minimize the upheaval to business operations.

Sources:

Karen Coffman, CMPE, "Safety in Numbers: Your Group's Emergency Preparedness Should Mesh with the Community's," *MGMA Connexion*, September 2009.

Lorraine C. Woods, FACMPE, "Disaster Recovery Plans: Develop Them Step by Step," *MGMA e-Source*, September 11, 2007, www.mgma.com/article.aspx?id=14468 (accessed January 23, 2011).

Medical Group Management Association, *Body of Knowledge Review: Risk Management, Volume 8* (Englewood, CO: Medical Group Management Association, 2009).

Thomas P. Peterson, MBA, FACMPE. "Know-How: Be Prepared — A Checklist to Help Ready Your Practice for an Emergency," *MGMA Connexion*, V. 2, No. 1, January 2002, www.mgma.com/articles/index.cfm?fuseaction=detail.main&articleID=11928 (accessed August 10, 2006).

QUESTION **86** I need to review and update our fraud and abuse compliance plan. Do you have any samples I can work from?

MGMA does have several online and print resources that provide information in developing compliance plans; however, each practice is different, so each compliance program must be written in alignment with a practice's size, specialty, state regulations, and culture. Use the following general information to assess your practice's current plan and the list of resources for more detailed information.

AUDIT ALERT!

The Patient Protection and Affordable Care Act (PPACA) requires physicians who treat Medicare and Medicaid beneficiaries to establish a compliance program. Ensuring that your compliance plan is complete and current keeps you ahead of the auditors.

There are several federal regulations that address fraud and abuse and apply to physicians:

> **False Claims Act (FCA) [31 U.S.C. §§3729-3733 and 18 U.S.C. §1341 and 1343 for criminal cases].** Prohibits the submission of claims for Medicare payment that are knowingly false or fraudulent. Fines for filing false claims may be up to three times Medicare's loss plus $11,000 per claim. The act includes actions that were the result of "deliberate ignorance or reckless disregard of the truth," as well as willingly and knowingly submitting a false claim. Private payers in civil court can also use the law.

> Actions that frequently lead to suits under the FCA include

>> Billing for services that weren't provided;

>> Billing for services provided by improperly supervised or unqualified employees;

- ➤ Upcoding or billing for a higher service than what was provided;

- ➤ Falsely claiming the medical necessity of services;

- ➤ Unbundling or billing for procedures separately that are normally billed as a single charge;

- ➤ Repeated overutilization of medical services regardless of patient's response, condition, or medical needs; and

- ➤ Improper or inappropriate use of billing codes in a consistent manner.

➤ **Anti-Kickback Statute (AKS) [42 U.S.C. §1320a-7b(b)].** Prohibits physicians from receiving remuneration as an incentive for patient referrals or other services for Medicare or Medicaid patients. Remuneration includes cash, free rent, trips, or excessive compensation for medical director or consultant services. There are specific safe harbors that protect physicians from AKS prosecution. More information is available on the OIG Web site/Safe Harbor Regulations page: http://oig.hhs.gov/fraud/safeharborregulations.asp.

Anti-kickback provisions apply to all referral sources, including patients. For example, it is illegal to routinely waive the payment of Medicare copayments. It is legal to provide free or discounted services to an uninsured or Medicare patient if it is an individual decision based on the patient's ability to pay. Accepting gifts from a drug company or durable medical equipment (DME) supplier is also prohibited.

➤ **Physician Self-Referral Law [42 U.S.C. §1395nn], also known as the Stark law.** Discussed in Question 88.

➤ **Exclusion Statute [42 U.S.C. §1320a-7].** Prohibits any individual or entity from participation in federal health programs if they've been convicted of Medicare or Medicaid fraud, patient abuse or neglect, other healthcare-related felony convictions, or felony convictions related to controlled substances.

The compliance plan in your practice should address these regulations as well as any applicable state regulations. You should also review contracts with your payers to ensure compliance with their specific requirements. The OIG has developed a "Compliance Program for Individual and Small Group Physician Practices" that can serve as a basis for your plan. Compliance plans in medical practices should include the following features:

➤ Corporate compliance officer or the person in a smaller practice who is responsible for overseeing the compliance program.

➤ Code of conduct that specifies appropriate behavior and the commitment to compliance. It should include the principles of complying with federal, state, and local laws and regulations; accurately documenting services; providing high-quality patient care; and acting in a lawful and ethical manner at all times.

➤ Training program to ensure employees and physicians understand the regulations, definitions of fraudulent behavior, and the organization's policies and procedures related to compliance. Employees should sign forms showing completion of training programs and commitment to codes of conduct.

➤ Communication channels for reporting behavior prohibited by regulations and in conflict with the compliance plan. Confidential channels are recommended.

➤ Procedures for auditing and monitoring to identify potentially fraudulent behavior. Accepted mechanisms for showing audit and review include testing billing and coding staff on their knowledge; confirming employee training; and reviewing previous compliance-related reprimands, analysis, or coding and billing activities. Auditors should be knowledgeable and objective.

➤ Consequences for inappropriate behavior, including disciplinary plans or potential penalties. Policies should specify planned disciplinary action to ensure consistent actions and should include reaction to committing offenses as well as failing to report an offense.

After the compliance plan is completed, the practice leadership should demonstrate its commitment to abide by the plan and support the compliance officer. It should be integrated with the practice's other policies, procedures, and operations rather than treated as an afterthought. The plan is an important step in documenting the practice's commitment to corporate compliance. The documentation should continue by accurately recording the provision of health services, employees' training, details related to auditing and monitoring actions, detection of any questionable behavior, and actions taken in response to the incident.

If gaps are found in the compliance program itself, it should be modified and updated. Be aware of regulatory changes by watching for MGMA Government Affairs or OIG alerts, including monitoring the OIG's annual work plans and fraud alerts that apply to medical practices.

ADDITIONAL RESOURCES

U.S. Department of Health & Human Services, Office of Inspector General, "A Roadmap for Physicians, Avoiding Medicare and Medicaid Fraud and Abuse," www.oig.hhs.gov/fraud/PhysicianEducation

MGMA Government Affairs Web page, www.mgma.com/policy

American Medical Association, *Avoiding Fraud and Abuse in the Medical Office*, MGMA Item #8316

Duane C. Abbey, *Compliance for Coding, Billing and Reimbursement, 2nd Edition*, MGMA Item #7083

Patricia A. Trites, *Compliance Guide for the Medical Practice: How to Attain and Maintain a Compliant Medical Practice*, American Medical Association, MGMA Item #6802

Sources:

John S. Cunningham, MS, MBA, FAMPE, "Doing the Right Thing Right," *MGMA Connexion*, January 2007, www.mgma.com/WorkArea/mgma_downloadasset.aspx?id=11034 (accessed January 24, 2011).

Lawrence F. Wolper, FACMPE, "Implementing a Physician Practice Compliance Program," in *Physician Practice Management: Essential Operational and Financial Knowledge*, 383–411 (Sudbury, MA: Jones and Bartlett Publishers, 2005).

Medical Group Management Association, "Healthcare Reform Creates New Enforcement Focus on Medical Group Compliance Plans," *MGMA Washington Connexion*, May 12, 2010, www.mgma.com/article.aspx?id=33645 (accessed January 24, 2011).

U.S. Department of Health & Human Services, Office of Inspector General, "A Roadmap for Physicians, Avoiding Medicare and Medicaid Fraud and Abuse," www.oig.hhs.gov/fraud/PhysicianEducation (accessed January 24, 2011).

QUESTION 87   What should we be doing to prepare for a RAC audit?

The HHS began the Recovery Audit Contractors (RACs) Program to address Medicare fraud and abuse. The RAC program began as a demonstration in 2005, became permanent and nationwide under a 2006 act, and expanded to include Medicare Advantage (Part C) and Medicaid under the PPACA.

The purpose of RAC audits is to use private contractors to identify improper payments in Medicare and Medicaid claims. Contractors will be compensated on a contingency basis dependent on the amounts of overpayment identified.

Improper payments can include payments for noncovered services, services not defined as medically necessary, and incorrectly coded or duplicate services. If a RAC finds both over- and underpayments from a provider, it offsets the underpayment with the overpayment. If the RAC finds only an underpayment, it notifies the Medicare claims processing contractor, which will process the claim adjustment and payment to the provider.

To prepare for a RAC audit, you should

➤ Identify a RAC contact person within the practice;

➤ Audit internal practices and documentation to ensure compliance with billing and fraud and abuse regulations;

➤ Review your compliance program (see Question 86); and

➤ Monitor information from CMS and MGMA regarding RAC audits. They will list issues and codes that will be targeted.

Reviews can be conducted by analyzing the claims data based on statistical norms (automated reviews) or detailed reviews of medical records (complex reviews). If your practice is identified for a RAC audit, the contractor will send a letter requesting medical records. If an auditor appears at your location without a letter, you have the right to refuse access and request a formal letter. The RAC may review Medicare claims up to three years old.

If violations were found during the audit, the RAC will notify you. This letter should state the following:

➤ The coverage, coding, or payment policy that was violated;

➤ A reason for conducting the review;

➤ A description of the overpayment situation;

➤ Recommended corrective actions;

➤ An explanation of the provider's right to submit a rebuttal statement prior to recoupment of any overpayment;

➤ An explanation of the procedures for recovery of overpayments;

➤ The provider's right to request an extended repayment schedule; and

➤ Information on the provider's right to appeal

If you decide to appeal the decision, you have a total of 120 days to request a redetermination. For appeal requests received within 30 days, the RAC must halt attempts to obtain payment for the violation. Interest will begin accruing 31 days after receipt of the letter declaring the violation. If the contractor confirms the violation, providers may file a request for reconsideration within 180 days.

RAC audits began with hospitals and are moving to medical practices. Group practices can learn from the analysis of the RAC audits that have been performed since the program began. Although review is intended to uncover both over- and under-payments, 96 percent of the identified violations have been for overpayments, not underpayments. As of October 2010, hospitals reported appealing 16 percent of RAC denials, and 13 percent of those appeals were decided in favor of the provider.

Sources:

Abby Pendleton, "Recovery Audit Contractors: The RAC Attack," presentation, www. mgma.com/WorkArea/DownloadAsset.aspx?id=40723 (accessed January 24, 2011).

Matthew Vuletich, "The Word on the Street about RAC Audits," *MGMA e-Source*, October 12, 2010, www.mgma.com/article.aspx?id=39646 (accessed January 24, 2011).

MGMA Recovery Audit Contractors (RACs) Resource Center, www.mgma.com/policy/ default.aspx?id=23052 (accessed January 24, 2011).

MGMA Government Affairs, "Frequently Asked Questions about Medicare Recovery Audit Contractors (RACs)," www.mgma.com/policy/default.aspx?id=28136 (accessed January 24, 2011).

QUESTION 88 We are considering a joint venture with another facility. What should we watch out for related to the Stark law?

The Stark law prohibits physicians from referring Medicare or Medicaid patients to a medical facility for certain health services if the physician has a financial relationship with that facility except under specific circumstances. The first "Stark law" was passed in 1989 and has been modified by several acts and regulations. The legislation can be found in the United States Code, 42 U.S.C. § 1395nn.

The designated health services covered under the law include clinical laboratory services, physical therapy, occupational therapy, radiology, radiation therapy, durable medical equipment, home health services, outpatient prescription drugs, parenteral/enteral nutrients, equipment and supplies, prosthetics, orthotics and supplies, and inpatient and outpatient hospital services. Each year, CMS updates the CPT/HCPCS codes for services that are considered designated health services (DHS) and are therefore subject to the Stark law prohibition on physician self-referral. In addition to updating current codes, CMS proposes additions and deletions to the list of DHS and publishes the updates in the annual Medicare Physician Fee Schedule final rule.

The major exception to the Stark law allowing physicians to refer to their own group practice is the in-office ancillary service. Among the requirements for group practices, the Stark law definition includes

➤ Two or more physicians legally organized as a partnership, professional corporation, foundation, not-for-profit corporation, faculty practice plan, or similar association;

➤ In which each physician is a member of the group and provides substantially the full range of services that the physician routinely provides, including medical care, consultation, diagnosis or treatment, through the joint use of shared office space, facilities, equipment, and personnel;

➤ For which substantially all of the services of the group's physicians are provided through the group and are billed under a billing number assigned to the group, and amounts so received are treated as receipts of the group;

➤ In which the overhead expenses of and the income from the practice are distributed in accordance with methods previously determined;

➤ In which no physician who is a member of the group directly or indirectly receives compensation based on the volume or value of referrals by the physician; and

➤ In which members of the group personally conduct no less than 75 percent of the physician-patient encounters of the group practice.

There are several additional categories of exceptions, including in-office ancillary services, services to prepaid health plan beneficiaries, academic medical center services, rental of office space and equipment, physician recruitment and retention payments, certain group practice arrangements within a hospital, payments to a laboratory for clinical laboratory services, and additional direct and indirect compensation exceptions. For a comprehensive list of exceptions and description of their definitions and applications, refer to MGMA Government Affairs at mgma.com/stark, or to the additional resources that follow.

PATIENT NOTIFICATION REQUIREMENT

The 2011 Medicare Physician Fee Schedule regulations included a new requirement for notifying patients about options for ancillary services. Beginning in January 2011, physicians must notify patients in writing at the time of a referral for MRI, CT, and PET services that they have the right to receive these services from an entity other than the physician or their group practice. The disclosure must be written in a manner that can be reasonably understood by all patients. The notification must also provide a list of five alternative "suppliers" within 25 miles of the physician's office or all of the alternative suppliers in the area if there are fewer than 5 within 25 miles.

STARK AND JOINT VENTURES

Medical practices should also be wary of entering into joint ventures because of the Stark regulations and other laws affecting physician referral and financial relationships. Stark regulations provide exceptions for financial and referral arrangements within group practices, but regulators are suspicious of joint ventures between physician groups.

Because of the Stark law's prohibition against referrals to an entity in which a physician has a financial interest (either an ownership or compensation arrangement), joint ventures that involve physician referrals of designated health services to the joint venture are illegal unless covered by one of these exceptions:

➤ The facilities are in a rural area;

➤ Agreements involving publicly held securities as defined in the Stark law; and

➤ Ownership or investment interest in a hospital if specific conditions are met.

The overarching rule in the Stark law and anti-kickback federal regulations is that joint ventures must be created for legitimate purposes. Acceptable reasons to form a joint venture include to aggregate capital, to purchase equipment, or to spread risk in connection with a new service. When a joint venture involves little more than a reconfiguration of the names and dollars in an existing service line, regulators may question its legitimacy and legal compliance.

The penalties for violating the Stark law can be extensive, including

➤ Payment of civil penalties of up to $15,000 for each service that a person knows or should have known was provided in violation of the Stark law;

➤ Payment of civil penalties for attempting to circumvent the law — up to $100,000 for each circumvention scheme; and

➤ Exclusion from Medicare and/or Medicaid.

ADDITIONAL RESOURCES

CMS Physician Self-Referral Web page: www.cms.gov/PhysicianSelfReferral

MGMA's StarkCompliance*Plus*: www.Starkcompliance.com

Sources:

Ed Bryant, "Capital Financing for Physician Group Practices," in *Physician Practice Management: Essential Operational and Financial Knowledge,* edited by Lawrence F. Wolper, MBA, FACMPE, 660–661 (Sudbury, MA: Jones and Bartlett Publishers, 2005).

"Exceptions to the Referral Prohibition Related to Ownership or Investment Interests, Financial Relationships between Physicians and Entities Furnishing Designated Health Services," 42 CFR §411.356, http://ecfr.gpoaccess.gov/cgi/t/text/text-idx?c=ecfr&sid=c2c182be4cad971907a4b5934ec595f0&rgn=div8&view=text&node=42:2.0.1.2.11.10.35.7&idno=42 (accessed January 25, 2011).

MGMA Government Affairs, "Federal Prohibition on Physician Self-Referrals: Stark FAQs," www.mgma.com/policy/default.aspx?id=5568 (accessed January 25, 2011).

MGMA Government Affairs, "Final 2011 Medicare Physician Fee Schedule Analysis," www.mgma.com/WorkArea/mgma_downloadasset.aspx?id=40300 (accessed January 25, 2011).

Powers, Pyles, Sutter, & Verville, PC, "Stark Regulations — A Year-End Review Memorandum," December 18, 2008, www.mgma.com/WorkArea/mgma_downloadasset.aspx?id=25296 (accessed January 25, 2011).

QUESTION

I've recently been hired to be the practice administrator of a group practice that doesn't have a HIPAA privacy and security compliance plan. Can you provide me with an overview of the regulations?

The Health Insurance Portability and Accountability Act (HIPAA) of 1996 included provisions designed to protect the privacy and security of patients' health information. The HHS Office of Civil Rights (OCR) administers and enforces the Privacy Rule and Security Rule.

AUDIT ALERT!

The HHS Office of Civil Rights (OCR), as part of its enforcement processes, has the authority to audit providers to ensure they are complying with HIPAA privacy and security regulations. The HITECH Act augmented OCR's enforcement authority related to HIPAA and the penalties for noncompliance. As an example, OCR auditors could require that the practice produce evidence of when the last risk analysis was conducted and what steps the practice took to mitigate any risks identified.

PRIVACY RULE

National privacy standards, included in HIPAA, specified the use and disclosure of individuals' protected health information by "covered entities." The goal was to ensure protection of citizens' privacy while allowing for the flow of information needed to provide quality healthcare. The final Privacy Rule became effective in 2003 and can be found at 45 CHR Part 160 and Part 164.

Protected health information (PHI) is information that identifies the individual or could be used to identify the individual. This includes common identifiers such as name, address, birth date, and Social Security Number, but it also includes information that relates to

> The individual's past, present, or future physical or mental health or condition;

> The provision of healthcare to the individual; or

> The past, present, or future payment for the provision of healthcare to the individual.

There are no restrictions on the use of the disclosure of information that has been "de-identified" by the removal of the individual's identifiers, the individual's family and employers, and any remaining information that could identify the individual.

The rule defines covered entities as

> Health plans, including Medicare, Medicaid, HMOs, and health, dental, vision, and prescription-drug insurers;

> Healthcare providers, including hospitals, physicians, dentists, and others, who electronically transmit health information including claims, referral requests, use of billing services, and so on; and

> Healthcare clearinghouses and all business associates that handle PHI as "covered entities."

Physicians and other covered entities are permitted to use PHI without an individual's authorization for its own treatment, payment, and healthcare operations. For disclosure of PHI for other purposes, the covered entity must obtain the individual's written authorization. Examples of authorized release of PHI include disclosure to a life insurer, to an employer for pre-employment information, or to pharmaceutical firms for their marketing efforts.

Physician offices and other entities must develop and implement policies to limit the use and disclosure of PHI to the minimum amount necessary "to accomplish the intended purpose of the use, disclosure, or request." The policies must identify who in the organization needs access to the information, the types of PHI within the organization, and the conditions for allowing that access. The practice should designate a staff member as a privacy official and designate a contact person for receiving complaints and questions from patients. All employees, volunteers, and others in the office must receive training regarding the practice's privacy policies and procedures.

The privacy official should review the flow of PHI in the practice, including its disposal. Any documents or electronic media containing PHI should be shredded or destroyed rather than disposed of in trash cans.

Medical practices must also provide all patients with a notice of its privacy practices that describes how the practice may use and disclose PHI and its responsibilities to protect the patients' privacy and rights, including the means to complain if they believe their privacy has been violated. The notice can be provided to the patient by e-mail or regular mail, or given to the patient at his or her first visit. The practice must also make an effort to have the patient sign an acknowledgment of receipt of this notice. In addition, the practice is required to post the notice in a visible location at the medical practice, where patients can see and read the notice, and post it on the practice's Web site, if it has one. Finally, the practice must provide a new notice to all patients should the notice be substantially revised.

The HIPAA privacy rule applied to business associates of the covered entities that perform certain functions or services, including claims processing, data analysis, utilization review, and billing, which involve use of PHI. Physicians and other entities had to ensure via written agreements that the business associates safeguarded the use and disclosure of PHI. With the HITECH expansion of business associates to covered entity status, business associates are now subject to enforcement actions and penalties. In its 2010 Notice of Proposed Rulemaking, HHS outlined an expansion of the "business associate" term to include patient safety organizations, e-prescribing gateways, vendors of personal health records, and subcontractors of business associates. The HITECH also states that business associates

➤ May not use or disclose PHI in violation of the Privacy Rule;

➤ Must directly comply with all HIPAA Security Rule administrative, physical, and technical safeguards and documentation requirements;

➤ Are now subject to HIPAA civil and criminal enforcement and penalties, in addition to contractual liability; and

➤ Must comply with new duties and responsibilities as specified in the Notice of Proposed Rulemaking.

HIPAA SECURITY RULE

The security regulations address a subset of PHI, the electronic protected health information (e-PHI) defined as the "individually identifiable health information that a covered entity creates, receives, maintains or transmits in electronic form." The security rule does not apply to orally transmitted or written PHI. The final regulation, effective in 2005, specifies the administrative, technical, and physical security procedures for covered entities to follow to ensure the protection and integrity of e-PHI. The security rule has the same definitions for covered entities, protected health information, and business associates as the Privacy Rule. OCR is also the government's enforcement agency for the Security Rule.

To comply with the Security Rule, medical practices and other covered entities must

➤ Ensure the confidentiality, integrity, and availability of all e-PHI they create, receive, maintain, or transmit;

➤ Identify and protect against reasonably anticipated threats to the security or integrity of the information;

➤ Implement policies and procedures to protect against impermissible uses or disclosures; and

➤ Ensure compliance by their staff and physicians.

Therefore, practices are required to comply with the Privacy Rule regulations for protecting all forms of PHI along with ensuring that e-PHI is not altered or destroyed in an unauthorized manner (integrity) and that it is accessible and usable when requested by an authorized person.

In order to comply with the security rule and prevent unauthorized access to PHI, medical practices and other covered entities must have in place:

➤ Administrative safeguards by implementing security measures to limit the use and disclosure of PHI to the minimum necessary. This should consist of policies and procedures limiting access to e-PHI to certain personnel, providing training on securing e-PHI, specifying consequences for violating the policies and procedures, and conducting periodic audits to assess the effectiveness of the policies and procedures.

➤ Physical safeguards that limit physical access to its facilities and limit access to workstations and electronic media. The policies and procedures should specify use and disclosure of passwords and the transfer, removal, disposal, and re-use of electronic media that contains or contained e-PHI.

➤ Technical safeguards that limit access to e-PHI to authorized persons, offer the means to record access and activity in information systems that include e-PHI, ensure the integrity of e-PHI, and protect e-PHI during transmittal over an electronic network.

SECURITY RISK ASSESSMENT

You must include Security Risk Analysis and Assessment as part of your HIPAA Compliance Plan and the CMS meaningful use requirements. The assessment should review practice policies and procedures related to employee responsibilities, physical and technical safeguards, backup plans, and so on to ensure they are in place and being adhered to. For more detailed information and assistance, visit the following resources:

➤ The OCR HIPAA Web site (www.hhs.gov/ocr/privacy) offers a HIPAA Security Information Series with detailed information including a Risk Analysis and Risk Management document; and

➤ MGMA and HIMSS Privacy and Security Toolkit for Small Provider Organizations (www.mgma.com/privacytoolkit). Select "Guidance and Resources."

EMPLOYEE TRAINING

Both the security and privacy rules require that employee training be included in organizational HIPAA compliance policies and procedures. Training ensures knowledge of requirements to protect PHI and instills a corporate culture of compliance. Training must be provided on an ongoing basis with periodic updates. Policies and procedures should state the consequences for not attending training and not complying with the regulations. Each training session should be documented with who attended and what was covered. The training can be modified based on the employees' roles with patients and their access to PHI.

Employees need to be aware of possible ways that PHI could be released accidentally and modify their behavior accordingly. Employees should be reminded to shred or otherwise destroy documents that contain PHI rather than throwing them in the trash. PHI should not be shared with others in casual conversations or in unsecured e-mails or text messages. Paper and electronic files with PHI should be secured and keys or passwords kept in secure locations.

Many states have laws that are more stringent or have applied for exceptions to HIPAA's preemption of state requirements, requiring practices and other entities to ensure compliance of state privacy and security laws. Although MGMA has urged HHS to ask states to conform their laws to HIPAA requirements, it is recommended that practices seek information to ensure compliance with state-specific regulations. Also, monitor information from MGMA, CMS, and the OCR for changes to and clarifications of HIPAA regulations.

KEYS TO ENSURING PROTECTION AND SECURITY OF YOUR PATIENTS' INFORMATION

➤ Conduct regular training sessions and follow up with informal reminders at meetings and elsewhere about HIPAA security and privacy regulations and practice policies.

➤ Randomly audit how employees control their passwords and monitor who accesses patients' electronic health records.

➤ Keep electronic data backups of patient information at secure but separate locations.

➤ Annually review the practices of key business associates related to HIPAA compliance.

➤ Conduct strict and thorough background checks of all new hires.

➤ Remove former staff from access to records.

➤ Use a multidisciplinary approach to assessing security threats, and deploy employee teams to audit how their peers carry out security and privacy policies.

➤ Be alert for new trends and emerging threats to patient health information and facility security.

Source: Bob Redling, MS, "What If: The One Question Every Administrator Should Ask," *MGMA Connexion,* August 2007, www.mgma.com/WorkArea/mgma_downloadasset. aspx?id=13982 (accessed February 4, 2011).

ADDITIONAL HIPAA RESOURCES FROM MGMA

Patricia Carter, *HIPAA Compliance Handbook, 2011 Edition,* Item #8360

Are You Ready for the New HIPAA Privacy and Security Mandates? CD format, Item #8158 or On-demand webinar, Item #E8158

Critical Privacy Changes under the HITECH Act: How to Bring Your Practice into Compliance and Reduce Enforcement Risk, CD format, Item #8229

American Medical Association, *Policies and Procedures for the Electronic Medical Practice* with CD-ROM, Item #8230

ADDITIONAL HIPAA RESOURCES

MGMA and HIMSS, *Privacy and Security Toolkit for Small Provider Organizations,* www.himss.org/ASP/topics_PS_ SmallProviders.asp

Healthcare Compliance Solutions, Inc., Employee Training Resources, www.hcsiinc.com

Sources:

HHS Office for Civil Rights, Health Information Privacy Web pages, www.hhs.gov/ocr/privacy//index.html (accessed February 7, 2011).

MGMA HIPAA Resource Center (under MGMA.com/policy, select Health Information Technology), www.mgma.com/policy/default.aspx?id=5108&kc=WAC (accessed February 7, 2011).

QUESTION 90 — What are recent changes to HIPAA, especially the new breach notification requirements?

The Health Information Technology for Economic and Clinical Health (HITECH) Act, Title XIII of the ARRA effective in 2010, included new requirements affecting medical practices. The regulations were not finalized as of this writing (May 2011). For current information, refer to the MGMA Web site, MGMA *Washington Connexion* newsletter, or federal government information resources (see the list of sources at the end of this answer).

HITECH included breach notification requirements, provisions for business associate liability, stronger limitations on the sale of PHI, augmented rights for patients' control over their health information, and restricted the disclosure of certain information. Under the Interim Rules, medical practices are required to

➤ Track all disclosures for treatment, payment, and health-care operations, if the practice is using an EHR. Patients have the ability to request disclosures for up to three previous years. Practices that acquired an EHR system after January 1, 2009, must comply with disclosure requirements beginning January 1, 2011, or the date they acquire a system. Those that purchased EHR systems prior to January 2009 must track PHI disclosures after January 1, 2014.

➤ Notify patients and HHS when PHI has been disclosed due to a breach. A breach is defined as the use or disclosure of information in violation of the requirements to protect PHI.

➤ Restrict the disclosure of PHI to a health plan for purposes other than treatment if requested by a patient who paid out-of-pocket in full for healthcare services or items.

➤ Use de-identified patient data or disclose only the minimum data possible to carry out administrative transactions.

➤ Apply HIPAA requirements to business associates under the new definitions.

➤ Provide patients with a copy of their EHR record in an electronic format (e.g., CD, secure Web site, or USB thumb drive), and take steps to accommodate the reasonable format request of the patient. Practices are allowed to charge the labor, supplies, and postage costs involved in copying and mailing the record but may not include costs associated with searching for and retrieving the requested information.

Monitor the following sources for the latest information on breach notification and other HIPAA regulations:

HHS Office for Civil Rights, Health Information Privacy Web pages: www.hhs.gov/ocr/privacy//index.html

MGMA HIPAA Resource Center: Under MGMA.com/ policy, select Health Information Technology

MGMA and HIMSS, *Privacy and Security Toolkit for Small Provider Organizations*: www.himss.org/ASP/ topics_PS_SmallProviders.asp

QUESTION **Do the HIPAA regulations allow us to communicate with our patients via e-mail?**

91

The HIPAA regulations do not prohibit medical practices from communicating with patients via e-mail. However, there are more factors to consider related to e-mail communication, including what type of communication is conducted and who may also have access to the patient's e-mail messages.

According to the HHS OCR,

➤ Yes, the Privacy Rule allows healthcare providers to communicate electronically, such as through e-mail, with their patients, provided they apply reasonable safeguards when doing so. (See 45 C.F.R. § 164.530(c).) For example, certain precautions may need to be taken when using e-mail to avoid unintentional disclosures, such as sending an e-mail alert to the patient for address confirmation prior to sending the message. Further, while the Privacy Rule does not prohibit the use of unencrypted e-mail for treatment-related communications between healthcare providers and patients, other safeguards should be applied to reasonably protect privacy, such as limiting the amount or type of information disclosed through the unencrypted e-mail. In addition, covered entities will want to ensure that any transmission of e-PHI is in compliance with the HIPAA Security Rule requirements.

➤ Note that an individual has the right under the Privacy Rule to request and have a covered healthcare provider communicate with him or her by alternative means or at alternative locations, if reasonable. For example, a healthcare provider should accommodate an individual's request to receive appointment reminders via e-mail, rather than on a postcard, if e-mail is a reasonable, alternative means for that provider to communicate with the patient. By the same token, however, if the use of unencrypted e-mail is unacceptable to a patient who requests confidential communications, other means of communicating with the patient, such as by more secure electronic methods or by mail or telephone, should be offered and accommodated.

➤ Patients may initiate communications with a provider using e-mail. If this situation occurs, the healthcare provider can assume (unless the patient has explicitly stated otherwise) that e-mail communications are acceptable to the individual. If the provider feels the patient may not be aware of the possible risks of using unencrypted e-mail or has concerns about potential liability, the provider can alert the patient of those risks and let the patient decide whether to continue e-mail communications.

The same precautions should be taken when e-mailing with other providers regarding patient care. Patient identifying information in e-mails should be limited unless e-mail communications are encrypted or otherwise secured.

MGMA Government Affairs advises medical practices to always use encrypting software when sending e-mail messages to patients or other providers if the message contains patient information. MGMA's Government Affairs also suggests that providers and patients be aware that others may have access to e-mail messages. This is especially true if an e-mail address is a work e-mail address because employers have the right to monitor employees' messages sent and received on employer-managed e-mail systems. Electronic messages regarding appointments can be considered differently than messages conducting an online consult or discussing treatment plans because of the different content. (See Question 67 on virtual visits.) Because of these concerns, practices are advised to use encryption and limit the content of e-mails or use secured patient portals for sharing more sensitive information.

Sources:

HHS Office of Civil Rights, "Does the HIPAA Privacy Rule Permit Healthcare Providers to Use E-Mail to Discuss Health Issues and Treatment with Their Patients?" December 15, 2008, www.hhs.gov/ocr/privacy/hipaa/faq/health_information_technology/570.html (accessed February 8, 2011).

Robert M. Tennant, MA, Senior Policy Advisor, MGMA Government Affairs, personal communication, May 16, 2011.

QUESTION 92 I'm hearing confusing information on the Red Flags rule and whether it applies to medical practices. What's the truth?

The status of the "Red Flags" rule as it applies to medical practices has changed several times and is subject to further change. The Federal Trade Commission (FTC) developed the Red Flags rule in response to concerns over identity theft. The Fair and Accurate

Credit Transactions (FACT) Act of 2003 required "creditors" to implement programs to prevent identity theft.

After release of the rule, the FTC maintained that the term "creditor" applied to any entity that defers payment, including healthcare providers who bill monthly or defer billing their patients until after submitting claims to insurers. Several industries objected to being considered creditors and launched advocacy and legal campaigns against this interpretation. As a result, Congress passed and the president signed the Red Flag Program Clarification Act of 2010, limiting the definition of creditor.

Shortly thereafter, a federal circuit court ruled in one of the many lawsuits against the FTC that the Red Flag Program Clarification Act superseded the FTC's interpretation of the term "creditor." Based on this ruling, if the FTC decides to include physicians and their medical practices in the definition of a creditor, it will need to go through a formal notice-and-comment rule-making process.

Therefore, at the time of this writing (March 2011), physicians and medical practices are not defined as creditors and are not required to comply with the Red Flags rule unless the FTC releases a new rule. However, changes to the Red Flag rule may have occurred since this writing. Continue to monitor potential changes to this requirement and other government laws and regulations for changes that may affect medical practices.

Sources:

MGMA Government Affairs, "Bill Limiting Red Flags Rule Passes House, Senate," www.mgma.com/article.aspx?id=40313 (accessed January 25, 2011).

MGMA Government Affairs, "Federal Trade Commission's 'Red Flags' Rule," www.mgma.com/WorkArea/linkit.aspx?LinkIdentifier=id&ItemID=26880 (accessed January 25, 2011).

QUESTION One of my new physicians wants to know if she should become a Medicare participating provider. What are the advantages and disadvantages? Can she limit the number of Medicare or Medicaid patients or patient appointments on her schedule?

If the physician enrolls with Medicare, she becomes a participating provider and agrees to accept Medicare's reimbursement rates as payment in full. As an incentive for providers to participate in the program, Medicare reimburses at 100 percent of the approved rate for any given service, pays more rapidly than nonparticipating providers, and includes the physician in the directory of Medicare providers. Participating providers receive 80 percent of this payment from Medicare and 20 percent from the patient.

Physicians are allowed to change their participation on an annual basis. The Medicare contractor will send a letter (called the "Dear doctor letter") each November informing the physician of the upcoming calendar year's payment rates and offering an opportunity to change his or her participation status. Response regarding the participation decision for the following year must be received by December 31. Unless CMS reopens this "open enrollment period," participation is binding for the entire calendar year.

If your physician chooses not to participate (non-Par) in Medicare, she has the option to accept assignment. If the non-Par provider accepts assignment, Medicare pays 95 percent of the participating amount, with 80 percent of that amount coming from the carrier and 20 percent from the patient. If the non-Par provider decides not to accept assignment, she must fill out a Medicare beneficiary's claim form and submit the claim directly to Medicare. Medicare then pays the patient directly, leaving the physician to bill the patient for services rendered. Physicians cannot charge Medicare patients for filing their claims, but by refusing assignment, non-Par physicians can balance-bill patients up to the limiting charge.

Federal law restricts Medicare nonparticipating providers from balance-billing more than 115 percent of the Medicare nonparticipating reimbursement rate. This is called the "limiting charge." Additionally, several states have enacted limiting charges. Effectively, the Medicare limiting charge translates into 109.25 percent of the participating amount, so a nonparticipating physician can, theoretically, realize higher income than a participating provider. This can only happen, however, if the majority of patients meet their financial obligations. In addition, the revenue stream will be slowed as practices wait for patients to reimburse them, and practices may incur expenses as a result of increased administrative work.

Physicians may also choose to stay out of the Medicare system entirely. You can then bill patients directly for the services at rates agreed to with the patient. To meet the legal requirements for the opt-out option, a physician must sign and file an affidavit agreeing not to bill or receive payment from the Medicare program for at least two years. This includes direct, indirect, or capitated payments. Indirect payments could come from an organization that receives direct or capitated payments from Medicare.

The physician must file this affidavit at least 30 days before the first day of the next calendar quarter and may rescind the affidavit within 90 days of the affidavit's effective date. The physician and Medicare patient must sign a written contract before any service is rendered. The contract must clearly state that by signing the contract, the beneficiary

➤ Gives up all Medicare payments for services rendered by the contracting physician;

➤ Is liable for all charges without Medicare balance-billing limitations or assistance from Medigap or other supplemental insurance; and

➤ Acknowledges that the beneficiary has the right to receive services from medical providers eligible for Medicare coverage.

Regarding the question about limiting the number of appointments for Medicare enrollees, Robert Saner II, Esq., MGMA member and Washington counsel, and Powers, Pyles, Sutter, & Verville, PC, Washington, D.C., provide the following advice:

There is no generally applicable federal law or regulation that requires a physician or group to accept Medicare or Medicaid patients, or to take all Medicare patients if some are accepted. Similarly, state laws are generally silent with respect to the issue. Thus, in the absence of insurance contract provisions applicable in individual situations, many groups have historically used scheduling practices to limit the number of patients from one or more payer classes, which may include Medicare or Medicaid.

There are, however, situations where restrictive scheduling policies can be problematic. For example, if a physician does treat Medicare or Medicaid patients, s/he can be sanctioned if that treatment does not meet "professionally recognized standards of healthcare" (Section 1128(b)(6)(B) of the Social Security Act). Failure to promptly schedule diagnostic tests or procedures, or follow-up visits, for existing Medicare patients in a manner that effectively produces lower quality care than the practice provides to other payer classes could violate this provision.

Similarly, Medicare managed care plans generally have obligations to provide reasonable and necessary care to their enrollees, and these obligations are generally passed through to practices with which they contract directly or through PPOs and IPAs. If restrictive scheduling practices effectively restrict access, the practice may be in violation of contract provisions to which it has agreed.

Other examples include hospital systems that have certain charity care obligations by virtue of Hill-Burton funding, tax-exempt practices that have community benefit obligations, state university–based academic practices that have "mission-based" restrictions on their ability to discriminate against Medicaid or other under-insured populations, ventures that seek compliance with kickback law "safe harbors," which sometimes impose nondiscrimination requirements, and organizations operating under corporate integrity agreements that include requirements that go beyond basic law and regulation.

Finally, payer-derived scheduling practices could in some circumstances look like race or age-based discrimination that runs afoul of state and federal civil rights laws to which some but not all practices are subject.

In short, this is a very complicated area of the law, and groups should proceed with caution when establishing restrictive scheduling practices.[1]

Sources:

1. Robert Saner II, Esq., and Powers, Pyles, Sutter, & Verville, PC, e-mail communication, November 8, 2006.

Medical Group Management Association, Government Affairs, "Medicare Participation Decision & FAQs," www.mgma.com/members/advocacy/medparticipationfaq.cfm (accessed February 4, 2011).

QUESTION 94 Are we required to have translators or interpreters for our hearing-impaired and non-English speaking patients?

Medical group practices are required by law to provide reasonable interpretive services in order to "have meaningful access to the health and social services" at no additional cost to the patient. Although this may seem burdensome, compliance with the regulations ensures patient safety and minimizes the liability risks. Studies by the Joint Commission on Accreditation of Healthcare Organizations have found that communication problems are a frequent cause of adverse events and that more serious outcomes were found among patients with limited English proficiency.

According to the Americans with Disabilities Act (ADA), providers are required to engage in "effective communication" with their hearing impaired patients. The type of accommodation for "effective communication" varies based on several factors. These include the nature of the patient's impairment, the patient's ability to communicate, as well as the complexity of the medical matter.

The ADA [28 CFR 36.303(b)(1)] requires healthcare providers to furnish appropriate auxiliary aids and services for people with hearing impairments. Appropriate auxiliary aids and services include "qualified interpreters, note takers, computer-aided transcription services, written materials, telephone headset amplifiers, assistive listening devices, assistive listening systems, telephones compatible with hearing aids, closed caption decoders, open and closed captioning, telecommunications devices for deaf persons, videotext displays, or other effective methods of making aurally delivered material available to individuals with hearing impairments."

If "effective communication" can be achieved by means other than an interpreter, then an interpreter is not necessary. If an interpreter is required, the interpreter must be qualified, meaning he or she is able to interpret effectively, accurately, and impartially both receptively and expressively, using any necessary specialized vocabulary. It is important to note that an individual does not necessarily need to be certified in order to be a qualified interpreter. Typically, the provider is responsible for the cost associated with providing "effective communication" unless the cost imposes an undue burden on the provider.

For patients with Limited English Proficiency (LEP), HHS regulations issued under Title VI require all recipients of federal financial assistance from HHS to take reasonable steps to provide meaningful access. An LEP patient, including pediatric patients, is one who "cannot speak, read, write or understand the English language at a level that permits them to interact effectively with healthcare providers and social service agencies." Receiving funds from Medicare Part B is not considered federal financial assistance. Therefore, most physician practices, unless they are part of a hospital, will not be subject to the LEP rules if they do not see Medicaid patients.

Although the regulations state that the interpretive services should be provided at no additional cost to the patient, a few states reimburse providers for the services as part of their Medicaid or State Children's Health Insurance Programs. Check with your state regarding its reimbursement practices.

MGMA's legal counsel, Powers, Pyles, Sutter, & Verville, PC, provides the following information based on the HHS guidance letter:

> *Physician practices subject to the LEP rules are required to apply and balance the following factors in deciding what steps can reasonably be taken to ensure meaningful access to their programs and activities by LEP persons:*
>
> ➤ *The number or proportion of LEP persons eligible to be served or likely to be encountered by the practice;*
>
> ➤ *The frequency with which LEP individuals come in contact with the practice;*
>
> ➤ *The nature and importance of the healthcare activity, or service provided by the practice to people's lives; and*
>
> ➤ *The resources available to the practice and costs.*
>
> *Physician practices are supposed to strive for a course of action that will provide meaningful access to information or services without imposing undue burdens on small businesses, including solo practitioners and small medical groups. Thus, a practice group that regularly serves a large Spanish-speaking population may need to make interpreter services available, assuming it can do so in a cost-effective manner. Whether it is reasonable for the practice to have an interpreter on staff or contract with an outside service will depend on the frequency of the need and the relative cost. By contrast, a practice that rarely if ever treats non-English speaking Hispanic patients may not be required to provide language services for a Spanish speaking patient who comes in for a routine exam unless the exam reveals a condition that requires follow-up attention.[1]*

The HHS guidelines do not require the use of a certified interpreter but do specify that the interpreter must be able to effectively communicate the information either orally or in written translations. The interpreter must be able to understand and translate medical terms and follow HIPAA privacy and other confidentiality requirements. Information of a more important or urgent nature will require greater accuracy and timeliness in the translation. Options for interpreter services include hiring a bilingual staff member, contracting with an interpreter, using telephone interpretation services, enlisting community volunteers, or relying on family members or friends of the patient. Family members cannot be required to provide these services. Family members often do not possess sufficient skills to effectively interpret in a medical setting. Even if they are skilled, family members and friends are often too emotionally or personally involved to interpret "effectively, accurately, and impartially." Using family members and friends as interpreters can also cause problems in maintaining patient confidentiality. If using a family member or friend, ensure the competency of the person to translate the medical terminology and that the patient agrees to the sharing of protected health information with the interpreter.

In addition, practices are required to provide translations of "vital" written materials including consent forms, HIPAA notices of privacy practices, standard policies regarding hours, and acceptance of insurance information. The practice should offer written translations for each language that represents 5 percent or 1,000 individuals of the population to be served or encountered in the practice. For nonvital materials, and if the 5 percent of a population is less than 50 individuals, the practice can provide written notice in that language stating that those individuals have the right to receive oral interpretation of the materials free of charge.

ADDITIONAL RESOURCES

ADA Home Page, U.S. Department of Justice: www.ada.gov

"Guidance to Federal Financial Assistance Recipients Regarding Title VI Prohibition against National Origin Discrimination Affecting Limited English Proficient Persons" available at www.hhs.gov/ocr/civilrights/resources/specialtopics/lep

Reference:

1. Powers, Pyles, Sutter, & Verville, PC, "Limiting English Proficiency Patients: Obligations of Physician Practices," memorandum to Medical Group Management Association, June 26, 2009, www.mgma.com/WorkArea/linkit.aspx?LinkIdentifier=id&ItemID=30325 (accessed February 4, 2011).

Sources:

Kimberly W. Parker, FACMPE, CMM, CPC, "Communicative Competence: Overcoming Language Barriers in the Healthcare Setting," ACMPE Fellowship Paper, October 2009, www.mgma.com/WorkArea/mgma_downloadasset.aspx?id=31772 (accessed February 4, 2011).

Medical Group Management Association, Government Affairs, "Guidelines for Hearing Impaired Patients," www.mgma.com/policy/default.aspx?id=30333 (accessed February 4, 2011).

CHAPTER 9

More Resources

QUESTION 95 What if I have a question that isn't addressed in this book? What other resources are available?

Although we have attempted to answer many frequently asked questions covering a variety of medical practice management topics, it is impossible to address all of the questions a practice administrator might ask. In addition to the resources used to support the answers in this book, there are many other resources, available in print and on the Internet.

MGMA offers many resources related to medical practice management:

➤ **MGMA's Government Affairs** department's detailed analyses of the latest healthcare legislation and issues about healthcare management are available via www.mgma.com/policy. The department staff can be reached by phone at 202.293.3450 or via e-mail at govaff@mgma.com.

➤ **MGMA Health Care Consulting Group** includes consultants specializing in all aspects of medical practice management and current healthcare trends.

➤ **MGMA Information Center** provides access to healthcare management and other online databases, assistance with frequently asked questions, and options for conducting in-depth research. The librarians can be reached toll-free at 877.ASK.MGMA (275.6462), x1887 or via e-mail infocenter@mgma.com.

➤ **MGMA Member Community** links medical practice administrators to share ideas and resources. The online discussion groups and blogs cover a variety of topics and the libraries provide links to checklists, surveys, job descriptions and other documents shared by members.

➤ **MGMA Store** lists books, manuals, surveys, webinars and other education programs by topic and product type.

➤ **MGMA Web site (www.mgma.com)** includes links to the above items plus other practice management solutions and tools listed by topic area, specialty, and resource type.

The MGMA Information Center recommends the following resources for healthcare statistics, regulatory information, or additional research sources:

➤ **Centers for Medicare & Medicaid Services Web site (www.cms.gov)** provides links to the annual Medicare physician fee schedule, provider enrollment forms and information, and regulatory guidance.

➤ **National Center for Health Statistics (www.cdc.gov/ nchs/)** conducts annual surveys and reports on diseases and conditions, healthcare status and insurance, and visits to physicians and hospitals. The National Ambulatory Medical Care Survey report includes frequently requested statistics.

➤ **U.S. Bureau of Labor Statistics (www.bls.gov)** has online tools that offer opportunities to analyze the Consumer Price Index, including medical care services cost indexes and wages and benefits by region or occupation. Among the online publications is the *Occupational Outlook Handbook* with break out of trends and earnings for most healthcare positions.

➤ **U.S. National Library of Medicine (www.nlm.nih.gov)** manages the PubMed database for searching clinical medicine and healthcare administration journals. The Web site also includes electronic medical record resources under LocatorPlus, clinical trials information, and MedlinePlus database for patients and their families.

INDEX